Praise for *Designing*

"Great web applications are like a best friend. They remember your birthday, anticipate your next move, and forgive your errors. Great web applications are now much easier to create, thanks to Mr. Hoekman's delightful book. Armed with this new edition, you'll design web apps that work the way your customers expect—fulfilling their needs and your business's goals. For site owners and designers, your next move is obvious: buy this book."

> **Jeffrey Zeldman**
> Author of *Designing With Web Standards*

"*Designing the Obvious* is my first reading recommendation to both designers who want to improve and non-designers who should have a baseline understanding of what a successful user experience means. Robert's insights are brilliant, common-sense, easy to absorb, and practical. The principles have become the basis of my own set of heuristics that I use to evaluate the success of all my work. You'll be smarter as soon as you finish the first chapter."

> **Jason M. Putorti**
> Lead Designer of Mint.com

"True Story: Just the other day, I went to grab *Designing the Obvious* off my shelf, only to realize it wasn't there. Again. The last person I lent it to never returned it; just like all the folks before that. It turns out I've bought myself seven copies and I have given each one away. Hopefully, I can keep the next copy for myself. (Probably not. It's just too good not to share.)"

> **Jared Spool**
> Founder of UIE.com, coauthor of *Web Anatomy*

"Hoekman's pragmatic, accessible insights in *Designing the Obvious* translate across disciplines because they focus on helping people get stuff done...quickly, easily, happily. The book's core principles can and should inform the way we make things for our users, period. And, as a content strategist, I especially appreciate the clarity of thought (and good humor!) in Hoekman's writing. *Designing the Obvious* is on my 'must-have' booklist for web professionals of all stripes."

> **Kristina Halvorson**
> Author of *Content Strategy for the Web*

"*Designing the Obvious* rocked my socks."

> **Brandon Hayes**
> @teh_viking on Twitter

Designing the Obvious

A Common Sense Approach to Web and Mobile Application Design

SECOND EDITION

Designing the Obvious:
A Common Sense Approach to Web and Mobile Application Design, Second Edition
Robert Hoekman, Jr.

New Riders
1249 Eighth Street
Berkeley, CA 94710
510/524-2178
510/524-2221 (fax)

Find us on the Web at www.newriders.com
To report errors, please send a note to errata@peachpit.com

New Riders is an imprint of Peachpit, a division of Pearson Education
Copyright © 2011 by Robert Hoekman, Jr.

Editor: Wendy Sharp
Production Coordinator: Hilal Sala
Copyeditor: Jacqueline Aaron
Research Assistant: Sunny Thaper
Compositor: Danielle Foster
Indexer: Emily Glossbrenner, FireCrystal Communications
Cover design: Mimi Heft
Interior design: Joan Olson

ISBN 10:   0321749855
ISBN 13: 9780321749857

9 8 7 6 5 4 3 2 1
Printed and bound in the United States of America

This book is dedicated to anyone who has ever used a web or mobile application and resented the experience.

Contents

Acknowledgments   x

Author Biography   xi

Chapter 1: Defining the Obvious   **3**

What Is 'the Obvious'?   6
    Qualities of a great application   8
How Do You Design the Obvious?   10
    Turn qualities into goals   10
The Framework for Obvious Design   12
    Know what to build   14
    Know what makes it great   14
    Know the best way to implement it   15

Chapter 2: Lead with Why, Follow with What   **17**

Know Your Motivation   19
    What follows Why   22
Make Authentic Decisions   24
    Audit the user experience   24
    Define the vision   28
    Plan the new design   31
    Implement it   32
    Measure everything   32
    Having vision   34

Chapter 3: Ignore the User, Know the Situation   **35**

    Designing for the User   37
    Designing for the Activity   44
Solve for the Situation   47
Understand How Users Think They Do Things   55
Understand How Users Actually Do Things   57
Find Out the Truth   61
    Contextual inquiry   63
    Remote user research   66
    Surveys   67
Write Use Cases   68

Task-flow diagrams 74

My advice 76

Chapter 4: Build Only What Is Absolutely Necessary 77

More features, More frustration 78

So what's a geek to do? 79

Think Different 80

The dashboard and New Invoice screen 81

The finished invoice 82

The result 83

Think Mobile 84

Hey, it's your life 87

Not present at time of photo 87

Drop Nice-to-Have Features 88

The Unnecessary Test 89

The 60-Second Deadline 90

Aim low 92

Interface Surgery 93

Reevaluate nice-to-have features later 98

Let them speak 99

Chapter 5: Support the User's Mental Model 101

Understanding mental models 103

Design for Mental Models 104

Making metaphors that work 107

Interface Surgery: Converting an implementation
model design into a mental model design 111

Eliminate Implementation Models 119

Create wireframes to nail things down 119

Prototype the Design 127

Test It Out 130

Chapter 6: Turn Beginners into Intermediates, Immediately 139

Use Up-to-Speed Aids 141

Provide a welcome screen 145

Fill the blank slate with something useful 147

Give instructive hints 149

Interface Surgery: Applying instructive design 153

Choose Good Defaults   160

    Integrate preferences   163

Design for Information   163

    Card sorting   166

Stop Getting Up to Speed and Speed Things Up   168

    Reuse the welcome screen as a notification system   169

    Use one-click interfaces   170

    Use design patterns to make things familiar   171

Provide Help Documents, Because Help Is for Experts   173

Chapter 7: Be Persuasive   **175**

Draw a Finish Line   176

    Ownership   177

Solve a Significant Problem   178

Make It Explainable   180

Know Your Psychology   181

    Reciprocity   181

    Commitment and consistency   182

    Social proof   184

    Authority   185

    Liking   186

    Scarcity   187

    Ethical persuasion   188

Chapter 8: Handle Errors Wisely   **189**

Prevent and Catch Errors with Poka-yoke Devices   191

    Poka-yoke on the web   192

    Prevention devices   193

    Detection devices   195

    Turn errors into opportunities   200

    Feeling smart   202

Ditch Anything Modal   203

    Redesigning rude behavior   204

    Replace it with modeless assistants   205

Write Error Messages That Help Instead of Hurt   207

    Interface Surgery   209

Create Forgiving Software   211

    Good software promotes good practices   213

Chapter 9: Design for Uniformity, Consistency, and Meaning   217

Design for Uniformity   220
Be Consistent Across Applications   229
  Understanding design patterns   230
  Intelligent inconsistency   233
Leverage Irregularity to Create Meaning and Importance   234
  Interface Surgery: Surfacing the bananas in a process   237

Chapter 10: Reduce and Refine   243

Cluttered task flows   244
The path to simplicity   245
Clean Up the Mess   246
  Reducing the pixel-to-data ratio   247
  Minimizing copy   248
  Designing white space   251
  Cleaning up task flows   255
Practice Kaizen   258
  The 5S approach   259
Eliminate Waste   262
  Cleaning up your process   263
Put Just-in-Time Design and Review to Work   265

Chapter 11: Don't Innovate When You Can Elevate   269

Innovation   270
  The problem with innovative thinking   270
  Elevation   272
Elevate the User Experience   272
  Elevation is about being more polite   273
  Elevation means giving your software a
    better personality   274
  Elevation means understanding good design   276
Seek Out and Learn from Great Examples   277
  Inspiration   278
  Elevate the standards   278
Take Out All the Good Lines   279
Get in the Game   280

Index   283

Acknowledgements

Words cannot express how much the first edition of this book changed my life. I can never thank you all enough for your part in what has been the greatest adventure of my lifetime. But I will try.

To my editor and friend, Wendy Sharp: you are a master. Without you, I am floating in space. Make no mistake, you're the reason this book is any good at all.

To Seth Godin, Jason Fried, Ryan Carson, Josh Williams, Jason Putorti, and everyone else who had a hand in the design of the best apps on the Internet: thank you for your contributions, your time, your excellence, and your dedication to your craft. The Internet is better because of you. Designers everywhere are in your debt.

To Hilal Sala, Nancy Davis, Jacqueline Aaron, Andreas Schueller, Mimi Heft, Amy Standen, Joan Olson, our esteemed publisher Nancy Ruenzel, and the rest of the amazing Peachpit team: thank you, once again and forever, for your diligence, patience, caring, and genius, and for making it a joy to be in this business. This book would be nothing without you, and this industry would be nothing without your work.

To my friend, colleague, and research assistant Sunny Thaper: your insight, knowledge, unending wit, and enthusiasm for this project have been invaluable. Thank you.

To my friends at CO+HOOTS (@cohootsphx on Twitter), the perfect downtown co-working space now serving as my office: thank you so much for your support and laughter. And the distractions. And the beer. And the donuts. You are the smartest people I know, and it is a joy to work alongside you each day.

To those who organized and attended all the amazing conferences I've been fortunate enough to be involved with over these years: you have given me a lifetime's worth of unforgettable experiences. I am eternally grateful. I hope to see you all again soon.

To the Phoenix design community (Twitter hashtag: #phxdc): I was wrong. You *do* exist. And you're brilliant. Thank you—*so much*—for making Phoenix great.

Finally, to all of you who read the first edition of this book and are about the read the second: thank you for your support, for caring about your work, and for fighting the good fight. And for being patient. Writing is 90% procrastination and 10% swearing. Thanks for sticking around while I got through it.

Author Biography

Robert Hoekman, Jr, is a passionate and outspoken user experience strategist and a prolific writer who has written dozens of articles and has worked with MySpace, Seth Godin (Squidoo), Adobe, Automattic, United Airlines, and countless others. He gives in-house training sessions and has spoken at industry events all over the world, including An Event Apart, Voices That Matter, Web App Summit, SXSW, Future of Web Design, and many more.

Robert is the author of Designing the Moment (New Riders) (www.rhjr.net/s/dtm), a collection of 31 stories on design solutions from real projects and the principles used to solve them. He also coauthored Web Anatomy (New Riders) (www.rhjr.net/s/wa), which introduces "interaction design frameworks" as an essential part of an effective reuse strategy, with revered design researcher Jared Spool.

Robert is the founder of the user experience consultancy Miskeeto (www.miskeeto.com). Learn more about him at www.rhjr.net. He is @rhjr on Twitter (www.twitter.com/rhjr).

IEXPLORE.EXE - Entry Point Not Found

The procedure entry point InternetGetSecurityInfoByURLW could not be located in the dynamic link library WININET.dll.

OK

Fantastic. I knew it was something simple like that.

1

Defining the Obvious

- ▶ What Is 'the Obvious'?
- ▶ How Do You Design the Obvious?
- ▶ The Framework for Obvious Design

Years ago, after people with me at a dinner party began relating horror stories about the difficult experiences they had with the websites and applications they used every day, I attempted to explain what I do for a living. I carried on for a little while. I tend to ramble when I think I'm saying something important. I tried to communicate that my work is about making software usable and useful so that people can benefit from it without having to become expert computer users. It's about improving the experiences people have with technology. It's about making the complex clear. I stumbled around these ideas for a bit until eventually, in a moment of Zen, I said:

"It's about designing the obvious."

It's been a few years since I wrote the first edition of this book inspired by that fateful conversation. In that time, I've spoken at dozens of conferences all over the world, met and worked with tons of people, read an absurd amount of books and articles and studies, been involved in hundreds of hours worth of usability tests, and worked with dozens of clients on hundreds of design and strategy projects (and boy am I tired!). I've worked a lot. I've researched even more. I've had several more years to think about and do this work. And while the job of designing the obvious is essentially the same as it has always been, I've solidified my thinking on a few more ideas, and significantly revised my thinking on some others. Besides that, the web is now better and more powerful than ever before, and we have now seen the beginning of the revolution of mobile technology. Undeniably, it's time for a new edition.

Now, all of what I said to my dinner guests back then is still true. Good design comes from understanding what your product is meant to support so you know what to build, and more importantly, what not to build, and even more importantly, why to do it in the first place. It comes from knowing (or *inventing*) the best ways to implement each feature so they make sense to the people using them. It comes from having a strong understanding of the possibilities of Internet technologies. It comes from understanding people, and having the ability to create something that works with them rather than against them. Great application design comes from understanding the qualities that make great applications great.

But I've learned in these years that there's slightly more to designing the obvious than I could articulate at the time. And while I still can't take on *all* the products my dinner guests were losing arguments to back then, or the ones they're losing arguments to now, I can do this:

I can tell *you* how to make *your* products better in hopes that someday developers and users will happily coexist, and communication between these fighting parties will be successfully bridged by the one thing they have in common: the interface.

See, the web has exactly three layers.

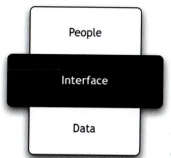

The web world is divided into three layers: people, data, and the interfaces that stand between them.

The first is the **people layer**. There's nothing in this layer but people. People, people, and more people. People who *have* information and things, people who *use* information and things, and people who *want more* information and things.

The third layer is the **data layer**. (I'll explain the second layer in a moment.) Everything in the virtual world that people need to know lives in the data layer: All the customer records, statistics, bookmarks, reference materials, finances, movie times, gas mileage, and popcorn cooking instructions live in the data layer.

The second layer is the one we deal with the most as web developers. It's the **interface layer**. The applications used to connect people with data are in the interface layer. Everything from Flickr to Amazon, from Google to Basecamp. These applications manage data and present it to us. They let us play around with it, churn it up, spit it out, translate it, decipher it, encode it, and sleep on it. The only difference between these applications is what kind of data is used and what people do with it.

Interfaces stand between people and their data, providing access to the data like a door from one room to another. But no application I've ever seen is as simple to use as a door.

It's time that changed. And that's what this book is about.

So let's get on with it.

▶ What Is 'the Obvious'?

In addition to designing software, I also, as you might guess, *use* software. And I, like many people (whether they realize it or not), tend to "hire" software the same way I would hire a person. I look for certain qualities, like a helpful nature, reliability, trustworthiness, and other things I'd expect to find in a good Boy Scout. Mostly, I look for software that can get work done in a smart and timely fashion so I can feel productive as a result of having hired the software—just what I'd want in a prospective employee. I look for characteristics that make me say, "Hey, you're swell. I'd like to work with you, take you under my wing, and invite you over for brunch. Come, join me in a game of Parcheesi."

Software, however, often interrupts me while I'm working, tells me I've made a mistake, refuses to help out in a useful way when I get stuck, spends a lot of time revealing things about how it works instead of simply telling me the job is done, and exhibits many other behaviors I find undesirable in employees. But usually I'm stuck with it. I can't find a way to live without the product because it's so valuable to my work, for whatever reason. I can't simply trade it in for something that may or may not be better, so I suffer through it. I yell at it, procrastinate dealing with it, and complain about it, but I live with it. This, of course, bugs me to no end.

These issues are not the result of an obvious design. An obvious design would let me get in, get what I need, and get out without spending any time at all thinking about how the software works or how to work with my data.

Every technology company should strive to design applications so intuitive that the people using them attribute their ability to use them effectively to pure common sense. The design should make things clear. The products should be simple to understand, easy to learn, well organized. Interface elements should be intuitive, streamlined, uniform.

That's what makes an obvious design.

Software shouldn't force users to understand how it works so they can learn to do things with it. It shouldn't make them wonder if something has gone wrong and all their changes are about to be lost. It shouldn't spend a lot of time and effort interrupting their work to tell them something is broken and there's nothing they can do about it but click OK. It's *not* OK.

The people using our software every day want to get what they need and move on. Usually, they're not like us. We're geeks. Normal people don't stare at desktop monitors and device screens all day because they enjoy it. They do it because they have to.

They put down their money and/or valuable time and make an investment in our applications. They have a reason for using the applications. They have goals. They have needs. They have expectations. And invariably, they have work to do.

We, the people who make the software, need to stop giving users excuses and start showing them results. We need to stop being accusatory and start being polite. We need to stop talking down to them. Our users should be able to walk away from our applications feeling empowered. Productive. Respected. Smart.

Fortunately, this is all possible. And no, it's not nearly as complicated as you might think. We just need to start *designing the obvious*.

At this point in Internet history, there are quite a few really great applications out there. Sure, they all have their own problems, but overall, many of them are swell. And we can learn from them. There are now countless examples of how applications can be made simple, effective, and most of all, *obvious*. Throughout this book, we'll look at the qualities that make applications like these so great, and discover how to create them in our own applications so our users can at last reach design bliss.

Blinksale makes it obvious how to perform the most common actions involved in creating an invoice, such as this one for, you know, writing this book.

Qualities of a great application

So what makes an application obvious?

When I sat down to write a list several years ago for the first edition of this book, it came very easily. Since that time, virtually every project I've worked on has strengthened my belief in that list. I've read countless studies and poured over an ocean's worth of site metrics. I've spent endless hours researching behavioral and social psychology and other social sciences. And in addition to being involved with the design of hundreds of applications, I've spent even more years now *using* web and mobile applications. Everything from slide creators to project management tools, from calendar applications to invoicing tools, from site builders to room planners—you name it, I've either helped design it or analyzed its usability and user experience, as a user and as a professional. Through it all, I am proud to say that this list has held up as my definitive list of qualities that make some products great and others miserable. One way or another, virtually every design problem I've seen a company come up with has tied back to one or more of these points.

That said, I have added two concepts to the list since writing it back in 2006— one that relates to *strategy*, the other to *persuasion*. They're concepts that should have always been there, but weren't. We'll discuss them in Chapters 2 and 7, respectively.

In the meantime, here's the list, including the two new additions.

A great web application, in my experience, has some or all of the following qualities:

- It is the product of intent. It has a clear purpose, a compelling benefit, straightforward usage, and a cohesive design that reflects the focus, passion, and purpose of the team that developed it.

- It conforms to the way users interact with the web, but focuses on the activity instead of a specific audience.

- It has only those features that are absolutely necessary for users to complete the activity the application is meant to support.

- It conforms to users' mental model of what it does.

- It helps users get started quickly so they can become intermediate users as soon as possible.

- It deliberately and ethically persuades users to take specific actions.

- It makes it easy to recover from mistakes and difficult to make them in the first place.

- It has uniformly designed interface elements, but leverages irregularity to create meaning and importance.

- It reduces clutter to a minimum.

Each of these qualities has been well documented as the result of human-computer–interaction studies, usability testing, and psychology studies. The interesting part is that these qualities usually go unnoticed. Why? Because good software makes itself invisible. It enables users to do what they need to do and gets its behind-the-scenes operations out of the way so they can do it well. That's what makes it obvious.

The good news is that the items in the preceding list are not only noticeable, if you know what to look for. They are also reproducible.

Yes, indeed. *You can design them.*

▶ How Do You Design the Obvious?

The answer to this question is pretty simple, actually. We already have a list of what makes designs obvious and effective. To define a plan of action for how to create obvious designs, we simply need to turn that list into a list of goals by restating each item as a call to action. It'll take the rest of this book to fully illustrate the following goals and how to accomplish them, but this section should give you a clear glimpse into what needs to be done, along with some details about where in this book we'll discuss each point.

Turn qualities into goals

The key to creating great web applications is to turn the list of qualities from the preceding section into a list of goals. In other words, our new mission should be to create software that does the following:

- **Reflects the intent–the focus, passion, and purpose–of the team that developed it.** Fragmented teams produce fragmented applications. Unified teams, however, produce the strongest brands in the world—brands we identify with, and that feel authentic and align with who we are. In Chapter 2, we'll look at the concepts of user experience vision and strategy, how they affect a user's experience, and how they can transform the way people within a company work together.

- **Supports the way users interact with the web, but focuses on the activity instead of a specific audience.** Understanding users is key to understanding how to approach application design, but as long as we have this understanding, it's best to ignore the demands of users and focus on the activity itself so we can create a feature set that makes sense for the product. In Chapter 3, we'll talk about how to understand users and why it's necessary to ignore their whims.

- **Has only those features that are absolutely necessary for users to complete the activity the application is meant to support.** Moving the "nice to have" features out of the "things to build right now" column is never easy, but it must be done. In Chapter 4, we'll talk about how to divide up the feature list and when to reevaluate nice-to-haves.

- **Conforms to users' mental model of what it does.** Allowing an application interface to reflect the inner workings of the program itself is a classic no-no in application design. We'll talk about the differences between implementation models and mental models in Chapter 5 and discuss ways to twist, contort, and mold your application into shape before you ever write a single line of code.

- **Helps users get started quickly so they can become intermediate users as soon as possible.** Once users understand how to work with it, the newbie stuff goes away so they can perform their regular operations with ease. Then it eases them into the advanced features. We'll talk about this in Chapter 6.

- **Deliberately and ethically persuades users to take specific actions.** It's not enough to deliver a usable application. It must also be designed to persuade users to take specific actions—to sign up, opt in, subscribe, edit, organize, manage, spread the word, and come back tomorrow. In Chapter 7, we'll look at the practical side of persuasion.

- **Makes it easy for users to recover from mistakes and difficult to make them in the first place.** Applications should avoid demeaning or interfering with the work of users in any way, instead offering polite interactions that keep things moving forward. Users have enough software issues to deal with—they don't need our modal dialog boxes interrupting their workflow, or error messages popping up to tell them they've screwed something up or that an application has failed in some way. This kind of negative feedback is just plain rude, and reduces a user's ability to explore an application. Software can become more polite, however, through the creation of *poka-yoke* (error-proofing) devices. We'll talk about these and more in Chapter 8.

■ **Has uniformly designed interface elements, but leverages irregularity to create meaning and importance.** Uniformity is core to good design, but knowing how to leverage irregularity is a little trickier. We'll explore this in Chapter 9.

■ **Reduces clutter to a minimum.** Finally, in Chapter 10, we'll examine the concepts of clarity and simplicity in web design, look at how to eliminate waste in the design process and in our interfaces, and put Just in Time design to work to iteratively create software that does its job well.

With this list of goals spelled out before you, the task of designing the obvious might seem much simpler than it did before. But, as you'd expect, it's much easier to *believe* you know how to do all these things than it is to actually do them. So the rest of this book is all about the things we need to know and do to make these goals a reality.

To get started, let me introduce you to what I affectionately call "The Framework for Obvious Design."

▶ The Framework for Obvious Design

The Framework for Obvious Design is like a 12-step program for people who produce web applications, except that there are no steps and the number of things to remember is much lower. In fact, there are only three parts.

Okay, so it's really more like a three-layer cake.

Each part of the framework is discussed in different contexts throughout this book. The framework isn't broken up into three major sections, each focusing on an individual piece, because it isn't that clear-cut. Each part ties itself up into every aspect of application design, so don't expect to read this section of the book while standing in the bookstore and walk out a genius. You really need to take the book home and read it all the way through.

That said, you may notice the three elements that make up the framework are, in fact, *pretty darn obvious*.

The three parts are, in their simplest form, as follows:

- Know What to Build

- Know What Makes It Great

- Know the Best Ways to Implement It

It doesn't take a rocket surgeon to realize that knowing these things will result in better products, but for some reason, it can take a long time to see the obvious. It took me about six years.

A key point to know about this framework is that it will still apply in the future, and there is no need to be an expert web geek to make good use of it. Not a jQuery guru? Doesn't matter. Don't know the difference between Web 2.0 and HTML5? No biggie. Don't know your Twitter from your Facebook? Fret not. The framework will carry you through. When all these things have come and gone, the framework will live on, guiding you down the path of web righteousness.

Also, it's important to understand that nothing in this book related to the *process* of application design is mandated in any way. This book is about the qualities of good web applications and how to create them. In support of achieving these qualities, I'll tell you about several process-related solutions that work for different people, but you shouldn't feel obligated to adhere to them, nor should you expect to learn about a specific development process in this book that outlines exactly how to create great web applications anytime, anyplace. Nothing works for everyone, no process works for every application, and no process in the world will tell you what makes applications great. Even the best development processes do not guarantee an application will be good. Use whichever methods are most effective for you. It's up to you to come up with the million-dollar ideas. I'm just here to tell you how to make them *work*.

To get things started, let's take a quick look at the three major elements of the Framework for Obvious Design.

Know what to build

Knowing what to build requires understanding the purpose of the application, the needs or desires of the people using it, and the product's scope.

With this knowledge, you can build the right tool for the job, whatever that job might be. An application that does a good job of filling a need will be desirable by potential users. Heck, it doesn't even have to fill a need. It could be aimed strictly at having some fun or providing a new approach to an old problem. Whatever the case, knowing the essential ingredients that will allow the application to do its job well will result in a design that is more obvious to users.

To start, the aim is to create an "elevator pitch." When you have 30 seconds to get the attention of your boss or a new client and present a new idea, you have to communicate the idea in a meaningful and attention-getting fashion, with very few words. From there, as long as the initial idea is clear and worth some extra attention, you can elaborate and talk about the target audience and feature set, and try to nail down the essence of the application and how it will work.

The knowledge of what to build, what not to build, and the underlying rationale for the application make up the *conceptual element* of the framework. The conceptual element creates desirability, because applications with a clear purpose that fill a void in an effective manner are always welcome.

Know what makes it great

You already know what makes web applications great because you read the list earlier in this chapter.

The list is by no means limited, however. If you discover something else that makes software really good, add it to your list. Just make sure it's a *quality* of the software and not a detail.

For example, drag-and-drop interactions cannot make a web application great. What makes it great is that the application offers real-time feedback based on user input. (In fact, maybe we should add that to the list now.)

iGoogle features drag-and-drop modules (called "Gadgets") that provide a real-time preview so you always know where the module will land when you let go of it.

These qualities may be hard to spot, so you have to look closely for them. When an application is designed badly, it tells you at every opportunity just how bad it is. But when it's good, you usually can't explain why it's good. You can't put your finger on it, but you know it when you see it.

All these qualities make up the *application element*. They help create a sustainable and positive user experience.

Know the best way to implement it

This part of the framework is the biggest variable. As we've all seen, the best way to do something usually changes over time.

At one point in history, for example, the best way to have a conversation with someone 100 miles away was to, well, walk there. Later, phones came into play (okay, *much* later). Now, it's as simple as typing a text message on a smartphone and waiting a moment for the recipient to reply.

Right now, jQuery and CSS 3 and HTML5 are all the rage, and they've enabled some clever developers out there to push web application interfaces further than ever before. Ten years ago, most of the things these technologies supported were impossible. Ten years from now, it will be a whole different story.

Regardless of what is the best way to implement a particular feature, these tools make up the *interaction element*, which enables the usability of an application and creates the *X-factor*. This is the part of the application with which people actually interact.

Throughout this book, I'll discuss ways to implement application elements in such a way that they make operations obvious and effective. I'll also provide some practical examples by showing you how to redesign several typical implementations of web interface elements so they are more meaningful, more helpful, and more effective.

2

Lead with Why, Follow with What

- ▶ Know Your Motivation
- ▶ Make Authentic Decisions

Recently, I sat down at a table of friends at a bar, and the one person I hadn't yet met asked, "What's your passion?"

It was a nice question. It's certainly easier to explain than my job title. "User experience strategist" just doesn't have the same ring of familiarity for people that, say, "firefighter" does.

"My passion," I responded, with far more eloquence than at my dinner party years ago, "is helping people empower themselves through technology by improving the quality of their experiences with it, whether on the web, on a mobile device, or in some other way."

I liked the question because she didn't ask what I did, but *why*. It cut straight to the source.

What you do is evidence of why you do it. Everything you do says something about you. Buying a moderately priced, used sedan says something different about you than buying a flashy red sports car. Store-brand lemonade says something different about you than gourmet, organic lemonade. A Saturday night at home with the dogs says something different than one spent at a downtown bar. People aren't random. They are the results of their own lives. You tell your story with every move and every decision. The books on your bookshelf, the rug on your floor, the food in your refrigerator, the car in your driveway, the shirt on your back—they all say something about you, your circumstances, the way you think, what you value, what you believe. People don't buy products. They buy their own identities. We are photographs of our own truths.

I want to help people empower themselves through technology, so I help companies create better applications. I write books and articles and speak at conferences for the same reason. If technology was my passion but I spent my days valeting cars for a living, that would say something about me as well. What you do is evidence of why you do it.

This applies to companies just as it does to people. Everything a company designs, builds, markets, and does says something about it. And the connection your customers make to your brand—your product, service, website, application—is largely based on how well they identify with it, and how well it aligns with who they are. *User experience strategy*, then, is important because it establishes the identity your customers will align themselves with.

User experience strategy is nothing more than a plan for how to achieve an end goal. But that goal is the arguably the most powerful thing a company can have. It's a vision for what kind of experience a company will attempt to create for its customers. It's a statement about how a company wants to be seen. It tells the company's story.

If you find this too esoteric, keep in mind that strategy also does something very practical. As stakeholders in the design and development of an application, strategy gives us direction. Knowing the Why behind a product, a company, or even a single feature, is crucial to making good decisions about it. It's crucial to ensuring that everything you do aligns with the larger product, the company, the vision.

I left a couple of important things out of the first edition of this book. This chapter is one of them. (The other is Chapter 7, about persuasion in design.) I didn't mean to. Strategy is not only a universal tenet for good application design, it's also first on the list. I just didn't know at the time that it was such a point of ambiguity for so many teams—for so many businesses. As it turns out, most companies suffer not from a lack of talent or skill or passion or ambition, but a lack of *vision*. And most of the time, this is the cause of all their other problems.

So let's talk about how to fix that.

▶ Know Your Motivation

First, to understand how strategy affects design, let's look at the symptoms of a weak design project:

- Decisions are made from the top down and executed from the bottom up.

- Different people have different ideas of what they should be working on.

- The primary ongoing goal is to *add* things to the product rather than *improve* it.

- Innovation is defined simply as anything the competition hasn't already done.

- Design initiatives are almost entirely driven by a reaction to customer feedback.

- No one on the team can clearly communicate the underlying motivation for design decisions.

- No one has considered how to measure the success of design decisions.

- Design decisions are neither justified nor validated—they're reactive and impulsive rather than deliberate and mindful.

Sound familiar? This is what happens when a design project lacks a user experience strategy—a clear and well-defined end goal for what the user experience should look like, why it should look that way, and how a team will achieve it—and it's typical. But more often than not, it's merely a symptom that the company *itself* lacks a clear strategy. And when a *company* lacks strategy, it can:

- Feel inauthentic to its audience

- Spend most of its time scrounging for ways to differentiate itself

- Disappoint customers along the way

- Fail to compete, stay relevant, or advance

- Fail to even stay in business

What most of the companies suffering from these problems have forgotten is why they got into their particular businesses in the first place. Even when the founders manage to keep their intentions pure for a while after the initial launch, at some point the obligation to shareholders and investors takes over, and rather than focus on a driving vision for a company and for each of its product offerings, the focus goes to whatever will produce the biggest bang for the buck. Short-term, this can of course work very well. Long-term, it leads to decisions that diminish a brand. That drive customers away. That fail to entice new ones. It leads to the constant creation and ineffective evolving of products that themselves lack strategy and have no larger strategy to fit into, resulting in entire brands that feel disjointed and disconnected from their customers, and that deliver displeasing user experiences.

When customers pull away, the allure decreases. When the allure decreases, they pull away even more. And on it goes. And the slide can happen very quickly.

Simon Sinek delivers his brilliant TED talk in May of 2010 on starting with Why.

In 2009, Simon Sinek wrote a best-selling business book called *Start with Why: How Great Leaders Inspire Everyone to Take Action* (Portfolio Hardcover) in which he states, "People don't buy what you do, they buy why you do it." He argues that by starting with Why rather than What when delivering a message to the world, organizations rally support and engage audiences. A brand fails when a company of vision becomes a company of symptoms.

In fact, this is often when a company calls me. As a user experience strategist, I help companies figure out their Why and how to make decisions that support it. I help them figure out what they believe and what they must deliver as a result. I help them become something their customers can align themselves with. I do this because you can't Know What to Build until you know *why* to build it.

When you start with Why, you get the right What.

What follows Why

We've all heard the classic axiom "form follows function." This gem has been the glue of countless projects for designers and architects and all kinds of other constraint-driven innovators.

The *form* is the thing that comes out of a process, whether industrial, digital, tangible, or conceptual. It's how the thing looks and feels and smells and tastes. And the *function* is the thing's purpose, whether emotional, practical, entertaining, or essential. The three words *form follows function* together explain the beauty of a world's worth of amazing objects and experiences. The phrase as a whole, however, is narrow. It casts no light on the belief or need or vision that gave birth to the function that the form is following.

If form follows function, what does function follow? Where does the function get decided?

The answer to this question is where most companies get into trouble. They can't always explain what justifies the function. Sometimes it's a function customers have said they want. Sometimes it's a whim to satisfy the CEO or marketing director. Sometimes it's nothing more than a shiny bauble that some developer got distracted by that has since morphed into a project.

A brand succeeds when What a company does is a result of Why it does it. It succeeds when it has a clear vision that is shared by everyone on the team. And when this is true for the company, it's true for the company's products. An application with a strong Why subsequently has a strong What. Yes, when it comes to design, form follows function. But when it comes to product ideation and development:

What follows Why.

When you start with What, you present a *thing*. When you start with Why, you present a *belief*.

And this is what strategy is all about.

I often ask people why their companies do what they do. Sometimes they answer by saying that the company does it *to make money*. I don't believe that. There are as many ways to make money as there are stars in the sky. Why choose this one particular thing over something else? Why did Tom Anderson and Chris DeWolfe get into social networking and start MySpace? Why did Larry Page and Sergey Brin get into the world of online search and start Google? If you're a business owner, why did *you* start the business *you* started?

I don't think you did it for the money. At least not *just* for the money. Something else drove you. Something about that particular field, that particular market, or that particular activity. What was it?

The answer to that question is what should be driving your design decisions. If it's not, you will one day become a company of symptoms. Without a higher purpose, you're just another business in a sea of competing businesses. With one, you're a brand on a mission.

User experience strategy is a big red target painted on the office wall where everyone can see it. It's a vision and a plan that unifies a team, justifies design decisions, and enables everyone within an organization to contribute to an application's future. It's a goal. It's a tangible thing you can all point to and say, "*There!* That's where we're going."

Say it with me, people:

"*What follows Why.*"

▶ Make Authentic Decisions

So how exactly does one devise a user experience strategy? By making sure your What supports your Why. By making decisions that support your motivation. By creating applications that support your belief.

In practice, there are five core activities involved in developing a user experience strategy, and they tend to happen in non-linear sort of way. While you can certainly inject burgeoning strategic thinking into current projects, you can't usually stop a project in its tracks while you step through a strategy overhaul one phase at a time. Hence, this isn't a list of steps so much as it is a list of activities sorted according to a preferred, but unlikely to ever actually happen that way, order.

And since the focus of this book isn't strategy but principles of application design, this is simply a high-level look at how to approach application strategy. It's only meant to be enough to get you started and inspire you to pursue more information on the subject.

Disclaimers aside, let's dive in.

Audit the user experience

I once had a client whose application suffered from severe strategic problems. (Actually, this is true for many of my clients.) It was losing customers by the second, and its most significant competitor was beating it to the punch, time after time, on compelling and much-needed innovations. The company, frankly, was having a bit of an identity crisis, and this was made abundantly clear by the fact that the company's homepage was a scrambled hodgepodge of content with an array of very disconnected purposes. An executive came to me to see how I could help. Specifically, the company was looking for a strategy for its marketing homepage—the homepage shown to visitors who had not yet signed up that was meant to convince those very people of the merits of joining the network.

When you're dealing with an existing application, the first essential activity is an **audit:** a thorough review and debriefing of an application to get familiar with the current state of things. You need to take the all-important step back, blur your eyes, and see what you previously could not. You need to build a big picture where previously there was none.

An audit is really just a solo debriefing to get yourself caught up so you know what the execs are talking about when they reference the Scratch-and-Sniff feature that has been a source of internal debate for the last six months. But it's also to form *hypercritical* first impressions (because, well, if you're running an audit, it means something has gone horribly wrong and the application may be fighting for its life). And performing an audit is really just a matter of paying close attention to those first impressions—enough that you can articulate them. Your job here is not to gather hard data (though you certainly can and should consider usage metrics as part of your inventory-taking), it's to give yourself a baseline understanding so you can drive the conversation forward.

Taking inventory with a cognitive walkthrough

To familiarize yourself with an application, start by taking inventory.

Taking inventory doesn't have to mean cracking open a spreadsheet application and painstakingly creating a categorized list of pages and issues. But it does mean taking a long stroll through all the various aspects of an application to see what's there and why so that you can start asking the hard questions. The idea, in other words, isn't to reverse-engineer your way to a comprehensive set of task-flow diagrams, but to familiarize yourself with an application when you're not already involved with it, to remind yourself of things you may have forgotten about when you are already involved, and to dig your way toward the center of the problem regardless.

What this really means, then, is performing a rather brutal version of a **cognitive walkthrough**, which is the process of assessing the set of current tasks that can be completed within an application, with the ultimate goal of compiling a list of potential issues.

These issues are not just usability issues, however. They are, more specifically, issues with the understandability, persuasiveness, explainability, flow, and scope of the application, and even its core value proposition. It's an assessment of all the things that can and will and do have an impact on a user's experience.

Evaluating the user experience

The goal of the audit is to come out the other side with a strong sense of the issues. The key word here is *strong*. If you've been part of the application's design and development team all along, critiquing an app objectively can be deceptively difficult. The more you think about and work on and use an application, the harder it becomes to see its shortcomings. But it must be done, and it must be done without mercy. The trick is to either approach it as if you're an outsider, or actually *be* one. The goal is to pick the thing apart so thoroughly and completely that you can pull out its bleeding heart, hold it up to the CTO, and ask how on Earth it got to be so damned *black*.

Reinventing a negative user experience requires a take-no-prisoners level of resolve. So, no matter how involved you've been, *be ruthless*. If you're only a little tough, the app will only improve a little bit. The tougher you are, the better the outcome.

My client's homepage presented a particularly heady case.

The content lacked focus. Virtually nothing on the page served to persuade users to become members. The navigation did little to illuminate what visitors could find on the site. Perhaps worst of all, the page featured a large ad that most of the site's visitors found annoying. And even registered members were required to visit the page—they weren't allowed to remain signed in after leaving the site.

Beyond these obvious problems, there were lots of little things. Weak copy. Hard-to-find entry points for signing in and signing up. These were the signs of a company that compromised too much, and that couldn't agree on how to handle the most important aspects of the design.

I wrote them *all* down. The tougher you are, the better the outcome.

Competitive analysis

It's also important to put an application into a larger context by considering how it measures up against its major competitors. This combined with your assessment of the app itself helps you shape the big picture that quite possibly no one else has and presumably everyone has been missing for quite some time.

A **competitive analysis** is an assessment of competing applications to see how yours compares in terms of features, scope, aesthetic, and other metrics. It's usually subjective, as it's pretty rare that you'll be able to get your dirty little fingers on actual usage stats for a competitor's app, but it can be very revealing.

A competitive analysis can reveal the differences between these two companies, and there are indeed differences.

Some of what you'll assess is entirely open to interpretation and judgment. If the competition has been open about the reach of its audience, you may have a number for comparison, but your competitor may also be an older and more mature company. You may be working in a long-established market with a lot of competing companies fighting for the same piece of the pie. You may be in a brand-new market and have only one competitor. It's vital to understand that you can't simply map numbers to numbers and expect useful answers. You have to see it for what it really means. Maybe it means you're new in town and have a hell of a fight ahead of you. Maybe it means you're in a position to grab some of the new customers in that market because you can operate more quickly. Maybe it means you're in bad shape and the little guys are creeping up on you. Maybe you'll learn you have less in common than you think.

What's important is that you inform yourself as much as possible so you can make a good guess. In the words of interaction designer Dan Saffer (in a 2007 session abstract), "The best designer is often the one who makes the best guesses."

That said, the notion of doing a competitive analysis also has more significant caveats. Namely, while it's certainly a good thing to know your competition, it can be inhibitive to know them too well, lest you get too focused on beating them one for one. As I discuss in Chapter 4, the goal is to avoid a feature war—to be better by being *different*—and it can be tough to resist the urge to start building out features simply because other companies already have them in place and you feel like you need them to stay competitive.

Get to know your competition, but not so you can copy them. Be better by being different.

Define the vision

While the ideas may already be flowing at this point of your strategy development work, it's far more important to establish a long-term user experience vision for the homepage than to dive into short-term designs (and let's face it, *most* digital design is short-term). Rather than throw some wireframes on the table and call it a day, the goal is to define a direction to follow for a long time to come. The goal is to start swinging the proverbial machete around to cut away the forest and open up a view of the sunlight on the other side.

Synthesize the story

To find that sunshine, I had to seek out the stakeholders and get their view of what were the site's strongest qualities and biggest problems and least-tapped areas of potential. I needed to find out where they thought it should be going. I had to uncover their Why. I had to ask:

"What is this company about?"

Only by answering that question could I then explain it to visitors through a focused homepage. The goal of this part of the strategy definition process is to find out where everyone who has a stake in the project thinks it should be headed and why. And this much is just a matter of asking a lot of questions and being a good listener. And taking good notes.

On my project, I collected bits and pieces from the company president, the product manager, the marketing director, and the lead designer, among others. We discussed what solutions the company had tried before, what succeeded, what didn't, why or why not, who or what might have gotten in the way, what the company's internal culture is like, what its external culture is like, and anything else that might contribute to helping me shape a wide view of the company. When I stopped hearing new ideas and insights, I knew I was done.

From there, it was a matter of turning all the input into something everyone agreed on.

I consolidated my notes, pulled out the recurring themes, and went through another round of phone calls during which I collaborated with all the same stakeholders to turn everything I'd heard and my own insights into a cohesive statement about the company's direction and, at a much lower level, the direction to be taken for this individual page.

Hang it on the wall

Once the vision is established, it's vital to make sure everyone understands it. Greatness doesn't happen in a vacuum. It takes a team. Make sure everyone involved knows the long-term goal and you'll have yourself a team full of people who can make decisions about how to get there. Yes, someone should continue directing the outcome—it's very easy for a car to veer into a ditch when no one's eye is on the road—but giving team members the autonomy to conjure up their own ideas and make decisions themselves can have the very positive effect of raising morale while inspiring great work.

The documentation of the user experience vision doesn't matter so much as the mindset. The culture. If the team knows why they're doing what they're doing, they'll do it better. If they know where they're headed, they'll get there faster and with better results. The documentation doesn't matter, the culture matters.

Every person on the team should be able to clearly describe the team's mission.

Write the rules

Next, start writing design criteria for the application. Design criteria are rules for a design—statements that express what the design must achieve so that decisions made about it can directly support the user experience vision.

For examples of design criteria, look no further than the table of contents of the book you now hold in your hands. The chapter titles themselves constitute a list of design criteria that is universally true for the design of effective applications.

- Lead with Why, Follow with What

- Ignore the User, Know the Situation

- Build Only What Is Absolutely Necessary

- Support the User's Mental Model

- Et cetera

And each chapter contains a set of top-level headings that form their own lists. The list for this chapter?

- Know Your Motivation

- Make Authentic Decisions

These are, of course, high-level criteria. Specific projects will have criteria specific to that project. For my client's homepage project, for example, the design criteria included:

- Make a promise

- Be persuasive

- Set clear expectations

- Make it mobile

(These criteria were accompanied by short annotations to explain their relevance and to prevent misinterpretations.)

These criteria are the rules for a design. They reflect the underlying vision, and they provide justification for all the decisions made about a design. If an idea can't be validated against the design criteria, it's the wrong idea.

Write design criteria for *everything*. Every product, every feature, and every screen. When you do this, the output reflects the input. The application that is built reflects the company that built it, and this time, it's a better company. It's a company on a mission.

What follows Why.

Plan the new design

The next activity is about **design thinking**—the brainstorming and ideation process of establishing what needs to be invented and what needs to be improved. It's also about planning what can be done now, in three months, six months, a year, and even further out. Here is where you shape the incremental evolution of an app over a long period of time by deciding what's urgent, what can wait, what *has* to wait, and when you can all start reaping the rewards of your hard work.

We couldn't rip out the marquee ad on my client's homepage—it was responsible for close to one-fifth of the company's revenue. To support the design criterion "Make it mobile," however, we decided to require that it be Adobe Flash–free. (While the mobile version of the site was seeing low traffic at the time, a dramatic spike in the smartphone and tablet market was about to change all that. Soon enough, a much higher percentage of users would be accessing the site via a mobile device. And as we all know, a couple of the biggest sellers don't support the Flash plug-in.)

We decided to allocate a large chunk of space on the page just for highlighting the benefits of joining the site to support the design criterion "Be persuasive." We could also show numbers that revealed the incredible amount of activity on the site at any given moment (more on persuasive elements like this in Chapter 7).

To satisfy our "Make a promise" criterion, we decided to decrease the amount of site content we exposed on the homepage and instead focus on making it really *relevant* content. We could, in other words, promise to give visitors something interesting and useful and compelling. (This would, of course, have to be delivered on throughout the rest of the site. Every design change affects the rest of the design.)

Finally, we plotted out how to make the content on the page more and more relevant over time as the company improved its recommendation system. Initially, we could show a more relevant ad. Later, we could recommend specific content. Later still, we could highlight the things the user would most likely want to know based on his prior activity.

Implement it

Depending on how you like to design, implementation can start with wireframes and prototypes or by going straight to code. Maybe you start with a sketch on a napkin and move through three other phases of iteration before you arrive at a final design. Maybe you start and finish in Photoshop. It doesn't matter.

What matters is that you constantly revisit the user experience strategy to ensure that the designs you create meet the design criteria and support the long-term vision. To justify your ideas. To validate your decisions.

Even if you're on the development end of things—laying down code, fixing bugs, and making the screen do magical things—this still stands. I know you have a lot to do. Add this to your list: be the last line of defense. Make sure everything you build supports the user experience vision. If it doesn't, you may be wasting your time.

Measure everything

Once a design has been fleshed out, built out, and launched, all that's left to do is measure its effectiveness.

Ideally, you'll have started establishing success metrics during the planning activity, but again, this isn't a linear process. They can be established and changed at any point.

Some of the things that can be measured include:

- Conversion rate

- Retention rate

- Active users within a certain time period, such as 30 days after registering

- Sharing activity (as on a social network)

- Participation

- Purchases

- Recurring activity

- And much, much more

There are also some very subjective metrics to measure, such as customer satisfaction rates and what percentage of people say something positive to others about your application. Unless these things can be answered within the app itself, you'll have to come up with some creative ways to determine their answers, but listening to what your customers *think* is essential to building good relationships with them. (That said, there are some caveats to listening to them too much. More on this in Chapter 3.)

Iterate

Finally, based on the outcome of whatever it is you decide to measure, you can (and should) start making adjustments in the design to improve upon those numbers. This can be difficult, because it's often very tempting to reinvent something when what it really needs is incremental improvement. Again, fall back on the strategy. Everything should be validated against the strategy. If an idea you have will truly help move things forward for your application, your users, and your business, it may be worth pursuing.

We'll talk more about improvement versus invention in Chapter 11, and more about the process of continuous improvement in Chapter 3.

Having vision

The idea of having vision is a recurring theme in this book. Most of what we'll talk about with respect to the principles of application design ties back to the importance of cohesive strategic thinking.

I used to focus on interaction design. Eventually, I realized that helping my clients nail down the reasons for doing what they did was the key to successful projects. Design without purpose is entertainment. Design without constraints is decoration. I shifted my focus to strategy.

It's vital to know your motivation for an application. For a feature addition. For your place in your customers' lives. For the business as a whole. Again, people don't buy products, they buy their own identities. What you do is evidence of why you do it. Have a fundamental belief. Customers will latch onto it, and everyone on your team will be able to point at the same goal line and work toward achieving it.

What follows Why.

3

Ignore the User,
Know the Situation

▶ Solve for the Situation

▶ Understand How Users Think They Do Things

▶ Understand How Users Actually Do Things

▶ Find Out the Truth

▶ Write Use Cases

Whether or not you want to believe it, the vast majority of software projects fail. They fail to live up to customers' expectations, fail to sufficiently support the activities they were conceived to make easier, and fail to gain the ever-elusive customer loyalty earned by companies like Apple, Google, and Amazon.

Many factors can be blamed for the ultimate failure of a product, but they tend to fall into the same few camps of thought. Sometimes a product fails because it doesn't stand up against the competition. Sometimes it's because the market isn't ready for your product. And sometimes it's because users just don't get what you were trying to do.

Of course, none of these complaints are the *real* reason. Sometimes the failure of a product doesn't seem to make any sense at all. Sometimes your product has all the same features as the other guy's product—and then some—and it still fails to capture the market the way its competitors have. Sometimes users understand completely what the tool is supposed to do but choose another one anyway. You ask yourself over and over, Why? Why can't my product do every bit as well as my competitor's?

There is no single answer. But some of them go like this:

- Typically, users latch onto the first website or tool they find that they can tolerate, and they stick to it. Most of the time users spend on the web isn't devoted to visiting new sites and discovering new things. Rather, users go to the same sites over and over. And you haven't given them a good enough reason to switch.

- Your product isn't better than the competition's just because you crammed more features into it (more about this in Chapter 4). Your long list of features may make for good marketing material, but it also adds up to complicated software that confuses and frustrates users. Most users never become experts who benefit from the more advanced features. The majority of users, in fact, become intermediate-level users quickly, and stay at that level as long as they use the product. I'll discuss this point further in Chapter 6.

- The difficulty of accomplishing tasks in your application means that users don't stick around to fight their way through it, and they don't bother coming back.

Whatever the reason (and there are plenty more to go around), the most important lesson to learn is that you need to know—from the very beginning, and throughout your project—*what to build, and why*. With that knowledge, you can overcome potential causes for failure and build an application that serves and benefits its users effectively.

Aside from the two new chapters in this edition of the book, this chapter is practically brand new as well, as my thinking on this aspect of application design has changed significantly in the years since writing the first edition. Here, we'll look at the ins and outs of some common methods for researching your users, and about why to then *ignore* your users and instead design for a situation.

To start, let's look at the notion of putting users at the center of the design process.

Designing for the User

In his revered book *The Inmates Are Running the Asylum* (Sams, 2004), Alan Cooper argues that a great way to keep the goals of your users in mind is to create a **persona** to describe each type of user. A persona is a fictitious, archetypal user profile based on research of actual users—a fake person based on the insights gained from interviewing and observing the real people who use or are likely to use your application. Each persona description document has a name, photo, and some personal details that bring him or her to life, and is focused on goals and activities rather than demographics. The idea is that attaching a name and face to the very flexible notion of a user helps lock down who the user really is, making him less open to interpretation when it comes time to decide whether or not your real customers will be able to decipher how the Data-Juicer application works.

Personas are also meant to help those involved with a project realize that the person on the other side of the screen is not made of rubber, and cannot be bent at random to fit arbitrary ideas of what a user can handle and will find useful. Programmers and managers alike are forced to look Molly from Sales in the proverbial eye and consider whether or not she'll really understand how a button labeled *Publish* translates to pushing her unfinished content to the intranet where the whole company can see it.

A persona description can be as short as a single paragraph or as long as, um, two or three paragraphs. The important part is that it describes a fictitious user who represents the real people who will be using your product, how savvy they are, how and why they'll be using the product, and so on, topped off with a couple of personal details, a name, and a photo, to bring the person to life, as it were.

The goal is to narrow your list of user types down to three or four and create a persona description (a document) for each of them. (Compiling too many persona descriptions, in fact, is counterproductive, because you end up trying to please everyone, which is not usually possible.) One in particular should serve as your primary persona—the one that absolutely must be satisfied for your product to be a success. Cooper recommends keeping these persona descriptions in front of everyone involved, all the time, throughout your design and development process. Everyone on the development team should know the users—let's call them Greg, Anna, and Mary—well enough to know exactly how they're likely to respond to the different aspects of the product.

For example, if you're designing a stock photography website, one of your personas might be described like this:

Greg is a 26-year-old print designer from San Jose, California. He has extensive experience with tools like Adobe Photoshop and Illustrator. He has very little experience designing for the web, but has been picking up more and more web projects in recent weeks and would like to expand his skills. However, he has to fight through his hectic schedule to make any headway. His design work, which often includes ads for trade magazines and brochures, has won several awards, and he is comfortable using stock photography sites, particularly Getty Images, where he frequently purchases high-resolution photographs. His No. 1 pet peeve with such stock photography sites is the time it takes to wade through thousands of images to find exactly what he needs.

This persona is Greg the Print Designer.

This simple description of the fictitious user Greg reveals several key points: he is comfortable with computers, he wants to focus more on web design, his time is limited, and he needs high-quality images. Despite being relatively new to web design, he'll be taking on web projects more and more, and he would love to have a one-stop shop online for all the images he needs. Greg could be a loyal, frequent customer if you design something that works well for him.

Pleasing Greg is critical to the success of your stock photography site.

To address his needs, you can do several things in the interface. First, you can point out which images, or which versions of an image, are suitable for the web. You can also provide links to relevant supporting material on the site to help him learn—for example, articles about the differences between designing for print versus the web.

Next, you can create a way for Greg to save the searches he performs, and a way to store groups of images so he can quickly access personalized categories of images and more easily find the ones he likes. This will save Greg huge amounts of time in the long run. When he first begins to use the site, he'll have to wade through images as he does on other stock sites, but each time he does so, he can add the images he likes to his libraries, even if he doesn't use them right away. The more he uses the site, the larger these libraries of images will grow, and the quicker he'll be able to find images he likes.

These few features will help Greg a lot, and the simple act of writing out a description of who he is has helped you take a big leap toward designing an effective application.

But one part of the feature set is still a concern: the first several times Greg uses the site, he still has to wade through tons of images, just as he would on any other site, and it will be difficult for him to see the benefit of having a personal library. Greg is already using other stock photography sites, and he may be hesitant to start digging through a new one. You need to give him a good reason to switch, and make the shift immediately beneficial. This issue might have never surfaced if you hadn't got to know Greg.

Now that you know him, you know just how to handle it: you can offer him ten free images in the first month, and guide him toward adding images to his library during each of his first few visits. (I'll talk about how to get people up to speed with an application in Chapter 6.) While browsing for his ten free images, he'll start creating custom libraries and adding images to them, and by the time he's used all his free photos, he'll have built up a small arsenal that he can use in the future. Now you've given Greg a reason to visit, a way to personalize what he sees on repeat visits, and a reason to keep him coming back.

Greg's happy. You're happy.

As you can see, having a persona like Greg by your side, so to speak, during the design process can be really helpful when you're starting to narrow down the feature list for an application. You know Greg, you know what his goals are as a designer, and as a result, you *Know What To Build.* You can refer back to the persona description again and again to keep yourself in check when considering new features.

Greg is not real, of course, but he enables you to leverage what you know about your real users as a result of personifying them through Greg, so you have a better idea of what to leave in, what to leave out, when to walk away, and when to run.

The upside, in theory

Personas are a vital part of **user-centered design** (UCD), a widely popular approach to design that aims to help designers better understand the needs and wishes of users so that interactive systems can better help them meet those goals.

The essence of UCD is to try to break down the wall that exists between our users and us. As a metaphor, consider a conversation between a developer and a user. The developer explains how and why something happens, and the user nods his head and says, "I don't care how it happened, or why—I just want to know it's fixed so I can move on with my life."

Developers tend to want to put up dialog boxes and error messages and all sorts of intrusive widgets that rudely reveal all the fanciness going on behind the scenes, but users don't care. They only want to know the thing is working so they can accomplish their goals. A user's goals live outside the application. Their goals are personal. Very few users have a goal of understanding how PeopleSoft works. That goal is usually encapsulated by a larger goal. Perhaps Molly wants to earn a promotion at work and thinks that understanding

PeopleSoft better will enable her to be more productive. The application itself is not a goal at all—it's an obstacle between Molly and her goal.

Acknowledging that the user's goals have nothing to do with your web application allows you to design something that pays more attention to the user's real needs. Thus, UCD involves performing thorough user research, developing personas through which to gauge how well a design holds up, and designing something that works for the target users, in the context in which they use the application. UCD means listening to users, getting to the truth of what they want, and creating applications from a more informed perspective.

The reality

A user-centered approach can be very effective, and it's one that is used effectively by many successful interaction designers. Personas can be fantastic to rely on, for example, when the application being designed is intended for a niche audience—it's relatively straightforward work to establish a core set of users when the user base is fairly small. Personas are also brilliant tools for building empathy. On teams where some people are simply too far removed from an application's real users to understand their needs, and are therefore prone to inject personal bias into design decisions, personas can work wonders. Persona descriptions can help everyone from developers to executives understand that the people on the other side of the wallets being used to pay their salaries do not necessarily share their passion for bad design. (A faster solution: tie these people to chairs in a conference room and force them to watch usability test sessions. If that doesn't cure them, go find another job.)

However, when your application's audience spans a wide array of user types (as we'll discuss in the next section), designing with a narrow set of persona descriptions in mind could actually prevent you from achieving the results you're after by alienating audiences not part of the persona pool.

But more specific than this, several things have always bothered me about persona descriptions. First, they almost always include personal details meant to bring the fictitious, albeit research-based, user to life—something to make the user real to the people relying on these persona descriptions. For example, Todd Zaki Warfel, interaction designer and author of *Prototyping: A Practitioner's Guide* (Rosenfeld Media, 2009), offered this example in a presentation titled "Data-Driven Design Research Personas":

> *Becky moved to Boston three years ago to work for a small law firm. With her recent promotion, she's ready to purchase her first home.*
>
> *Living in the city, a Vespa is her primary mode of transportation. On rainy days, or in winter, she commutes into work on the subway.*

It's just a couple of sentences, but details like this can be more distracting than insightful. For starters, these details can't contribute directly to design decisions—they don't translate into features, or even into more subjective elements such as the tone of a site's copy. Because of this, they're immeasurable. There's no way to check back in with a fictitious user to see if the application that was launched felt in line with Becky's Vespa-riding lifestyle. The inclusion of these details in persona descriptions makes me think, "Frankly, Becky, I don't care who you *are*. I care what you're *doing*."

Only a couple of the faux factoids offered in the typical persona description actually *do* contribute directly to design decisions: for example, her job/role and her requirements to complete the activity (often expressed in terms of the user's current challenges). Most of the other details—name, age, location, beliefs, life and career goals, and so on—are demographic factors, which are more pertinent to marketers than to application designers (more on this in a moment).

Finally, personal details, strangely, can cause designers to feel incapable of confidently making decisions of behalf of their users, at least without then *validating* those decisions in various ways, whether by going back to the users originally researched, through usability tests, or by other methods. I'm not suggesting we stop validating design decisions, but we are far more *like* our users than *un*like them, at least in terms of our basic hopes for a productive user experience.

Our users are human beings, after all. We're designing for different *people*, not a different *species*. While some designers condemn the idea of generalizing about audience behaviors and needs, it is not only possible but extremely *useful* to see commonalities among our users, and to recognize patterns. (If it weren't, the psychology profession would be in a world of trouble.) Odds are, you aren't the only person on the planet who loves corn chips on roast beef sandwiches, nor are you the only person who thinks it's insane that scissors come in packages that require scissors to open. But what's the first design criterion to appear in virtually every design project in recent tech history?

"It must be dead simple."

As if this is some sort of revelation.

Beginning users will want it to be simple so that they can understand how to use it. Expert users will want it to be simple because they have other things to do and just want to get this out of the way. Of course it needs to be simple! (More correctly, it needs to be *clear*. Simplicity is not always possible. Clarity is.)

Persona descriptions, in other words, are simply too broad. Several aspects of them are more prone to throw you off the track than put you on it.

Furthermore, personas are meant to be used in conjunction with *scenarios*, which are essentially short stories about how a persona might interact with the system designed for him. And it's at this point that the practicality of using personas starts to become a little, well, *fuzzy*.

I, for one, am no character actor. I can't easily pretend to be someone else—not in any realistic way. And I can't safely pretend to know how I, as this other person, would handle the interactions laid out before me as a shiny, new application, or whether or not the application would even be interesting or relevant to me.

When you start imagining how a fictitious character would respond to a hypothetical situation using an imaginary interface, it's probably time to put down your little plastic army men and crack open the playbook.

We can do the research, get to know our users on a personal level, and dream up something we think will work very well for our intended users, but time spent on fiction will eventually begin to interfere with reality. When the fuzzy starts to get too fuzzy, it's time to try something else.

So let's look at another approach. A very different one.

Designing for the Activity

To understand the notion of designing for the activity, there's something else you should understand about people. And it's a fact that really changes things.

You ready?

People adapt to technology.

I know—it's surprising. But think about your average day. You wake up to a digital alarm clock, use the remote control to turn on the television, hit the start button on the coffeemaker, push another little button to open the garage door, get in your car and fidget with the stereo while plugging in your Apple iPod, and drive to work glancing at the speedometer, gas gauge, and stereo controls the whole time. Then you get to work and pop on to your computer, where you crank out email, code, web pages, whatever, until it's time to go home. Once there, you set the DVR to record your favorite show while you make dinner (on a stove full of timers and heat settings, mind you) by following along a cooking video on your Apple iPad, simultaneously answering your iPhone so your spouse can tell you he is running late.

You've adapted nicely to all these things. You may have had to read a manual or two along the way, but you figured them out at some point, got them up and running, and now, with any luck, you don't even have to think about how these things work.

What this tells us is that it's possible to design interfaces that support the needs of our users without knowing anything about their life stories and dreams and ambitions and other things movies are made of.

Sure, having a strong understanding of some target users can help you see more easily what features and functionality might really help them. But thorough user research is time-consuming and expensive. In fact, of all the projects I've personally been involved with, very few allowed a long enough time line that user research could be done *at all*. Most projects are quick, dirty, and painful. Entire applications are often designed and built in six weeks rather than six months, and believe me, six weeks is not enough time for a deep dive into your audience's touchy-feely side. You're usually far too busy cranking out wireframes and prototypes. So, while it's nice to have the option of getting up close and personal with users, it's not an option very often. Time constraints, budgets, lack of interest, and many other factors get in the way. And even when it *is* an option, a common tendency is to listen only to the loudest users, which can result, contrarily, in products that are *more* difficult for everyone else to use.

To remedy this, we need to be able to trust ourselves to design good applications without being able to get friendly with our users. Here, renowned user-experience master Donald Norman offers a solution. It's called **Activity-Centered Design** (ACD).

Norman's article "Human-Centered Design Considered Harmful" (**www.jnd. org/dn.mss/human-centered.html**) points out that many technologies and products have become great not as a result of a deep understanding of users, but rather because of a "deep understanding of the activities that were to be performed." He cites everything from clocks to musical instruments as examples of products designed only through an understanding of the activities they were meant to support. He states the following:

> *One concern is that the focus upon individual people (or groups) might improve things for them at the cost of making it worse for others. The more something is tailored for the particular likes, dislikes, skills, and needs of a particular target population, the less likely it will be appropriate for others.*

His insight is both fascinating and true. Many applications have been designed to accommodate niche markets with specific needs, and while many of them are quite successful in their respective markets, a product is often more successful when driven by an authoritative, take-charge designer who almost completely ignores its specific users. And this phenomenon extends well beyond the web world. In the same article Norman states the following:

> *Sometimes what is needed is a design dictator who says, "Ignore what users say: I know what's best for them."*
>
> *The case of Apple Computer is illustrative. Apple's products have long been admired for ease of use. Nonetheless, Apple replaced its well-known, well-respected human interface design team with a single, authoritative (dictatorial) leader. Did usability suffer? On the contrary: its new products are considered prototypes of great design.*

Norman's article doesn't offer much insight about how to gain such a rich understanding of an individual activity, but it does illustrate very well that one does not need a through knowledge of users to design products that work for them.

It's easy to see how the same conclusions can be drawn from understanding the *activity* of searching for and purchasing stock photography online, the example in my discussion of user-centered design. Anyone who has used online stock images knows it's cumbersome at best to troll through the millions of images on any one site, and some creative thinking could very easily have produced the same feature list as what we extrapolated from the Greg persona.

Activity-Centered Design can be effective from the beginning, as the team starts with a construct—an activity—that the application must support. The team can then focus its efforts on the more practical aspects of design by breaking down the activity into a collection of tasks. Tasks are tangible. You can design ways to complete them without knowing anything about your users. Norman continues (in his second article on the ACD, at www.jnd.org/dn.mss/hcd_harmful_a_clari.html):

> *Tasks are situations with a single, well-specified goal, such as "respond to this email." Activities are larger groupings, comprised of multiple tasks that fit together, such as "get caught up on the day's correspondence," which means reading email, responding, looking up information, sometimes to copy and paste into emails, checking calendars, and other associated, related tasks.*

Not everyone has the vision and design chops of Apple's Steve Jobs or Jonathan Ive, but regardless, understanding the activity you're designing to support can lead to creating products that work well not only for a niche audience, but also the public at large.

Solve for the Situation

Still, while Donald Norman's case for ACD may seem strong and well-considered, arguing for it in design circles can make you appear nuts. Yes, *nuts*. How is it possible, other designers will ask, to design something for your users when you don't *know* your users?

When I wrote the first edition of this book, I believed strongly in Activity-Centered Design, so much so that I argued endlessly for it in conversations with other designers, with clients, and in my conference presentations. I could talk about ACD all day long, with anyone willing to listen, and I launched into epic riffs about it virtually every time someone dared mention the word *persona* in my presence. This went on for, oh, four years. All the while, despite the fact that ACD seemed to solve everything I disliked about personas, a few things about it bothered me. And they were like little cracks in a dam I was constantly trying to fortify with chewing gum. And as time passed, the cracks got worse. As cracks do.

Then one day, I couldn't stave it off any longer. The fact is, I was wrong. Where user-centered design is too broad, Activity-Centered Design is too narrow. Where UCD looks at too much of a person, ACD looks at too little.

To explain why, I need to wax philosophic for a moment.

The persona descriptions of UCD include details that aren't actionable and can be a distraction. But the narrow focus of ACD swings the pendulum too far the other way by discounting the circumstances that comprise the user's need for your application, and your application's role in his life at the moment it comes into play.

In his bestselling book *Blink* (Back Bay Books, 2007), Malcolm Gladwell illustrates that human behavior can be motivated more by situational factors than by who an individual is in general. This is an expanded look at what social psychologists refer to as the **fundamental attribution error**. Also called *correspondence bias*, the fundamental attribution error is the label given to the human tendency to over-value personality as an explanation for behavior and to undervalue situational factors. To paraphrase the Wikipedia entry, we tend to attribute freely chosen behaviors to a person's disposition, and chance-directed behaviors to the situation the person is in. That much seems perfectly rational and fair. The problem is that this occurs even when a behavior that appears to have been freely chosen was in fact spurred by situational factors, and when a behavior that appears to have been situational was in fact freely chosen.

When we look at the whole user to understand his needs, we give too much credit to his disposition and not enough credit to his situation. In truth, the commonalities between our users aren't in their lifestyles or backstories or personal details, but in their current and very transient circumstances. Likewise, when we look only at the user's actions as they relate to a specific activity, we discount the situational factors driving his behavior. In truth, activities aren't performed in a vacuum. They are motivated by the who, what, when, where, and why of a given situation. The circumstances are the unifier. Situation is king.

It isn't a type of person who uses an application, it's a person in a type of situation. Five completely different types of people can be in the same situation. They can even be in it *together*. Imagine five librarians. One is 62 years old, another 34. One is a married mother of two, another is a single 20-something working on his doctorate. One is from New York, another Kentucky. One plays Texas Hold 'Em, another Dungeons and Dragons. These five people can be completely different from each other and still have the same requirements for an application you're designing because they're in a shared situation—the situation of being a librarian, helping patrons do research and renew items and connect to the Wi-Fi network and download e-books. What's common between them are not their lives, but their situations. Only in the context of the library are the who, what, when, where, and why the same for all five people; but because they share these circumstances while doing their jobs, the same application can work for all five.

The applications we design are solutions to problems. Problems are situational. People are not. People are much more than the sum of the applications they use. Most of what is knowable about them is irrelevant to the design process. We don't need to be their best friends, we need to help them do things better. We don't need a holistic view of the lives they lead, but a situational view of the problems they face.

When Donald Norman points to the disbanding of Apple's human interface design team as evidence that designers at Apple focus only on activities, he takes too narrow a view. The iPod is not a success because it does a better job of supporting the activity of listening to music on the go, but because it does a better job of supporting the situations people are in when they use it. Lots of people thought Apple was nuts for releasing a player so light on features when the market was already flooded with more robust options. What most overlooked was the difficulty of using those more robust options. A feature-light player worked better in the situations it was designed for—jogging, taking the train to work, washing dishes, driving, walking the dogs, and being interrupted (when, after all, it has to be "dead simple" to stop the music). That big, white scroll wheel with the single center button was like magic compared with the tiny buttons and menus that riddled other players. At last, MP3 players were suddenly easy to use when the last thing you had a free brain cell for was figuring out how to use your MP3 player. Many people who only read about the first-generation iPod thought it was a terrible idea. The people who *used* it thought it was brilliant.

"Frankly, Becky, I don't care who you *are*. I care what you're *doing*."

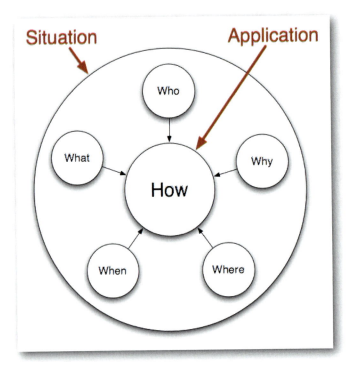

Application design starts where situations can be aided by software. It isn't user-centered, nor is it activity-centered. It's *situation*-centered. And if situations are comprised of who, what, when, where, and why, then applications are the *how*. The circumstances of the situation belong to the user. The *how* is where designers come in. It's what they can address. It's how they contribute. It's how they affect the world.

Self-design explained

One reason the notion of situation-centered design is important is that it explains another notion of design—a much-debated notion—known as **self-design**.

Self-design is what user-experience professionals call the act of designing an application referencing only yourself or your own team, as opposed to external users, as the basis for design decisions. But trying to find a designer who thinks self-design is a good idea is like trying to find a chicken in a fox-house. (That's a thing, right?) Most web professionals dismiss it as amateurish and naive. But there are instances of it working well.

For example, the designers at 37signals have seen tremendous success despite claiming to design their products entirely for themselves. (37signals is the company responsible for the wildly popular web applications Basecamp, Backpack, Highrise, and others.) This has never been easy for user-centered design advocates to explain. "How is this possible? Are they just pretending? Aren't they *really* designing for users in the end?" I don't think so. But I'm also unconvinced that calling what they do "self-design" is accurate.

In the case of Basecamp, a project management tool and the first commercial application launched by the small company, the team recognized that traditional project management software, which focused on organization and structure and planning, wasn't working for them. They believed they needed a system that focused on communication and collaboration. So they built one that featured tools to support those needs, such as a message board, a file manager, a to-do-list, and an activity dashboard.

Basecamp steers away from charts and graphs in favor of communication in plain English

They may not have designed Basecamp with outside users in mind, but they also didn't focus on themselves as their user base—at least not in the way that a user-centered designer would have them do. What they did was design something for the situation they were all in. They were a small team. They were juggling projects. Their communications were all over the place. They were disorganized. They needed to get out in front of their work.

Sounds like a lot of small teams I know. Like, *most* of them.

The founders of 37signals didn't design Basecamp to support *who they are*, they designed to support *what they were doing*. They solved for a situation—one that, it turns out, a boatload of other teams face every single day.

"Self-design" sounds bad. But if you are indeed a person who faces the very situation you're designing an application to address, it's more like *first-person* design, akin to telling a story using first-person narrative. If you are one of the people who can and will gain from the application—if you would pay for it, use it, and benefit from it even if you were not involved in its design—use that fact to your advantage. Research the situation from the inside out. You are part of your audience. Don't be ashamed of it. Self-design can be sel*fless*.

Interestingly, this fact opens up another possibility.

Situational immersion

The notion of self-design can be a powerful temptress—what better person to design for than *you*?—but don't fool yourself. If you're not really part of the target audience, your biases don't count.

Now, disclaimers aside, nothing says you can't temporarily *become* part of the audience in the interest of research. When you design to address a situational need, it becomes possible to do research from the inside—by *immersing your-self in the situation*. It's a line that must be treaded carefully—self-design versus designing from a first-person point of view—but walking a mile in your users' shoes can earn you insights you simply can't get any other way. And a vast range of situations can be recreated or otherwise constructed exactly for that purpose. While it's unlikely you'll be able to transform yourself into a foodie if your most frequent dinner guest is a guy named Swanson, there are plenty of situations you can research through direct participation.

Situational immersion is what Morgan Spurlock did in his docudrama *Super Size Me* and his television series *30 Days*, in which he put himself into various situations and reported on them from the inside, as an active participant, facing all the same challenges as someone who really faces that situation (albeit temporarily, like a tourist). For this, he was named one of the top ten "Best Journalists in the World" by *Time* magazine, and *Super Size Me* was an Academy Award nominee for Best Documentary feature film. All you have to do is apply the approach to the job of application design.

Imagine, for example, that you're designing a mobile application that helps people find and choose nearby restaurants—a simple, straightforward solution to a common problem. The personal details found in personas would be superfluous. Perhaps even just plain weird. (How does knowing that you went to school at Georgia Tech affect how you'll use your smartphone to find a restaurant?) But situation research would be ideal. To get an inside look at the specifics of the problem, you decide on a *situational immersion* approach. You spend a Saturday night in a part of town you're not usually in and avoid eating until you're just about to pass out from starvation. Then you grab your phone. Go!

"Let's see—what restaurants are nearby? Okay, there are seven places within a few blocks of here. Two are fast food. That's out. Two are Chinese take-out. That could work. One is pizza. Not in the mood. Two are bar-and-grill joints. You know, a cheeseburger would rock my world right about now. Are these places still serving food at 11:17 p.m. on a Tuesday? Are they expensive? Is one better than the other? Ratings. I need ratings and reviews. Okay, found some reviews. LawnGnome264 says the wait staff is nice and the food is good. Is LawnGnome264 a reliable source? Leap of faith, man. Leap of faith. Four and a half stars on average. Good enough for me. So, do I call for directions or can I get a map up in here?"

What we can learn from that experience is that our app needs to answer the following questions:

- What restaurants are nearby enough to get to in a few minutes using your current transportation option (car, taxi, bike, on foot)?

- Which of those restaurants are open right now?

- Which of them have food that sounds desirable at this moment?

- Which of them are in line with how much money you're willing to spend?

- Which of the restaurants have enough positive reviews to make me believe they're a good choice?

- How do I get there?

The answers to these questions easily translate into a solid feature list. Simply by immersing yourself in the situation, you can glean enough insights to cover the basics, and even some of the subtler details.

Research options

That said, you can certainly gain some other insights by talking to and observing *other* people who have been in the situation. When you were in need of a cheeseburger at near midnight, there were certain factors that were true for you that may not have been true for others. Let's say you went to a place that accepted credit cards and you had your debit card handy. No problem. But let's say someone else in that situation discovered that there was a local dive nearby with killer taquitos, but it didn't take credit cards, and he wasn't carrying any cash. Suddenly, he needed to know something else: the location of the nearest ATM.

Situation research can be done three ways.

- Observation

- Immersion

- All of the above

It will be best in most cases to do both observation and immersion. If, however, you're on a tight budget and have no access to the application's end users (and this happens *a lot*), then immersion is a solid approach. It's a cheap, legitimate, and often *fast* research option through which you can glean tremendous insight.

Situation-centered design enables you to take whichever research approach works best for you without having to get into a religious war about which way is better. Want to observe and interview people and create a set of personas? Go for it. Want to immerse yourself in the situation and then design from an insider's perspective? Assuming it's possible, then do that. It doesn't matter. No need to get into an argument about it—when you focus on the situation, either approach will work.

▶ Understand How Users Think They Do Things

Regardless of which approach you take, the research you do on a project will be pivotal to its outcome. It's essential not just that you research the situation you're designing for, but that you do it the right way, and that you have the wisdom to know when and how to read between the lines.

People, it turns out, aren't as truthful as you might think. In fact, we are notoriously bad at being honest. With regard to how we *think* we act and how we *actually* act, we are born liars.

I once heard an interesting story that did a nice job of revealing the differences. The story was about a new sandwich from a fast-food restaurant that wanted to launch a low-carb version of the their best-selling sandwich.

Before launching the product, the marketers for the restaurant chain asked a bunch of people if they would find the low-carb sandwich appealing. Resoundingly, people said they would indeed love to take their usual trip to the establishment and order something they know is good for them and their families. The marketers knew they were on to something. So they whipped up a plan, sent the recipe-makers into action, and released the sandwich, sure that their hours of hard work would pay off and earn the company big dividends.

Reality kicked in a short while later. The sandwich failed miserably and quickly disappeared from the menu.

Why, you ask?

People often don't do what they think they would do. They don't act the way they think they would act. We can talk for hours about we would respond in any given situation, but who knows what will happen when the hypothetical becomes real. The sandwich failed to live up to its promise because the promise was based on meaningless conversations with people who thought they would do the smart, responsible thing and make the healthy choice.

The marketers, I'm sure, didn't mean to have meaningless conversations. It's more likely that they asked leading questions such as, "Would you choose to eat the healthier version when given the choice?" It's a question designed to make the person who says "No, I wouldn't" feel like an idiot for doing so. It's a question designed to get a "Yes, I would."

And even if the questions were presented in an unbiased way, you can't just walk up to people on the street and ask them what they would do. No one really knows what they would do. History shows us that people don't always make the right choices. They make comfortable choices. They make safe choices. More to the point, they make the choices they *know how to make*.

It's difficult to predict how we'd make decisions in hypothetical situations. Hardly anyone can do this well. When we intentionally begin making better choices, we usually do so in increments, making small improvements for a short time. At some point we find ourselves in a stressful situation and immediately revert. We fall back on the types of choices we've been making our whole lives. The ones we know how to make.

One kid starts screaming or crying, another starts begging ruthlessly for a kid's meal with the shiny new toy from his new favorite cartoon movie, and the money in hand goes toward whatever will get them to settle down. Forget the healthy sandwich—one kid's meal, please.

When people use computers and mobile devices, it's because they need or want to do something. Your application stands between them and their mission. And while many people boast of their self-determined compe-tence, we all know someone—someone close—who can never quite figure out whether or not the one-click purchase they just made on Amazon.com is going to ship to the new house or the old one.

"One-click purchase? Now let me just sign in. And double-check my address. And credit card information. And shipping preferences. Okay. Click!" My purchases take closer to 20 clicks. But I'd never admit that to an Amazon usability specialist if he asked me outright.

People prefer to think they know how they would act in any given situation. But very few of them chose the low-carb cheeseburger.

You can't ask users outright what they want. You get theoretical answers. You don't get the answers that result from real choices in real situations. You don't get the truth about how people think and work.

Now you know.

▶ Understand How Users Actually Do Things

So what do you need to know about how people *really* act? Well, several things.

First, instead of becoming gurus of the applications we use every day, we tend to learn about 20 percent of what an application is capable of doing. Some-times we even intentionally hide some or all of the other 80 percent of fea-tures (if we can figure out how to hide them), or at least ignore them, because they get in the way. I can even point to my own behavior as an example of this:

To write the first edition of this book, I used a Microsoft Word template supplied by my publisher, New Riders. While using it, I hid almost all of the other tools Word had to offer. I didn't need them because I knew the keyboard shortcuts for the things I did regularly, such as creating and saving documents, making text **bold**, *italicizing* it, or <u>underlining</u> it. The toolbars that offered these commands, via some cute little icons, just took up space. As a result, I had nothing on my screen but the document, the Styles toolbar, which took up very little room over on the right, and the Zoom tool.

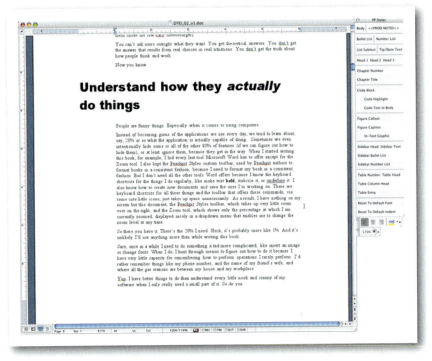

This is how clear Microsoft Word *should* be.

So there you have it—the 20 percent I needed. Heck, it's probably more like 1 percent. And I rarely used anything more.

Sure, once in a while I needed to do something a tad more complicated, like insert an image or change fonts. When I did, I'd hunt through menus to figure out how, because I have very little capacity for remembering how to perform operations I rarely perform. I'd rather remember things like my phone number, and the name of my friend's wife, and where all the gas stations are between my house and my office.

Yup. I have better things to do than understand every little nook and cranny of my software when I only really need a small part of it. So do you.

Want to know a secret? Our users are just like us. They have things to do as well. Loads of things. They don't have time to comprehend every nook and cranny either.

Humbling, isn't it? For all the time and energy we put into creating robust applications that do everything but wash the dishes, only a very small percentage of people ever even venture into the nooks and crannies. They stick to the 20 percent (or less) that they need, and they rarely advance their skills. (There are exceptions to this, of course, but I'll talk about that later on.)

Also, people tend to learn one way to use their application and stick to it. Some prefer menus, some prefer icons, and of course, some prefer keyboard shortcuts. Very few of these people bother remembering more than one way to complete a task beyond those basic operations (in which case, they might know two or three methods). And why should they? Is there any benefit to knowing more than one way to change a tire? No, not really.

Further, people tend to form one idea of how something works and latch onto it. For example, someone once told me that Word is much better for creating tables for printed documents than Microsoft Excel. This surprised me.

I have a fairly typical mental model for Word. In my mental model (what I *believe* to be true), it's a word processor. Nothing more, nothing less. When I need to process words, that's where I go. When I need a table, I go to Excel. If the tiny calculator application that comes with my operating system isn't enough to do what I need, then as far as I'm concerned, I'm in over my head. But it seems Excel can also be thought of as a giant calculator, and Word as a word processor with a strangely cunning ability to print tables.

Huh.

The point, of course, is that I use these tools for the purposes I think they're best equipped to handle. It's human nature. We search for the easiest explanation we can find and we latch onto it. It doesn't necessarily matter if it's true or not. (I'll talk more about mental models, and how they play into our ability to design the obvious, in Chapter 5.)

All these ideas, of course, apply to our users as well. That is, our users also tend to:

- Learn 20 percent or so of what an application can do

- Learn one way to do something and stick to it

- Form their own understanding about how applications work

Contrarily, people tend to wish the applications they use had *more* features. Other features. Features that would, according to the comments that riddle blogs and forums all over the web, compel some people to do all sorts of crazy things, like "pay twice as much if only the software did *this*," or "get my entire company to switch to this application if only it did *that*." In truth, it may not be more features they want. It may be *better* features.

So how do you find out what users really need?

▶ Find Out the Truth

There are several ways to uncover what will be most beneficial to the people who use (or will use) your applications. The first way is simply to *assume* you know how your users work—what challenges they face and how they deal with them. I don't recommend this approach.

Every day—every minute—someone, somewhere, does something we can't imagine. A man enters his email address into the Address bar in Internet Explorer and wonders why he can't check his email. A woman adds *.com* to the end of her username in her web-mail program and wonders why she can't access her home computer. If only it were so simple!

These people are not dumb. Not by any means. They're business owners, and sales managers, and master organizers, and stellar employees. They're experts at something. They're just not experts at using computers. And frankly, they shouldn't have to be.

You probably don't know these people. You are surrounded by people who know the web extremely well because they spend most of their time building it. And you are probably surprised to hear that the less computer-savvy out there can have such a difficult time performing basic operations. But these people are real, and they might one day use *your* application. Don't assume you know anything about them without finding out firsthand. The second you do, someone will come along and ask why he can't scan his printed document by holding it up to the monitor. (Yes, this has happened.)

If you want to know how users work, don't assume anything. Find out the truth.

The way to uncover reality should seem obvious. After all, if you're like the rest of us, you've had at least one argument in your life about whether you were listening to your spouse, your parents, your best friend, or [*insert person here*]. But it's not obvious at all.

When we communicate with our spouses, we have a history to rely on. We know how to talk to and listen to our spouses. Our users, on the other hand, are alien to us. We have no history with them, we've never hung out with them at a bar on a Friday night, and we don't typically have long conversations over dinner with them. So when we're faced with trying to understand what our users really need, it's very easy to forget everything we know about communicating with other people.

For example, if I were designing and building an application used to track sales trends for the sales department in my own company, my first instinct might be to hunt down Molly from sales and ask her what she would like the application to do. Tell me, Molly, how should the Sales Trends Odometer display the data you need?

I would never ask my father—someone I have history with—the same type of question. My father knows next to nothing about how websites are built, what complicated technologies lie lurking beneath the pretty graphics, or the finer points of information architecture. He wouldn't even be able to pick a web application out of a lineup, because he doesn't understand what I mean by the word *application*. Is Amazon.com an application? He doesn't know. He just knows it's a web page and he bought a book there once.

What my father does know is that the model rockets he builds for fun on weekends require several parts that he has to hunt down on a regular basis. He has to make sure he gets to the model rocket store on time every week so he has the parts he needs to complete his rockets, so he can head off to the airstrip and boost a few with his friends. (These are big, professional-level rockets that are often upwards of 8 feet tall and use small explosives as engines. The Federal Aviation Administration regulates the launching of such rockets because they can fly high enough to actually hit planes that have recently taken off; hence the need to use an actual airstrip.)

If I told my dad he could buy these parts online, he'd be interested. If I asked him how the application should filter the online catalog and allow him to make purchases, he'd look at me like I was nuts.

Molly from sales would likely do the same thing.

Molly has no idea what your software might be able to do, and she almost certainly doesn't have the language to explain it. She likely doesn't realize that your product could make the task of creating a client birthday list (for mailing out discount coupons) a matter of two clicks, and therefore, she might never mention that this task is particularly gruesome and ask if your software could do it for her. Thus, you need to look a little deeper to find out what Molly needs.

To find out what Molly wants and needs the software to do, don't look to her words for answers, look to her reality. Study her situation.

One of the best ways to do that is through contextual inquiry.

Contextual inquiry

Again, most project time lines and budgets are too constrained for you to have time to really connect with end users. And besides, most of us don't have the time, will power, or energy to go live and work with a bunch of accountants so we can better understand how to build an effective web-based invoicing system. But when it's an option, you can learn a lot through **contextual inquiry,** an abbreviated version of ethnographic research, which comes in the form of short, observation-driven interview sessions. The goal of these sessions is to observe target users on their own turf so you can see how they really do things. (Note the similarity between the ideas of *context* and *situation*. This could just as easily be called "situational inquiry.")

This method can be especially useful when the people you're observing are already using an existing version of the application you're working to improve.

For example, I once worked on an application that was meant to support the development of e-learning courseware. The first round of users for this application were internal employees—a group of instructional designers who created audio scripts and guidelines for the company's own courses—so there were daily opportunities for contextual inquiry. Endless amounts of quality information could be extracted from simple conversations with those users. This application had no road map at all—no design work had been done to plot it out—so contextual inquiry became a primary method for determining how to evolve the tool. Most of the people working on the application had no experience as instructional designers, and the best way to understand how to create the application was to spend time with the people who did instructional design for a living to study their realities.

To better understand the situations our users faced, I could simply walk over to an instructor's desk and ask to observe. From watching her perform tasks in the application as she worked, and by talking to her along the way, I could learn how she used the tool, why and when she might need to do so, who else might need to be involved in course decisions, and so on. I wasn't on the court, but I still had a front-row seat to the situation these users faced, and could make decisions based on what I learned.

There's nothing complicated about contextual inquiry. It's just a matter of hanging out with a few users for a while to see how they work, how they think, what issues arise while they're working, what situational factors affect their decisions, and, ultimately, how they interact with your application so you can see how effective or ineffective it really is.

At the interaction level, if a user is interrupted by a phone call in the middle of a complicated task, is it easy for him to jump right back into the task when the call has ended? Does he get interrupted like that a lot? Can he move quickly to another part of the tool (perhaps to check a setting) and come back without missing a beat? If this happens, why does it happen? How can the application address this need?

At the application level, is the tool meeting the user's expectations? Does it behave the way she thinks it will, or does she often end up muttering at her screen while trying to understand what just happened? Is the tool organized well, making things easy for her to find? Does she have to perform the same tasks over and over again, and are those things easy to get to and complete on a frequent basis?

Contextual inquiry can actually be very similar to usability testing. The key difference is that the users being observed are in their own environments, in their own contexts, dealing with all the distractions and frustrations they would normally deal with, making it a very real glimpse into their challenges.

Contextual inquiry is perhaps most effective when a tool is still in its conceptual phase because it helps you determine what tasks it needs to support in the first place so that, once again, you can *Know What To Build*. Far better to establish the core requirements before an application launches than after.

Shadowing

Now, I realize that if you're a programmer, the last thing you want to do is talk to those peppy salespeople down the hall who ring a big gong every time they make a sale, but if your product is aimed at salespeople, you can gain tremendous insight by spending some quality time with them. Try to find a few who don't completely clash with you and latch onto them. These folks are your users, and they have the most information about how their jobs are done and what they need to know to do it well. If you're building a product for a client company and can't simply wander down the hall to perform such inquiries, make arrangements to spend a few days at the company so you can talk to users there and learn what you can on-site.

Set up a time to **shadow** several users individually, and go have some fun bonding with your new best friends. Shadowing is the act of quietly hovering over the shoulder of someone who knows what they're doing, with the goal of learning to do that person's job so that you, too, may one day become a Jedi Master. Contextual inquiry is really just a fancy name for shadowing.

Shadowing doesn't have to be overly formal. In fact, the more rapport you have with the users you observe, the more likely they are to open up and tell you about the things they struggle with all the time—things your application can help resolve.

Naturally, there are a few tricks to shadowing. You can't just waltz in and expect someone to tell you exactly what the application needs to do.

- First, make it clear that you are not trying to build a tool to replace them, but rather one to make their jobs easier. You certainly don't want your users thinking you're stealthily finding ways to make them homeless for the holidays (unless, of course, you *are*).

- Next, follow them around and see what it is they do, how they do it, why, and what external factors influence their actions. Take notes, and sketch ideas along the way. The notes app Penultimate for iPad (Cocoa Box Design) is excellent for this—it's like having a digital Moleskine. I've heard that something called "pen and paper" is also fantastic. It's supposed to be very cheap.

- Ask questions, but not so many that you become a major distraction. Just ask simple questions to clarify anything that isn't perfectly clear.

- As you're doing all this, quietly think of all the ways a good application could eliminate Redundant Task A, Annoying Task B, and I Hate This Part of My Job Task C.

- Keep things casual and light. Spend a day with one or two people, or half a day with each of several people. If time is tight, spend two hours with five or six people over a two-day period and stop there.

- Go the immersion route—if you're able, try *doing* the job your application is supposed to support. No one can explain the subtleties of a situation better than you can after actually dealing with them directly for a while.

Remote user research

If you don't have direct access to your users, you can perform remote research using web-based tools like WebEx (Cisco Systems) and GoToMeeting (Citrix Systems), or by making a few simple phone calls to some of your customers.

You won't get the same in-depth knowledge you would from contextual inquiry, and the environment will be less natural than if you were stalking a coworker in person for a day. But you can still get information that helps you build an organizational structure and a feature set that make sense for your application. You can do this by interviewing people over the phone about what they do and what situations they find themselves in, or by having them perform tasks in the current version of your application or a related product and taking notes about how they work, what trips them up, what distracts them, and what you can do to help them. (That said, don't make any promises.

Promises backfire big-time when whatever it is you promised doesn't make it into the next release.)

Surveys

Finally, a low-effort way to get some quick feedback is to survey the people who face the situation your application is meant to support. If you're developing a sales support tool, for example, look to your own company's sales department. Put together a quick screening survey and send it out to the whole department to determine who might have the most useful information. If your product is aimed at senior salespeople, the survey should weed out the trainees and leave you with a shortlist of qualified sales veterans.

SurveyMonkey.com makes quick work of creating nice, easy-to-use survey forms, and it offers a set of tools to analyze the results. I highly recommend it, but you can use whatever survey tool makes you happy and gives you the information you need.

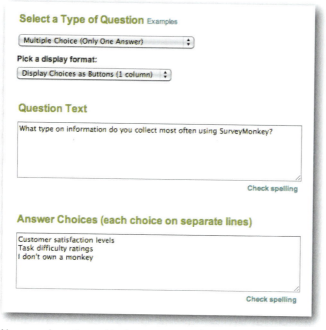

You can rely on SurveyMonkey.com as a tool to more fully understand your target user.

Surveys are effective for acquiring high-level information; for example, they can help you determine satisfaction levels in regard to an existing application, or the order of events in a process and how much time is spent on each one. It's difficult to pinpoint what situational factors have the biggest impact on users' decisions or which ones take the most time, but surveys can help you gather insights about the challenges they face. You shouldn't expect to learn the subtle details of how a person interacts with the shopping cart on a site, but you can gather focus-group–style information pretty easily.

▶ Write Use Cases

When you're ready to start creating something tangible, a **use case** is an excellent way to capture the workflow that you will eventually build into an application. More than that, it's a powerfully effective way to think through your ideas—to solidify them, discover what's missing, and just start sorting through the mess of notes on your iPad.

A use case is a set of step-by-step instructions for how an interaction or a task might be accomplished within your application. You may have heard the term *use case* thrown around in your office a few times, and may even understand what it means. If you're a programmer, you probably know better than most, as use cases are often written to explain a procedure before writing the code, to bring it to life.

A use case can be kept at a high level, describing general situations in which the application will be used (for example, Mary goes to Target.com because she needs furniture items for her new home office), or it can include more detailed descriptions of what actually happens on the screen when the user performs each operation, and of how the user interacts with the application along the way.

Faster than code and capable of producing real results

Writing use cases is, perhaps strangely, one of my favorite things to do. In just a few minutes, typically, I can list out the exact process for how a set of interactions will work once it is built. This exercise invariably exposes potential problems and brings to light any assumptions I was making about a task prior to writing it. It also provides a common ground for the developers and myself. When we communicate through use cases, we're speaking the same language, and that's a good thing.

Just yesterday, in fact, I wrote a use case for a task that enables users to submit personal recommendations for products. To do this, I wrote out several steps that looked like this:

Write a recommendation

Step 1. User clicks the Write a Recommendation text link, and a short form is displayed immediately beneath the button. Tech note: This form resides in a hidden <div> and loads with the rest of the page.

Step 2. User completes the form.

Step 3. User clicks OK to submit the recommendation, and the form disappears.

Then I thought to myself, That doesn't sound right. If the form just disappears as soon as you click OK, the user would have no idea whether or not the recommendation was successfully submitted. So I revised Step 3, opting to keep the form visible after clicking OK, and displaying a message above the form to tell the user the submission was successful. Then I realized that there would have to be a way to close the form once the user was done with it. So I added a fourth step, in which the user clicks a Close button. But I had to decide where to put the button. I asked myself, Should I make a new button and display it as part of the form? Nah, I think I'd rather make the Write a Recommendation link toggle based on context. This link can't be used once the form is displayed, for obvious reasons, so instead of disabling it and displaying another Close button, why not reuse Write a Recommendation in a new context? Once you click that button, its label and function could *change* to a Close button. If I combine the two buttons, I enable the user to open and close the form without moving the mouse (should the user decide not to complete the form, that is).

So, great, now I have a four-step use case that says the user will click the button, complete the form, click OK to submit the form, and (optionally) click Close to make the form go away. I now have a single button that has two purposes, the user has access to the form right in the page instead of being sent to another page in a round-trip process, and the whole interaction is "as simple as possible, but not simpler" (Albert Einstein). Perfect. That's my use case.

Wait. What happens if the user decides not to complete the form?

Writing exceptions

Exceptions are sub–use cases that detail what happens when the main use case cannot be followed from end to end. This is very common in web applications, and it's extremely important to address the alternative workflows because no one—and I mean *no one*—uses an application exactly the same way you do, or how you might have intended them to use it.

(Quick story: I once spent several days using and testing an application to see how it held up against the latest changes. I didn't come across any major problems, so I set up an account for someone to let her try it out. The *very first thing* she did was break it. It didn't even take two minutes. The lesson to learn? No two people will use a web application the same way, so you can't test only the *ideal* way of completing a task. You have to test *all* the ways it can be completed.)

In Step 3 of the use case above, a user could decide not to complete the form. To explain how to deal with this, I added a simple exception to the use case.

The final version looked like this:

Submit a recommendation

Step 1. User clicks the Write a Recommendation link, and a short form displays immediately beneath the button. Tech note: This form resides in a hidden <div> and loads with the rest of the page. The button toggles to read *Close* instead of *Write a Recommendation*.

Step 2. User completes the form.

Step 3. User clicks OK to submit the recommendation, and a success message displays above the form.

Step 4. User clicks the Close button to close the form.

Exceptions

Step 3a. User clicks the Close button without completing the form. Tech note: This resembles a "cancel" action, in which input data would be stripped from the form and the form is hidden, but since this is just a <div> whose visibility is being toggled, the data is retained by default and will therefore be displayed again if the user clicks Write a Recommendation a second time.

"3a" indicates that the exception applies to Step 3 in the use case. It means that if the user decides not to complete the form, another workflow begins, which is detailed in Step 3a. Simple as that. Use cases can get rather lengthy, of course, when detailing complicated or large sets of interactions, but each use case often ends up very similar to this example. No matter how complex the app (and many apps are complex out of necessity), its individual use cases can and should be clear and concise.

Traditionally, use cases don't include the details of what buttons appear where or anything else that specific, but I find it incredibly useful to add these details, because it gives graphic designers and developers a more exact idea of how the interaction should look and work. It also forces me to think through whether the interaction is technically possible, and how simple or complex it will really be before I move on to working it out in actual screen designs. In this use case, I was able to find a way to consolidate three buttons into a single button with three purposes. (In the real version, I also included information about the form itself—how the fields were labeled, how big they were, and all that jazz—but such details aren't important for this example.)

As you can see from the initial use case, I was making a big assumption about the interaction. I was assuming I could just throw up a simple form that would drop into place on demand and call it a day. And the developer who would eventually build the thing would have made other assumptions—for example, that the form should have two buttons: one that opens the form and one that submits the data. He would have built exactly what I said to build, *as he understood it*, and the interaction would have turned out pretty badly.

Then, I would have written up a review of the interaction, explaining to the developer that it was all wrong, and he would have had to rework his code, rather substantially, to correct the interaction. And in my review, I might have left out another detail, and thus the process could have gone on for days, adding to the developer's growing frustration, increasing my stress level, and wasting many hours of expensive and valuable programming time. By taking 20 minutes to write an effective use case at the start, I avoided most of the pitfalls.

The rather obvious secret is this: It's far easier to change a sentence in a Word document than it is to rewrite code that runs conditional logic to perform a specific operation in an interactive system (what a mouthful!).

It takes much less time to write a use case than it does to create an interaction in HTML, with the JavaScript and CSS needed to make it all work. And more often than not, a use case is all you need to explain to another person—like a developer—how a task will be completed in an application.

Get the picture? Use cases rock.

Applying kaizen to use cases

Before we discuss the arguments against use cases, I'd like to share some quick, practical advice about how to make them as effective as possible:

Programmers often enjoy the task of "refactoring" their code to make it cleaner, run better, and contain fewer bugs. I'm a former programmer myself, so I may be a bit biased, but I enjoy making similar improvements to use cases (as in the example above).

Whenever I write use cases, I like to apply a little kaizen to the process. **Kaizen** is Japanese for "change for the better," or, more simply, " improvement." It was originally used as a management technique (it is credited as the reason Toyota consistently builds high-quality, long-lasting vehicles and can justify higher costs as a result), but I find kaizen can be applied to just about anything.

For every interaction I spell out with a use case, I go back over it several times, each time trying to find a way to make it smoother, faster, easier—more *obvious*. It doesn't matter whether the use case ends up changing at all. What matters is that time is spent trying to improve it. Any little detail that can be modified to improve the intuitiveness of the interaction is fantastic, but not every "improvement" is really an improvement.

For example, in the use case about submitting product recommendations, one thing I could do to make the activity easier to complete is to simply show the form by default instead of hiding it away until the user clicks the Write a Recommendation link. This translates to at least one less click for every user who decides to submit a product recommendation. Easier, no?

The downside is that the form would be displayed all the time, cluttering up the page for the 98 percent of people who will never use it. This translates to a more cluttered page every single time it's viewed. No, not easier.

However, one improvement I could make is to have the form "remember" (via a JavaScript cookie) the user's name and email address the next time she writes a recommendation, so she only has to enter the information once. This feature wouldn't be apparent the first time she used the form, but repeat submissions would enable her to complete the form more quickly.

Another improvement would be to auto-focus the first empty input field. If the user's name and email address are retained from previous visits, those fields will already be filled out when the user accesses the form again, so the first empty field would be the one in which she would write the actual product recommendation. If I created the form so that the cursor went immediately to that field, she could click Write a Recommendation and begin typing without having to click in the field first.

This would be a definite improvement. I wish I'd thought of it before I sent the use case to the developer.

Kaizen is a simple concept that can produce great results. Remembering the user's name and email address is a tiny detail, but it makes completing the form a breeze. Users may not even realize the form works this way, but as they see how easy it is to write a recommendation, they will be prone to do it more often.

Funny. That's exactly what you *want* users to do. See how well that works?

In case you missed the point: Improving usability means improving the chances users will do what you want them to do. A little kaizen can take you a long way.

The argument against use cases

Some people dispute the merits of doing anything that doesn't directly contribute to the final product. They say it's bad to spend your time on anything but code. Instead of learning about your users, design products for which *you* are the target audience. Instead of creating wireframes (which I'll talk about in Chapter 5), create a sketch and go straight to HTML.

This approach has its merits, but many of us work in environments that simply don't fit with this style of development. My job, for example, used to be to design interfaces for and perform heuristic evaluations on several major applications, none of which were targeted at someone like me. Different development teams were in charge of building and maintaining each one. There were far too many interfaces, interactions, task flows, and applications to deal with to go straight to code, and it would have been difficult to maintain a sense of consistency between the applications without the support of a large design team.

Again, use whatever design and development process you like, but give use cases a whirl before dismissing the idea. You'll likely find they're a fast, cheap, and easy way to get all those fuzzy ideas on paper and start seeing the possibilities and problems.

Task-flow diagrams

In his argument for Activity-Centered Design, Donald Norman advocates the use of task-flow diagrams. So do I. They're the logical next step after writing use cases, and they can help you refine your ideas.

A task-flow diagram is a flowchart that details how a user will complete all the tasks in an application from beginning to end. Drawing up such a diagram can put you on the path toward an obvious design, because an effective task design is one that makes it obvious how to get from one step to the next in a process, and that process follows an obvious logic.

The diagram below is an example of how a typical shopping experience might go on an e-commerce site. In the diagram, the user wants to buy a desk lamp. To complete the task, the user needs to go to the Products section, drill down into the Desk Lamps category within the Products section, locate a particular desk lamp, add it to the shopping cart, and check out.

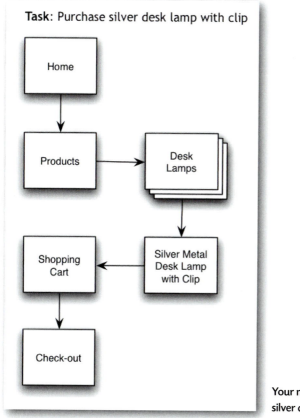

Task: Purchase silver desk lamp with clip

Your mission is to purchase a silver desk lamp with a clip.

The task-flow diagram not only details how the task will be completed in the application, it also can be used as the basis for a prototype later on. And prototypes can be helpful in usability tests to determine how well the design guides users through the process. (I'll talk about prototypes and usability tests in Chapter 5.)

My advice

In sum, my advice is this:

- Learn as much as you can about how people think and work and make decisions. Read fewer design books and more psychology books.

- Design to support a situation, not a specific user base. It's not a type of person who uses an application, it's a person in a type of situation.

- Research situations through contextual inquiry and situational immersion whenever possible. Don't guess.

- If you insist on creating a set of persona descriptions, skip the personal details. They're silly.

- Write use cases.

By taking a situation-centric approach to research, you're well on your way to designing the obvious. The rest of the work is figuring out how you implement interfaces that support the qualities of great web-based software, and I'll spend the rest of this book talking about how to bring those details to life.

4

Build Only What Is Absolutely Necessary

▶ Think Different

▶ Think Mobile

▶ Drop Nice-to-Have Features

When applications evolve based on the demands of users (or of CEOs), they tend to take a bad turn. Features used by only 10 percent of users or used only 10 percent of the time are added and get in the way of the remaining 90 percent of features. They clutter an otherwise clean interface. They interfere with the features used most often.

And when "featuritis" takes over, you quickly find yourself permanently providing tech support for things that shouldn't be in the tool to begin with, fixing more bugs, writing more Help material, and neglecting other, more important features. And while this may sound like a lot of fun to certain (slightly crazy) programmers, it's clearly the wrong approach.

The focus should not be on features, the focus should be on *focus*. An obvious application is a focused application. It's easy to explain to other people. It makes sense to those using it because the purpose of the tool is self-evident, and nothing in it strays from that purpose. Every feature supports the single situation the application is designed to support.

More Features, More Frustration

A user's frustration level doesn't map directly to the number of difficult features in an application. Frustration increases *exponentially*. For every additional feature, there is more to learn, more to tweak and configure, more to customize, more to read about in the Help documentation, and *more that can go wrong*.

For you, it's one more feature. For users, it's one more thing that adds to the already long list of frustrating things to deal with while using a computer. It's not just your application—it's everything else, too. It's the operating system, which hides files away in obscure directories and is constantly popping up little dialog boxes and error messages that you are forced to address before you can get on with your real work. It's the browser, which has no graceful way of indicating whether or not the link you just clicked is going to show you what you want to see. It's the email client, which offers no insights into how long it will take for the message you just wrote, with the rather large photo of your cat, to be sent to your grandmother.

Users contend with all these things and more during the same stretch of time they try to deal with your application. And the frustrations add up quickly.

I know, I know—none of these things bother you at all. They don't really bother me either. But that's a sad fact. It means we've become desensitized to things that are otherwise maddening. It means we've gone numb.

In short, we've become "computer-savvy."

So what's a geek to do?

You have to have killer features or your application won't be able to stand up to its competitors. Right? You have to keep adding things to new versions or no one will purchase upgrades and sales will stagnate. And you have to match the competition one-for-one so no one can ever say your application is light where the other guy's is robust. *Right?*

To paraphrase Alan Cooper, however, trying to match competing products feature-for-feature is like running through a battleground under cover fire. You can run all you want, but you have to keep shooting to get anywhere. Dishing out cover fire keeps you alive for a few minutes at a time. Long enough to hide. Companies that fight all the time to stay ahead fall into the endless cycle of trying to outdo the enemy (if the enemy has a big gun, you need a bigger gun). This goes on and on until someone falls. It's not a fun way to do things. It's a method that works only as long as the people fighting the battle continue to come up with bigger guns. They spend all their time spraying out cover fire while they run 3 feet to the next safe position.

Many companies live and die this way. To get into the fight, you have to stock up on venture capital, go into major debt, hire a bunch of rock star developers, go straight to code because there's no time to plan or design anything, and rush, rush, rush to market with a 27-page list of features. And if the enemy starts to catch up, you have to add more features, call the next version "the most robust release ever," and try to maintain your market share. Until, of course, the enemy puts out a new version with even *more* features.

It's exhausting.

It's also exhausting for users. The more features you offer, the more the user has to learn. The more options you provide, the more users have to do to get anything done. The more you allow customization, the more users have to fidget and tweak and manipulate your application. They spend more time configuring the tool than using it. As a result of fighting the fight, complicated applications often end up much less usable than one would hope.

To stay alive, you eventually have to get out of the line of fire. It's the only real option.

▶ Think Different

A few years ago, Firewheel Design (www.firewheeldesign.com) got out of the line of fire by creating Blinksale (www.blinksale.com), a web-based invoicing system. The simple application contains only the features that are absolutely necessary for the largest percentage of its users to successfully create, submit, and track invoices.

Firewheel's decision to minimize Blinksale's feature list might look like a mistake because it seems as if it won't be able to compete in the rat race with the big boys of invoicing systems. But the small crew at Firewheel did something the big boys hadn't done: it created something that stood out.

Blinksale is aimed at contractors who don't need to do anything fancy with their invoices. Many people who need to submit and track invoices need only a few basic tools. These include a way to create the invoice, submit it, mark it as closed when payment is received, and perhaps send a receipt confirmation to the client. When the folks at Firewheel Design set out to create Blinksale, they realized they could keep it simple and satisfy the vast majority of user needs. They may have even realized that making it more complicated would decrease their chances of satisfying user needs. So they designed a web application that does one thing, and does it very well: it gives people a fast and effective way to create, submit, and track invoices.

(See how easy it is to explain? That's a good sign.)

Since Firewheel created Blinksale, it's been taken over by Doublewide Labs. It's even been completely redesigned. Amazingly, it's *still* one of the best applications around.

The system can be used by plenty of people besides contractors because it's so stripped down that a trained monkey could use it (assuming the trained monkey could type). The application contains just a few key features.

The dashboard and New Invoice screen

When you sign in, Blinksale shows you a summary of your recent activity (open invoices, past-due invoices, and so on) so you get a quick, at-a-glance, dashboard-style view of the state of your invoices. It also offers an easy-to-spot New button, to start creating a new invoice.

You simply choose the client the invoice is for or create a new one—right there, on the same page—and hop over to the New Invoice screen. This page actually *looks* like a real invoice, so you maintain context the whole time you're creating it. All the fields you need to complete are displayed as form elements, so you can simply edit the invoice onscreen and click the big Save button.

Blinksale's main invoice-editing screen is easy to use.

When you're done, you see the final version of the invoice and a few new buttons, which let you send the invoice, edit it, or delete it. One click of the Send Invoice button produces an in-line form in which you checkmark all the people in the client company to whom you want to send the invoice and write an optional message.

The finished invoice

The invoice itself is an HTML-formatted email that looks great right out of the box (well, the browser), and you don't have to configure anything at all to send off a professional invoice to a client in five minutes or less.

Blinksale generates easy-to-read invoices and lets you email them to your clients in a click.

Simple as that.

Blinksale offers a few basic templates from which to choose how you want your invoices to look. You can also send reminders to clients about late payments and create thank-you messages to send to clients who pay their bills on time.

The whole application takes less than 30 minutes to learn inside and out, and just about pays for itself every time you create an invoice (at the time of this writing, Blinksale offers a $6 per month plan for up to 6 invoices, with plans of up to $24 per month for 250 invoices.)

Firewheel built only what was absolutely necessary for most people to successfully handle the activity of invoicing clients. And Doublewide Labs has lovingly maintained that tradition. There are no obscure configuration options, no redundant functionality (there's exactly one way to complete each task in the tool, which makes it easy to learn), and no fancy interface widgets to figure out. It just does exactly what it should, and does it within a simple, clean interface that somehow makes invoices seem friendly, like someone you'd want to take to lunch. (We'll talk more about software personality in Chapter 10.)

The result

Josh Williams, one of the creators of Blinksale, was justifiably proud of how things turned out. Back in 2004, he told me:

> *As a small design company we did our fair share of client billing. Unfortunately we've always been less than enamored with the off-the-shelf invoicing and billing software that is available at your local office supply store. After a few years of frustration we set out to build our own web-based invoicing service. Goal number one was ease of use. Goal number two was keeping our cost of design and development of the service low. Remarkably, these two goals often go hand in hand.*

Firewheel could have designed Blinksale to be chock-full of features that did everything from integrate with Intuit QuickBooks in 12 easy steps to preparing tax information and letting you export it to Intuit TurboTax at the end of the year. They could have built a product that rivaled its competition feature for feature. They didn't. They built the 20 percent people actually need. Nothing more. Nothing less. Even after a change in ownership, with Doublewide Labs at the helm, Blinksale is still hyper-focused on only the most essential features.

While there are a few extra gadgets thrown in for more computer-savvy users, Blinksale keeps things simple and focused. If all you want to do is create an invoice and send it to a client—the single task most people will spend most of their time completing in Blinksale—you can do it in just a few minutes and be on your merry way.

▶ Think Mobile

One of the best ways to avoid feature battles is to focus your attention on designing for mobile platforms such as Apple's iOS and Google's Android. Strategically, it's also one of the best things you can do for your business. Consider this story:

Recently, after boarding a flight to San Francisco for the Voices That Matter conference (hosted by New Riders, of course), a man in his early 30s sat next to me and pulled out his iPhone. The older gentleman who sat on the other side of him asked about it. What was it like to use it? How easy was it *really*? Wow, it sure does look fast, and neat. The younger man answered every question with growing enthusiasm. I'd seen it a hundred times before— the iPhone frequently turns otherwise perfectly jaded people into vehement, adept Apple sales representatives. But then the younger man said something that surprised me. When the older man asked the younger man what he did for work, he replied:

"I'm a cop."

He wasn't a designer. Or a marketing guru. Or a social media expert. Or an entrepreneur. He wasn't heading to a tech conference or a sales seminar. He wasn't at all the kind of person I normally see have a conversation like this one. He was a cop—a middle-class guy who puts on a blue uniform every day and relies on walkie-talkies to communicate—heading off to meet some old college friends for the weekend.

"I hardly ever use my computer anymore. I can do it all on this thing."

Touchscreens and gestural interfaces have taken rise. Long gone are the days when the Internet was considered the new frontier. Personal tech has taken over. Devices are the *new* new frontier.

And this, my friend, is a very good thing.

Over the next few years, as the obstacles to the adoption of mobile devices are eliminated, more and more people will trade in their desktop and laptop computers and start using devices exclusively. Apple and its competitors in the smartphone and tablet markets will make sure of that. And while many people in the tech industry still see some of these gadgets as luxury items—often even wondering what on Earth they would do with a tablet—these devices are designed for the other 99 percent. They're designed for that large segment of the population that uses computers for paying bills, social networking, making plans, watching videos, checking the news, listening to music, digging up recipes, learning new skills, creating spreadsheets for work, writing memos, and of course, checking email. These people use computers primarily for media consumption, web browsing, and basic document-creation. And that's exactly what the iPad and other tablets are designed to do best.

As these products evolve and get cheaper, it will simply be more affordable and more useful to buy a touchscreen tablet backed by a catalog of cheap and easy-to-use apps, with its ever-expanding array of possible use cases, than it will be to buy a desktop, laptop, or even a netbook. More people than ever before will be able to empower themselves through the Internet, and they'll be able to use it anywhere they want. The air will be completely filled with Wi-Fi signals, and all the world's information—all *your* information—will be quite literally at your fingertips, anytime, anyplace..

Personal tech is now affordable by the masses, useful for the masses, and usable by the masses. And this will only become more true in the years to come. If you're not designing for it now, you're already late.

But even if you ignore this fundamental shift in personal computing, devices are good for application designers for other reasons—specifically, because they force designers to follow the principles of good application design.

The people designing for devices right now are doing a better job of embracing these principles than most people designing for the desktop *ever* have. The constraints of the medium—the limited screen space, risk of network slowdowns, difficulties of multitasking, and so on—are having the happy side-effect of encouraging designers to design more concise applications.

Southwest Airlines offers a great example. Here's the site in a desktop browser.

Naturally, the site offers a way to book a flight, car, or hotel. In fact, in this desktop version, there are two sets of tabs that offer this, one of which lets you fill out the reservation form on the homepage, the other of which takes you to another page to do it. Why? Well, because the larger tabs at the top are more than just links—they're menus. The Air tab, for example, offers a menu chock-full of links to other information, including a list of destinations Southwest flies to. And yes, plenty of people will seek out this information. But the natural effect is that the design takes up a lot of space, offers a lot of options, and requires a lot of scanning and decision-making.

The Southwest Airlines iPhone app, however, focuses only on what's absolutely necessary. On the iPhone, users can find this information by checking the To Where option on the Book a Flight screen.

Now, let's say you want to see how your Rapid Rewards stockpile is coming along. On the desktop version, there is a large Rapid Rewards tab-like link near the top of the page, an accordion tab labeled My Rapid Rewards, and a sign-in form that asks for your Rapid Rewards number. Which one is right? Which step do you take first?

In the iPhone app, you tap *Rapid Rewards.* It leads to a sign-in screen.

One of these things is so much clearer than the other.

Hey, it's your life

So if you still wonder what on Earth you'd do with a tablet, there's your answer. You'd secure your own future as a designer. As a marketing guru. A social media expert. An entrepreneur.

Don't neglect to see the significance of mobile computing because you're busy sitting at a desk with a souped-up PC, a killer video card, and 8 feet of monitor space displaying 75 open Photoshop files. Yes, you'll have to continue doing a lot of your design work there. Yes, it will continue being *easier* to do design work there. But don't delude yourself that your customers will always and forever be sitting at a desk when they use your products. They won't be.

Use your desktop computer. Just use it to design for *devices.* And make sure a tablet is sitting next to it.

Throughout the rest of this book, I'll discuss mobile-specific considerations alongside our discussion of design principles for effective applications.

Not present at time of photo

Sadly, at the time of this writing, there is no device-friendly version of Blinksale. Hey, nobody's perfect.

A competing invoicing application, Ballpark, does offer a mobile-friendly dashboard. It's not much, but it offers a cursory view of your recent activity.

▶ Drop Nice-to-Have Features

Almost every mature application in existence contains at least a few features that were probably first described in a statement that started with "Something that would be really nice to have is *<insert description here>*." But most of these things are exactly what clutter up interfaces all over the web and on our devices, and it's our job to fend these things off with a big stick. They need to be removed from your next application before it's even built. An obvious interface is one that is focused on what's most important and leaves out the things that are simply nice to have.

In its book *Getting Real,* 37signals has this to say about focusing on only the important features:

> *Stick to what's truly essential. Good ideas can be tabled.*
> **Take whatever you think your product should be and cut**
> **it in half.** *Pare features down until you're left with only the*
> *most essential ones. Then do it again.*

The statement is similar to something Steve Krug said in his book *Don't Make Me Think,* one of the greatest books out there on web usability. It's Krug's Third Law of Usability:

> *Get rid of half the words on each page, then get rid of half of*
> *what's left.*

And Krug's law can be traced back to William Strunk, Jr., and E. B. White's *The Elements of Style*:

> *Vigorous writing is concise. A sentence should contain no*
> *unnecessary words, a paragraph no unnecessary sentences,*
> *for the same reason that a drawing should have no*
> *unnecessary lines and a machine no unnecessary parts.*

Say it again, brother.

All these people are in the business of simplicity. Simplicity makes the point clear. It lets messages stand out. It offers communication that cuts through the noise.

The Unnecessary Test

To create applications that cut through the noise, you have to be willing to slice your application's feature list down to its bare bones, and you have to recognize what's most important.

With that in mind, try the following exercise, which I call the Unnecessary Test:

Open an application you've worked on recently and find a feature you thought was really important a long time ago, perhaps before you started building the application.

Ask yourself the following questions:

1. Is there more than one way to complete the task this feature supports?

2. Does this feature contribute directly to the completion of the task?

3. Is the task this feature supports vital to the activity this application supports?

If you answered no to any of these questions, the feature may be unnecessary. You've found yourself a likely candidate for the cutting room floor.

If, on the other hand, you answered yes to all of these questions, you're either looking at a rock star feature or you're not looking hard enough at the feature to be objective. Try your best to detach yourself from all the work you did and ask these questions from a more objective point of view.

Regardless of your answers, it's likely there are several features in your application that could be scrapped, so you should take the time to go through every feature and run each one through the Unnecessary Test.

When you're done with the testing, close the application and ask yourself three more questions.

1. What are the circumstances of the situation my application is meant to support?

2. If this application didn't exist and I needed to handle the same situation, and I could wave a magic wand to create an application that helped me with this situation with the greatest of ease, what would the application do? (Hint: You should limit this answer to a few very big-picture statements that relate to the principal desired outcome.)

3. How long will it take to rebuild my application to make it do that?

Sorry—that last question is a joke (sort of). After all, you're likely to have answered one of the first two questions in a way that prevents you from having to admit you were wrong. I know—I've done this myself. It's difficult to admit your application may not be living up to its promise.

If this is true, have someone else answer the same set of questions and see if the answers are different. Even better, ask one of your users.

I'm not suggesting you start ripping functionality out of an existing application. Doing this could have the rather negative side effect of making some of your users extremely upset. To the people using the more obscure features, removing them would be a huge mistake. I'm only suggesting you learn from what you've already done so you can create more focused applications in the future.

The 60-Second Deadline

Here's another quick way to learn to effectively aim low and keep your application focused on the 20 percent that matters:

Pretend I'm your boss. I walk into your office and very matter-of-factly state, "The project time line has been cut in half. We have about 60 seconds to decide what to keep and what to throw away before we meet with the client in the conference room."

How do you respond to this statement?

Whatever you do, don't impulsively offer up the theoretical answer—the one where you say how much you'd love the low-carb sandwich. *Figure out the real answer.*

Grab a notepad and a pen, write down the list of features you have planned for an upcoming application, and see what you can cut in 60 seconds. Draw a line through each feature you can cut without completely destroying the application.

The goal is to leave yourself only with what is most essential for the application to serve its purpose.

Bells? Gone.

Whistles? Gone.

Show me only the pieces you absolutely have to keep for the tool to do its job.

When you're done, cut one more feature, just for good measure. Cut the one you're holding onto only because it's really cool. C'mon, I know there's at least one on your original list. Draw a line though it.

Your 60 seconds are up. Good job.

Now, take out a second sheet of paper and write a new list that shows only what you have left, just so you can see it sitting there all nice and clean. Looks much better, doesn't it? I know, it probably hurts a bit to have lost so much stuff, but I bet your application is now easier to explain.

Finally, take out another sheet of paper and write down the list of things you drew a line through earlier. Title this page "Nice-to-Have Features," stick it in your filing cabinet, and forget about it. We'll look at it again later.

The first time you do this, it can be quite revealing. You may find you've been wasting a lot of your time and energy on things that don't really contribute to the application in any meaningful way. Of course, this may be a bit unsettling, but hey, knowing is half the battle. Next time around, you can use the Unnecessary Test and the 60-Second Deadline exercise before you start coding, to see what really needs to be built—and you can spend all your time working to make those things as good as they can be.

And since building what's most important takes much less time than building what's not important, you can get more sleep, take more vacations, get more weekends off, and live a happier, healthier life.

Or you could do what I do and use all that saved time to design more applications. I know that's what you *really* want to do.

Aim low

Regardless of how you do it, the ultimate goal is to determine what's most important to the application by whittling your list of features down to about 20 percent of what was built or what you were planning to build. Yes, some of the remaining 80 percent of your features may be useful somehow, to someone, some of the time, but they are most likely useless to 80 percent of your users, 80 percent of the time. And you probably spent 80 percent of your development time building things that aren't essential to the application.

This is because the 80-20 rule has made its way into the world of software.

Known formally as the Pareto principle (named for Vilfredo Pareto), the 80-20 rule was originally suggested to indicate that 80 percent of the effects come from 20 percent of the effort.

In terms of good, clean application design, it means that 80 percent of an application's usefulness comes from 20 percent of its features. It also works the other way around, to illustrate that 20 percent of the development work produces 80 percent of an application. The other 80 percent of the work satisfies only 20 percent of the outcome.

To create more focused applications, stick to building the 20 percent of features that are essential—the ones you'll stick on the mobile version—and you'll take care of 80 percent of the user's needs. Let your competitors worry about the rest. While they're floundering around trying to one-up you by fleshing out the other 80 percent of the application, you could be taking 80 percent more vacations and enjoying 80 percent of the market share.

Less is more. Aim low.

Interface Surgery

A job application form I saw once was composed of two windows. One window got the user through the first few screens of the process, and then it launched a second window to complete the bulk of the application. The first window was connected to the user's log-in session, which was timed and was designed to log out the user automatically if the system remained inactive for 20 minutes. However, the second window was not tied to the session. So, when a user tried to complete the job application in the second window—the part of the process that took the longest amount of time—the system invariably logged the user out after 20 minutes, rudely doing so without any notification whatsoever.

The company's solution was to add a bit of text in the original window warning users that they would be logged out after 20 minutes—a weak attempt to get their pesky users to stop complaining. This was a band-aid. It did not solve the problem, it just told people what to expect. Users would still have to complete the job application in 20 minutes or less. The company was essentially saying, "Sure, we've created a terrible system that will likely terminate your session before you can complete your job application, but hey, we're warning you before you start, so it's okay!"

I don't like band-aids.

Instead of putting band-aids on problems, I perform surgery on them. Interface surgery.

In this first installment of Interface Surgery, we'll cut out a bunch of unnecessary features from a fictitious web-mail application. Instead of finding ways to make a ton of unnecessary gadgets easier to present and use, we're going to rip them out and leave only what's absolutely essential for the application to do its job.

This application has a ton of features. In addition to being able to simply check your email, you can search the web, see how much storage space you've used, make sure you're logged in using a particular user name, reuse saved searches, apply actions (such as set up an automatic response email), move email to other folders you create yourself, configure options for the Inbox (such as font settings), and even change how many messages should be displayed in the list before having to switch to a new page.

Some of these things are necessary, some are not.

To get started, let's strip out the part of the Search feature that lets users search the web. There are already plenty of ways to search the web, and most modern browsers feature a built-in search bar, making this action accessible 100 percent of the time the user has the browser open. There's no need to replicate what's already ubiquitous. And since we're leaving only the option to search mail, we can remove the two radio buttons and shrink down the space this piece takes up.

Let's also get rid of the ability to save searches. It's more difficult to save a search, find it again later, and rerun it than it is to simply reenter a few keywords. This might be nice for some users, but it's not going to seriously benefit *most users, most of the time.* And since we're getting rid of it, we can lose the tabbed interface that displays it. Since the Folders view is now the only option, it no longer needs a label or a tab.

Next, let's get rid of the percentage indicator that tells users how much storage space has been used up. If we decide this is essential later, we can move it into the Settings screen. There's no reason to give it a permanent position in the main interface.

Next, let's get rid of the text that indicates which user is currently logged in. This is unnecessary most of the time, because most users will only ever have a single account, and since they have to manually log themselves in before they can see this screen, it's pointless to show them something they already know.

Also, let's kill the option to change how many messages display in the list at once. This can certainly be retained as a feature, but it's not the kind of thing users are going to use every day, so we can move it to the Settings screen.

And since a Search bar is provided in the left-hand sidebar, we can remove the Search link from the top of the page.

Showing a title bar for which folder is currently being displayed is redundant, because the label for the folder in the sidebar is made larger and bold when that folder is displayed. And if we remove the Folder title bar, we can free up some vertical space for more important content—like *mail*.

When an email is being displayed, another small bar appears above the email offering Reply, Reply All, Forward, and Delete functions, as well as a way to mark an email as junk.

Delete	Move to folder ... ▼	Move	Create Filter

From	Subject	Date Received
☐ John Smith	Check out our new email application	Thurs, 11:00 am
☐ Christine Pearson	9-ball on Sunday night?	Thurs, 11:00 am
☐ Yoshi the Dog	Can you please throw me a bone?	Thurs, 11:00 am

Message

Reply | Reply All | Forward | Delete | This is Junk

This is the content of an email. The Reply, Reply All, and Forward options are in another horizontal bar located just above this message.

But there's already a Delete button in the bar above the message list. If we remove the button and tidy things up a bit, we can consolidate the bar and unify the message options into a single interface element, which means less code, less interface, and less confusion.

Reply | Reply All | Forward | Delete | Junk | Create Filter   Move to folder ... ▼   Move

From	Subject	Date Received
☐ John Smith	Check out our new email application	Thurs, 11:00 am
☐ Christine Pearson	9-ball on Sunday night?	Thurs, 11:00 am
☐ Yoshi the Dog	Can you please throw me a bone?	Thurs, 11:00 am

Message

This is the content of an email. The Reply, Reply All, and Forward options are in another horizontal bar located just above this message.

Finally, let's add some logic to the application and have it disable the Reply, Reply All, and Forward links if more than one message is selected at a time. Delete, Junk, and Create Filter can all be applied to multiple messages, so we'll leave those active. In doing this, we make the message options more functional while still taking up less space.

Ahh, that's much better. We stripped out a few features, removed a few interface elements, cleaned things up, and came out with an application interface that is easier to understand at a quick glance and easier to use on a daily basis.

We'll perform interface surgery throughout this book as a way of improving applications one step at a time.

Reevaluate nice-to-have features later

So, when is it time to take the list of nice-to-have features back out of the filing cabinet? The simple answer is this: not one second before your application has been released.

Once your application is out there, being used by real users, and you've given it some time to stabilize by fixing a lot of the immediate bugs that have inevitably come up since the release, then it's time to review the list of nice-to-haves. It's also time for a good laugh.

What usually happens is that users start to speak up about what they wish your application did, things that bother them, and so on, and no one ever mentions the items on your list of nice-to-haves. Users very quickly form different perspectives on your application than you may have ever had, and since none of them use the application exactly the way you thought they would, the complaints and wish lists that emerge are usually different than what you thought was important.

If this is the case for you, feel free to put that list of nice-to-haves into the *other* filing cabinet—the one shaped like a trash can—and call it a day. The things we often think are so important at the beginning of a project usually prove to be about as useful as adding another color to a logo. And more often than not, adding them way back when would have meant putting the rock star features at risk by making them harder to find, harder to configure, *harder to use.*

Let them speak

Once your application is being used out in the wild and you want to hear all the little screaming voices of your users, you need to give them a way to talk to you. This means providing a way for users to offer feedback about your product or talk to others about it, getting out of the way so they can speak freely while you take notes and carefully interpret.

Something as simple as setting up a forum on your site and directing people there from your Support page can dramatically lower your customer-support costs (a forum costs extremely little to maintain), while greatly increasing the amount of information you get from customers.

Note, however, that you will probably not like everything that gets posted. Invariably, there will be some dissatisfied and possibly rude users who scream about your "horrible" application and say nothing constructive, but you have to let this happen. If you moderate user comments to filter out the negative, you'll defeat the purpose of the forum, which is to hear the complaints. The goal is to feel the pain.

When you allow your users to speak up, you'll quickly come up with a whole new list of nice-to-haves. Put those in the filing cabinet as well.

Avoid bending to users' whims if the high-demand features don't fit into your grand vision for the application. You might try pooling a few beta users together and have them try out a prototype of the proposed functionality to see how it really works before unleashing it to all your customers. There's no shame in pulling the feature back out if it just doesn't work. Better now than later.

Focus only on the features that are the most essential. *Build only what is absolutely necessary.*

5

Support the User's Mental Models

- ▶ Design for Mental Models
- ▶ Eliminate Implementation Models
- ▶ Prototype the Design
- ▶ Test It Out

When we consider how to organize papers, we may think of filing cabinets. We fill filing cabinets with hanging folders, and fill those with manila folders, each with its own stack of files. We use labeling systems to help us remember what each folder contains.

In modern desktop operating systems, we can glance around a virtual desktop full of folders (represented by icons), spot the one we need, open it up, and scan its contents to find the file we need.

In reality, though, computers use addresses to tell them where each specific bit and byte is stored. The addresses on the hard disk don't need to correspond to a filing system—in fact, two files stored in the same folder do not necessarily exist in consecutive spaces on the hard drive.

As another example, when we think about throwing something away, we usually think of trash cans. Trash cans sit in every room in our houses and offices, and do nothing but give us a place to toss items we no longer need.

Today, instead of entering obscure terminology into a command-line tool to delete a file—which is how it used to be done—we throw it away. On the desktop, we drag a file icon to another icon shaped like a trash can or recycling bin. In a device app, we may tap a trash can icon. Either way, the visual metaphor of the trash can has replaced the typed command, and deleting files has come to mean throwing them away.

Much like throwing something away in real life, the trash metaphor used in Pages for iPad (the Apple iWork word processing app) lets us visualize the removal of an item in a way that supports our mental model.

In actuality, the metaphor of throwing something away bears no resemblance to deleting a file from a computer. But which makes more sense to you? A trash can icon or a typed command? Both have the same effect—they delete an address from the hard drive's index so the storage space can be overwritten the next time the computer needs to save to the hard drive—but again, one is so much better than the other.

The useful, concrete mental metaphor has effectively replaced the reality of what occurs, and no one cares! The metaphor works, and is much simpler than the reality.

In both of these cases, users have been given visual metaphors that adhere more closely to our knowledge of the world outside of our computers. Trash cans are used for trash, and filing cabinets are used for organizing files. This is how we do things in real life, and now, this is (more or less) how we do things on a computer. What we believe about what happens has nothing to do with the reality of what happens on the computer. But we rely on our real-world experiences to help us assimilate and understand.

Understanding mental models

A mental model, in other words, is what we believe to be true, generally based on our experiences, and how we assimilate new things into our existing knowledge. It doesn't have to be the truth, and it usually isn't. It just has to settle in our heads well enough to let us sleep at night. It has to help us understand how to *use* a computer and understand what it *is*, but not necessarily what it really does.

For users to feel good about an application, they need to feel as if they understand it. Making it as simple as possible for them to understand—even if that simple understanding is technically inaccurate—is designing the obvious. Of course, the inaccurate understanding has to be useful as a way of thinking and simplifying, but as long as that's true, the design has a better chance of succeeding.

In other words, it's okay if the user is completely wrong in her perception of what is happening as long as her sense of understanding makes her feel good and competent, and she can accomplish her goals with her understanding, regardless of how faulty it might be.

An implementation model, on the other hand, is something that has been designed, usually by not being "designed" at all, to reflect the underlying details of a system. Implementation models have no regard for a system's users. They aim, usually, to please the geeks that create them.

That old DOS prompt, which required us to understand how to forcibly remove a file from the dark shadows of the hard drive index, is an example of an implementation model. We were expected to know how the hard drive worked, how to remove an item from it, and so on. Now, we just throw the darn thing away.

In web applications, many implementation-model designs appear even when there are far better ways to represent the functionality the interface elements are intended to handle. This chapter is about how to avoid implementation models and design interfaces that make sense to users without forcing them to understand the underlying technologies.

▶ Design for Mental Models

When an application is designed to reflect its underlying functionality, a few common trends emerge.

First, error messages tend to read like bug reports written specifically for the developers who wrote them. Programmers often need to add code to applications during development that helps them debug issues as they arise, and the error messages are written in words that help the developers narrow down the issue. Before the application is released, this is fine, but these cryptic messages often live on into released applications and mystify users to no end. These messages reveal the system from the developer's perspective instead of revealing the system's benefits by improving a user's understanding.

This error message is not only meaningless to users, it also interferes with their ability to learn how the application works and their ability to be productive.

Second, application interfaces often become overly complicated. Because programmers enjoy exposing every option and setting a system could possibly contain, interfaces offer up buttons, configurations, settings, dialog boxes, panels, and menus that do everything but wash the dishes.

Instead of focusing on focus, implementation-model designs focus on covering all the bases. They sacrifice ease of use in favor of the fine level of control a system is capable of allowing.

Programmers, who are usually the first to admit they are more computer-savvy than the rest of the world, often want incredible amounts of control over the applications they work with, so they surface everything they can in the applications they build, regardless of how difficult it makes a tool to learn for someone who lacks the experience of a programmer. Their users typically don't want this fine level of control. They want to understand how to get their work done and go home to their kids and spouses and dogs.

Just yesterday, I was shown a design for a blog template that featured a small section in the sidebar used to display a list of keywords associated with the post currently being viewed. The list could be shown in two ways. One way was as a tag cloud (which uses varying font sizes to illustrate the relative popularity of a set of linked keywords). The other way was as a plain list where each item used the same font and font size. Two buttons, labeled Cloud and List, were offered so users could switch between the tag-cloud view and the list view. When I asked why the buttons were there, the designer told me a developer had said something like, "It would be nice if users had a choice to display the list both ways."

I understand where the developer was coming from. Developers like to cover their bases and offer everything they can. If it's *possible* to show the list in two ways, we think the choice *should* be offered. But most users viewing this particular page online will not know what a tag cloud is, nor will they find any compelling reason to switch between the two views. Providing them the choice is pointless. Users who see a tag cloud and understand it will benefit from being able to quickly discern between the relevancy of the various keywords, and those who don't understand it will still see a list of links. No harm, no foul.

But when presented with the option to switch between the two views, every user without preexisting knowledge of a tag cloud would have to try to figure out what was meant by the two buttons. Users would be forced to learn something they don't need to know to become comfortable with the page. The choice doesn't help anyone, and actually distracts users from the task of making sense of the page's functionality.

Thankfully, the designer decided to scrap the two buttons and just show the tag cloud.

A third trend that results from the use of implementation-model designs is that tasks often become cumbersome and frustrating, because the system needs all sorts of particular bits of information to complete an operation, and it forces you to tweak and guide it at every step so it can complete the operation in the exact way you tell it. It doesn't work to help you form a simple understanding of how to make it work, it forces you to understand it so it can get what *it* needs. To this end, it pokes and prods at you until it gets everything out of you it can.

This approach manifests itself as labels that mean nothing to someone who doesn't know how the system works, positioned next to pieces of functionality that should never have been surfaced in the first place. Like a button labeled *Cloud*.

This behavior is, well, rude. It's about making users do everything they can to make the system happy and not doing what makes *users* happy. Applications like this try hard to be all things to all people, and end up failing to be anything great to anyone. Yes, these applications can still succeed, but it is often because of other factors, such as the lack of any other application in the market that fulfills a similar purpose. This sad fact doesn't make it okay for applications to be rude, but they end up that way far too often because the mighty implementation model rears its ugly head.

When applications work well, however, and allow users to easily form their own, more comforting mental models, everybody wins.

Making metaphors that work

Backpack (**www.backpackit.com**), created by 37signals (**www.37signals.com**), is a wonderful and very simple tool for managing small projects and chunks of information. Backpack allows you to create web pages you can fill up with . . . stuff. You know, like you can fill up a backpack.

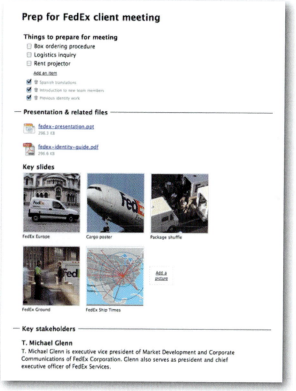

This sample page from Backpack shows to-do list items, notes, files, and images all managed in a single page.

In Backpack, you simply click a button to create a page, name it, and then start filling it up with anything you need to get yourself organized. Notes, images, files, and to-do lists can all be kept in a single page.

Prior to Backpack, sinking your teeth into some new research or small project invariably meant compiling information until it became a mess. Maybe you'd start by creating a folder on your desktop and throwing some files into it. Maybe you'd create a bookmarks folder in your browser and start adding bookmarks to it. Maybe you'd collect images. Write lists. Write more notes. Go crazy with disorganization.

With Backpack, you can keep all that information in one place, just as if you were a student throwing books, homework, notes, and perhaps even your lunch, into your backpack. Instead of the implementation model of the operating system, which says that bookmarks, files, to-do lists, and images are all different things that are stored in different software applications and folders, Backpack supports a mental model of how information like this is organized in real life. A real-world backpack lets you keep it all in one place. Now, a web-based backpack can do the same thing.

And for the record, I use Backpack myself. It helps me get organized in a way that allows me to maintain structure and relationships between formerly disparate bits of data and see it as a single collection that has meaning and context for me. Information and ideas tend to come in sporadic waves, and Backpack lets me work within this free-flowing state, without forcing me to use phrases like "maintain structure and relationships between formerly disparate bits of data." It lets me keep my own model of how all these bits of data go together where I used to be stuck with the operating system's methods of organization.

When I asked Jason Fried, the fearless leader of 37signals, about the inspiration for Backpack, he said:

> *Like every product we build, the motivation is to scratch our own itch. We needed Backpack to "keep life's loose ends together" so we built Backpack. Our experience with organizational software was that it was too complex. It asked you too many questions and imposed too much structure. The truth is that information comes in chaotic streams and you just need a place to capture it all. You can organize it later, but if you don't get it out of your head and into a central location you'll forget about it. So Backpack was designed to bring all this loose information together in one central location. Then you can use Backpack's simple to-do list, notes, text, image, files, and reminder tools to shape it into something that makes more sense to you.*

Rolling over the page title displays a Rename link. Clicking it converts the page title into an editable text field, in which you can simply type a new page title. Then you just click another button to save it.

Another compelling aspect of Backpack is that everything on the page can be edited *right in the page*. Creating a new Note, for example, drops a text field into the page so you can just start typing. Creating a to-do list is as simple as clicking one button to create the list and typing the first item into another editable text field. Upon saving the to-do item, it converts to a check box so you can check off your to-do item later on. Adding files is a small matter of browsing to a file and uploading it.

The fields you need to add a new note are dropped right into the page so you can create it without leaving the page.

You never have to wait for a new page to reload, never have to remember which link takes you to which page, never have to remember how to perform a task.

Backpack immediately became invaluable because it lets me get on with doing whatever I need to do and stays out of my way. I never see error messages while using the application, and it doesn't expect me to learn anything remarkable about its inner workings to understand how to use it. There are exactly zero hoops through which to jump.

Are you sure?

The only implementation-model piece of design I've seen while using Backpack is the JavaScript alert message that intrusively appears when you attempt to delete something from a Backpack page. It asks, simply, "Are you sure?"

While the message is a pretty standard confirmation message—which we're all used to seeing—it's a sign of the underlying system. It's a big ol' banner that says "I don't have an undo feature and the only way I can deal with you deleting an object from your page is to interrupt your workflow with this message to make sure you know what you're doing."

Yes, yes, I'm sure. Oh, wait. What did that message say? I clicked OK out of habit and didn't even bother looking at it.

An ideal solution would be to design an undo function for the application and get rid of the confirmation message. There's no reason to require confirmation if an undo function exists—maybe a simple text link that appears in the page whenever the user performs an action that can't be undone some other way. This text link could remain available until the user performed a different action, at which point the link would change to enable an undo of the more recent action. The ability to undo the action would remain available for more time than the JavaScript alert message, and it wouldn't get in the user's way when he was trying to work. Two benefits in one. It would not only hide the system from users, it would further support their mental models of how things are thrown away.

Overall, however, Backpack does a fantastic job of communicating its purpose. In addition to letting users do exactly what they want with it, it's aptly named. Just like a backpack in real life, Backpack is the place you throw all your stuff so you don't need to keep it in your head. I use it at work to jot down interface ideas, and at home to organize articles I'm working on and plans for personal projects. And since it's web based, I can bring it with me wherever I go. Just like a backpack. It's quite effective at supporting my mental model of the concept of organization.

With the one exception of the JavaScript confirmation message, Backpack never reveals how it works or bothers me to confirm every little decision. It just works. For that, I thank 37signals. Every time I use Backpack.

When was the last time someone thanked you for creating such a great application?

Interface Surgery: Converting an implementation model design into a mental model design

One of the peskiest implementation-model approaches around today is the attempt to port a website to a touchscreen device *as is*. This approach is a lot like the shift from designing for print to designing for web, wherein many designers have an irresistible urge to simply recreate printed brochures online, detail for detail, without making them work well for the web, and link to PDF files stuck up on a server somewhere rather than create legitimate web pages. This is a problem because we expect different things from different mediums. In print, we crumple up paper and toss it out when we're done with it. On the web, we interact and then click away. On a touchscreen device, we tap and swipe and pinch and then move to another app.

In this second installment of Interface Surgery, we'll look at how to convert an implementation-model design into a mental-model design by examining a company that tried to turn its desktop site into an iPad app: Netflix.

When the super-popular video streaming and rental company made its leap onto the iPad, it moved fast. The company was able to do this by simply stuffing the existing website into an iTunes-friendly shell and shoving it out into the burgeoning video-on-demand-for-mobile market.

Browsing categories on Netflix for iPad is just like–no, *exactly* like–browsing categories on the website.

In theory, this was a fine move. The site was friendly enough to use, and Netflix had enjoyed unmatched success with it so far. So why pick on this approach? Well, because what works for the web doesn't always work in an app. The desktop browser has a click interface. The iPad has a gestural interface (an interface that responds to touch). The expectations are different. The user's understanding is different. The possibilities are *very* different. And in this case, interactions that were clearly designed for the web, while certainly still usable to anyone who had already used the desktop site, translated to a clunky and sluggish iPad app nonetheless.

To trawl the Netflix catalog of streaming media for, say, a movie to watch while you're supposed to be working, you have to traverse the same collection of pages you find on the site. This means you start at your member homepage, perhaps move to a genre page (for example, *Drama + Independent,* a gallery of movies in that subgenre), then onto a content page where you decide whether or not to watch the movie you selected. That page, of course, offers ratings and reviews, a synopsis, and much more, but it's also a little slow to load. To alleviate this annoyance, especially when you're already sure of which movie you'd like to watch, Netflix offers a Quick Look style overlay that gives you a glimpse of what's on the full content page before you tap through to it, the idea being that if you decide you're not interested, well, at least you didn't have to tap through to that other page.

Actually, I've seen this one a hundred billion kajillion times. Just play, please.

If you do visit the content page for a movie, you can see why it takes so long to load: it's a full web page featuring all the information you could ever want about the movie, including what everyone in the world has to say about it. And while this is most definitely useful information in all kinds of use cases, the page displays *all* of it by default rather than organizing it into bite-size chunks that can be accessed through a few quick gestures.

Boy, it sure does take a long time to load this page. If only I could get smaller samples by default and gesture for more information when I want it.

Throughout the app, clicks are replaced by taps, and scroll wheels are replaced by scroll gestures. Again, while this may be quite usable, especially for those who have used the desktop browser version of the site before, it completely fails to leverage what works best on a touchscreen device, and in doing so, it abandons the mental model that touchscreen users expect.

This is an implementation-model design.

To counter it, let's look at an approach Netflix could have taken by examining what Apple itself wanted us to know about how to use its touchscreen iPad.

The Photos app is divided by category.

In the pre-installed Photos app, photos are cleanly divided into named photo albums. With a *spread* gesture, a photo album becomes a gallery of photos.

With a quick spread gesture, a thumbnail becomes a full-size photo.

And with another spread gesture, a thumbnail photo expands to full-size. Beneath the photo, a filmstrip of the photos in the album sits just begging for you to scroll through them.

That's my dog, Max, by the way. Max on, Max off. (C'mon. What are the odds of my ever being able to make that joke again?)

To slide from one photo to the next, just swipe your finger from right to left, or from left to right to go backward in the series.

And just like that, you move from category to gallery to content. Now, imagine applying these ideas to Netflix.

For the purpose of this exercise, I did just that: I imagined what Netflix for iPad might look like if it had used the interaction model from Photos, supporting the mental model people have of how to interact with a touchscreen iPad. No, I haven't worked out every detail. No, I don't expect anyone to be able to add water to my design and serve up a delicious Netflix stew. But I do believe I can get my point across—that it's better to support the user's mental model than it is to present an implementation-model design.

First is the Genres landing page, just a tap away from your user homepage. Much like Photos, it offers up groups of related items.

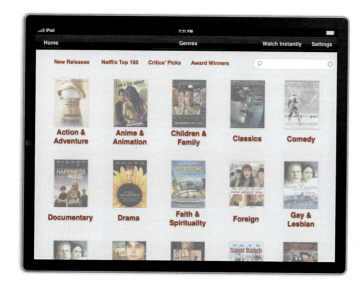

From here, you use a spread gesture to expand a genre into a gallery of the items within that genre. These are thumbnail images accompanied by Play buttons. You can also choose subgenres here via a toolbar menu.

Next, you expand an individual item into a full-size content view. Note, though, that this version of the Netflix content view has been reduced quite a bit. This is to make it load faster, and to surface the most relevant information and functions while still keeping everything else handily within reach. Wow, it's difficult to talk about gestural interfaces without using a lot of puns.

Suddenly, Netflix works the way Apple imagined it could. You get the satisfaction of gesturing your way into a movie's content view, and you can easily grab more information when you want it without being inundated by it when you don't.

Yes, there would be some issues to resolve in trying to apply this interaction model to Netflix. Here's a list of things we'd need to figure out how to do:

- Keep users entertained during the load time between content screens (movie quotes, perhaps)

- Pare down the information on a content screen to hide most of it

- Maximize the use of the title bar to provide context-sensitive information while retaining app-level access points, such as a link to your account information (one solution might be to supply a menu)

- Show a glimpse of what's coming next so you can decide whether or not to skip back to the gallery rather than flip through the genre one movie at a time

■ Convince Netflix executives that we don't have to prominently display the logo every single second the catalog is in use

But caveats aside, it's not bad for a concept sketch, right?

My favorite part of this concept is the filmstrip interface at the bottom—the row of tiny images with the "Shades of Ray" text. The idea is this: you tap any film's thumbnail to see its title, then tap the text overlay to go to the content screen for that film. In a perfect world, you could simply scroll through the content screens by running your finger across the display, but the loading time required to show all of these content screens with such immediacy would be too significant, especially over a slow network connection. Hence, this technical limitation means requiring two taps to access the content view: one to see the title of the movie, one to access the content view for that title.

Now, a few disclaimers: Netflix has done a great job on its site, the iPad was its first real foray into the world of touchscreen devices, and it's entirely possible that by the time you read this, the company will have completely overhauled its iPad app. I mean no offense to Netflix with this exercise. My point is only to illustrate the difference between an implementation-model design and a mental-model design.

▶ Eliminate Implementation Models

The rest of this chapter is about how to find implementation-model designs in your application plans and eliminate them before they get built. Most of these solutions, such as creating wireframes and running usability tests, are also great as general design methods, but we'll focus on them here as a way to ensure our applications support users' mental models.

Create wireframes to nail things down

When an architect goes to work on a new building, the first major design step is a blueprint. Likewise, when a designer begins a new application, wireframes are often the best place to start. A wireframe is the interface equivalent of a blueprint.

Wireframes come in many shapes and sizes, but they all aim to illustrate the initial design ideas for an end product.

Generally, they're not much more than stick-figure versions of future interface designs. They illustrate layout and spatial relationships, allude to the content that will eventually be added to the interface, and in some cases, show how contrast is to be used to set certain interface elements apart from others.

Various tools can be used to create wireframes, the most popular of which are OmniGraffle for Mac; Apple iWork Keynote, which I'll talk about more later in this chapter (note there are quite a few toolkits out there for designing for mobile devices with Keynote); Microsoft Visio and PowerPoint; and Axure RP Pro. Each of these tools has its own benefits and shortcomings, but each is a viable option.

A wireframe of a simple log-in screen has in-line validation to catch user-name and password errors.

The principal benefit of wireframes is that they help us *design understanding*. An entire interface can be designed in just a few minutes and changed just as easily. You can quickly create a document that shows you exactly which design elements will impede a user's ability to understand the application's purpose. With no idea at all about how the interface should look, you can simply start tossing various interface elements onto the screen because you know they'll need to be there, then gradually refine the layout, organization, and inter-action of each element until you have a design that makes sense. And you can keep going over it until you think the interaction works for users instead of working only to satisfy the system. (You can ask yourself, for example, Does the user actually need to know when this background operation fails, or is there a way the application can stay on track without warning the user? Does this screen need to appear here or somewhere else? Can we get rid of it entirely? Would getting rid of it make the application easier to understand?)

The Three Rs

When creating wireframes, pay close attention to the following three focal points, which I call the Three Rs.

Requirements. It may seem obvious that you need to pay attention to the requirements of the project, but this R is here as a constant reminder, because it's very easy to let someone else's pet feature (or even your own) make its way into your work. Far better to stick to what's absolutely necessary for the project, to support the activity that the product is meant to support and meet users' goals.

Do not—I repeat—do *not* let things that end with "that would be nice to have" get into your product in the first round. As discussed in Chapter 4, put the nice-to-haves on a separate list and see what's still important later on. For now, when you're staring at your screen and drawing out all the little boxes and widgets that make up your interface, stick to your guns. Stick to what's required. The items that are required are the most important, and are the only ones that should get any attention. The less there is to know about an applica-tion, the easier it is to understand.

Reduction. This is my favorite R. Along with sticking to the requirements for the project, be sure to reduce interfaces to their core as much as possible. Reduce clutter, reduce redundancy, reduce the possibility of user error, reduce verbiage until it's only as long as it absolutely needs to be—reduce, reduce, reduce. Then reduce some more. If you can find a way to make a single interface element serve three purposes while maintaining an obvious usage model, do it. If you can turn seven words into two, do it. If you can get rid of an entire interaction because the information it's intended to acquire can be obtained another way, do it, do it, do it.

All of this reduction will result in a significantly clearer and more understandable interface. Remember Einstein's rule:

> *Everything should be made as simple as possible, but not simpler.*

We'll talk about reduction in greater detail in Chapter 10.

Regularity. Regularity is about making it look like you did things intentionally. It's about using the same font and font size for all form labels, lining up input fields so they create a consistent design, using the same spacing in all blocks of text, the same colors for similar or related interface elements, and so on. Regularity means that if one text field is 20 pixels in from the left edge, and the next one is part of the same form, it should sit 20 pixels in from the left edge as well. Regularity is the notion of organizing, aligning, synchronizing, and optimizing interface elements so that they provide a clear, clean, aesthetically pleasing interface.

Chapter 9 has more on the subject of uniformity, and discusses how to leverage irregularity to create meaning and importance in a design.

The Three Rs are your support system. They keep you in check when your mind starts wandering and you start imagining how cool it would be to add a talking paper clip to your interface that answers help questions. Microsoft tried that once. It wasn't cool. Stick to the Three Rs.

The ultimate goal is to identify places the application can avoid reflecting how the system works. Find ways to avoid asking users questions that satisfy the system's needs instead of theirs. Present the options most likely to be chosen instead of forcing users to choose them manually—default options help illuminate the application's purpose and support the user's purpose. Provide a good starting point instead of forcing users through complicated setup screens, which often ask users tough questions without letting them know they can change their minds later on. Let the application explain itself instead of making the user explain how the system should work.

Wireframes can bring to light a lot of issues you simply can't see otherwise. So create your wireframes, look for the implementation models, and replace them with things that make sense for users.

Kaizen, applied to wireframes

Before you even start creating wireframes, you can grab the nearest notepad and sketch out your ideas there. Firewheel Design did so with Blinksale, and when I asked about the approach back in 2004, Josh Williams said:

> *We designed 75 percent of the product with ink on paper before we began working on the HTML code itself. This was incredibly helpful as our reasoning was that if the service couldn't be drawn simply on paper it was too complex for most people to use. The ink sketches also served as a wonderful reminder of what we wanted the service to be when we were tempted to add more features later. Of course, since we launched the service we have added features here and there, but our goal has always been to keep Blinksale easy to use for everybody.*

The first step I usually take is to sketch several design possibilities on a whiteboard (a dry-erase board). I sometimes do this in collaboration with other people involved with a particular project, but often it's just me and a marker. I simply swing my chair around from my desk and start frantically drawing something out on the large whiteboard conveniently (and intentionally) located as close to me as possible.

Some people stop there. If you're designing and building the application yourself, you can certainly go straight from a sketch to the real thing, even if you're only coding the HTML end of things.

The problem with this is that few people, if any, can consistently design the best possible interaction on the first try by simply sketching it out on a piece of paper once and going straight to code. The people who can do this understand complicated systems and have a far deeper knowledge of computer interactions than the average computer user. (A colleague of mine, Sunny Thaper, can stare at a piece of graph paper for 20 minutes and then proceed to draw—with a Sharpie, mind you—a complete interface, with annotations, as if it were his tenth try and he just finally got it perfect. It's so impressive, it's practically a party trick. Your results may vary.)

Use cases, sketches, and wireframes help designers see problems with an interface early on in the process and help them think through it. Designers are forced to think about each and every screen, how they relate to each other, how they flow, and how users might grasp them. As a result, creativity is given a bigger seat at the table.

Ideas emerge when designers give themselves the space they need to come up with them. If you only give yourself one shot to sketch something out before you start coding, you risk missing out on the other possibilities. But if your goal is to lay out an entire application and hand it off to a team of developers, then the entire process may begin and end with wireframes.

For example, I sketch ideas on the whiteboard, then move to Keynote or OmniGraffle, or whatever tool might be best that day, and create a fairly detailed wireframe there. Then I go into kaizen mode.

Kaizen, again, translates to "improvement," which is synonymous with iterative design (discussed in Chapters 3 and 9).

Before I present wireframes, I go over them several times, just as I do with use cases, each time trying to find ways to improve task flows, make user-interface widgets more clear, and error-proof the screens (we'll talk about this more in Chapter 8).

Once, while revamping the editing features in a web-page–builder application to improve usability, I immediately saw many ways that menus and tool-bar options could be consolidated to clean up the interface. So I created a text document and started making notes about all the things that could be grouped together, options that could be removed from the main toolbar, and pop-up windows that could be eliminated. I also took out my sketchpad and sketched out what the interface would look like if all these things were done.

Yes, it was much simpler than before, but it just wasn't enough. There were still two different modes for editing a newly created web page, and neither of them kept users in context—they both either took users away from the main interface or changed the view of the interface substantially enough that it was difficult to understand how edits would affect the page when they were completed. So I started looking for ways to combine the two editing modes and keep them in the main interface so that users would only have to learn that *what you see is what you get.* Plus, if a user could edit the page directly instead of moving into another mode, she would be able to work with the tool with a much simpler mental model.

In doing this, I saw a way to create a main toolbar that offered up a few common features and a couple of menus, and show it every time a user clicked into an editable text block. But after creating a first draft of a wireframe, this still seemed a bit awkward, as it meant this toolbar would appear in a different place every time the user edited a different area of a page.

Because users tend to rely on spatial memory—that is, they memorize where something is located on a page and continue to go back to the same spot for the functionality they found there last time—moving the toolbar around all the time wouldn't be an effective solution. After a little toying around with the wireframe, I moved the toolbar into a permanent spot within the main interface, and then added tabs to it. Each tab contained the editing tools for different page elements. One contained text-formatting tools. Another contained form widgets so users could add a form to their page and edit the properties of each form element. Another tab contained image-editing tools. Each tab provided a way to add elements to a web page a user would create himself, and the toolbar as a whole was contextual, so that when the user clicked inside a text block, he would see the text-formatting tab, and when he selected an image, he would see the image-editing tab, and so on.

This solution was by far the best of the possibilities, as it eliminated several implementation-model designs (such as the pop-up window used for one of the editing modes, which took users *away* from the page being edited); provided the right tools at the right time; and allowed me to get rid of many points of duplicate functionality. By doing these things, the new design made the tool easier to understand.

I never would have seen this possibility if I had drawn up one sketch and had gone straight to code. The moral of the story is that even if you do decide to go straight from sketch to code, don't rely on the first sketch. Go through a few and give yourself room to see the possibilities in a design before committing to anything.

Once I'm comfortable with a design, I like to talk it over with another interface designer to get a second opinion. When that's done, it goes to that application's product manager so we can hash out any other issues. (Eventually, the wireframes are approved and I start working with the graphic designers and developers to bring the application to life.)

All in all, the wireframes are probably changed a dozen times before they go to the development team. (Doing the same thing with code could take hours. In more extreme cases, two hours spent on wireframe revisions can eliminate weeks of coding. Unlike code, wireframes and sketches are extremely simple and inexpensive to change.) Each iteration is an incremental improvement over the previous version, and each one is a step closer to an obvious design that reflects a user's model instead of one that reflects only what the underlying system needs to perform its routines.

▶ Prototype the Design

A prototype is essentially the interactive version of a set of wireframes, by which other people can see how an interaction might work; how they might navigate a site to get through a series of screens; or how a particular widget, such as a drag-and-drop shopping cart, might behave. Prototypes come in varying degrees of quality, and it doesn't really matter how you build your prototypes, how nice they are, or whether they're exact simulations of a future design. What matters is that they demonstrate how something should work to some reasonable degree of accuracy.

The prime benefit of a prototype is that it brings to the surface all the instances where the system's logic is dictating how a design comes together. It also gives you something to show clients and coworkers that simulates real functionality, and the benefit of doing this can't be underestimated. Clients, and you, can click or tap on interface elements, see what happens as a result, and begin to get a real sense of what an application or site will do. This makes it quite simple to spot implementation models in a design, because they're right in front of you, and there's no way to escape them. And seeing them is the first step toward getting rid of them. Prototyping gives weight to a design that you can't deny. If it works well as a prototype, it has a good chance of working well as a real app. If not, things are only going to get worse. Prototypes are a cheap litmus test.

In addition to giving clients something that they can touch and use, a prototype can be used to solicit feedback about an interface before you get too deep into the process to make adjustments. Writing code is expensive, and it takes valuable time and energy to make changes to a working application. Making substantial changes late in the game causes missed deadlines and overblown budgets, but changing the entire behavior of an interaction in a prototype is fast, cheap, and easy. And usually it only takes one person to build and maintain the prototype, so it doesn't even interrupt a project.

The simple fact is that a prototype allows you to get valuable feedback and put it into action immediately to see how the new version is received. If people don't like the next version of the prototype, you can easily change it again. In fact, you can change it several times in a matter of hours, exploring different solutions to each problem the prototype is meant to address, and nail down a final solution before getting into coding.

Another key advantage to prototyping is that you have an interface in front of you throughout the entire development process, which helps limit the addition of new features that might obscure the basic purpose of the tool and therefore impose on the user's mental model. It also provides a clear picture of how the final project will work so everyone knows exactly what needs to be done, and it gives you a chance to work with the product directly very early in the process so you can gradually refine, step by step by step, until it shines.

One last benefit of a prototype is that you can create usability tests around it early in the development process. As long as your prototype clearly shows what will happen at each step in a process, you can run it past some actual users and find out very quickly what problems exist, what questions come up, and what can be improved. We'll talk more about testing your application later in this chapter.

There are quite a few ways to create a prototype, and each style has its own pros and cons. Following is a breakdown of some popular prototyping styles.

Paper prototyping

A paper prototype is made up of interface elements sketched on different pieces of paper so that various application states and screens can be shown without redrawing the interface each time. A paper prototype can be used for early usability tests by having one person act as the computer and another as the test moderator. The user "clicks" (touches) the parts of the interface he wants to interact with, and the person acting as the computer manipulates the paper sketches to show what would happen in the application as a result. To learn more about paper prototyping, pick up Carolyn Snyder's book *Paper Prototyping: The Fast and Easy Way to Design and Refine User Interfaces*, (Morgan Kaufman, 2003), and read every last word.

HTML

HTML prototypes are actual web pages, often put together without regard for color, fonts, or anything else that qualifies as a detail. The goal is to simply get the major elements of a screen into a basic HTML format and have users test it out to see if they understand the application's basic purpose and flow and interaction model. Various WYSIWYG (what-you-see-is-what-you-get) editors like Adobe Dreamweaver can be used to create these incredibly stripped-down versions of application screens in very little time, and it's a great way to see how an application might really work once it's completed so you can rapidly shape it into something that supports a user's mental model.

Note, however, that it's best to avoid using prototype code in a finished application. Prototype code is generally hacked together quickly and is unlikely to provide the scalability needed to create a stable application.

Click-through mockups

A click-through mockup is a series of mockups that illustrate various application states or screens, each of which has triggers (such as a button) to transport the user to the next screen and illustrate a basic task flow. Prototypes like this are great for illustrating a single course of action, but simulating multiple interactions within a single interface, or multiple states within a single screen, can certainly start to get time-consuming. It's often best to stick to the essentials. Still, click-through mockups can help you see where implementation models are being used so you can change things now instead of later.

Apple Keynote is a remarkable tool for click-through prototypes, especially with the array of toolkits now available for prototyping iPhone and iPad apps, such as Keynotopia (keynotopia.com) and the Keynote Wireframe Toolkit (keynotekungfu.com).

Flash

Macromedia Flash can be a fantastic tool for prototyping, but only if you know your way around ActionScript and can whip up interfaces quickly using the Flash UI Component Set that ships with the authoring tool and any prototype elements that need to be built from scratch. If you're willing to dive in, or already have some Flash skill, it's definitely worth testing to see if it's right for you. Create a prototype for something simple, such as a contact form, and see how far you have to take things to create an effective sample. The benefits you gain from the rich interface capabilities of Flash can outweigh the extra time you'll need to create prototypes with it.

▶ Test It Out

The number one way to explore the user experience of an application once it's created—and find any remaining implementation-model designs—is to test it. You've heard the hype about usability testing, you've read an article or two, and you may have even tried it, but odds are you're not testing your applications as often or in as many ways as you should be because, you might think, usability testing is typically very expensive and time-consuming. But there are plenty of ways to perform tests and get the information you need to build a better application, and the benefits reach far and wide. Abe Fettig, the man behind JotSpot (purchased by Google in 2006 and morphed into Google Sites), said:

> *Having users involved throughout the process was very helpful because it helped us identify any problems with the product. If we were missing an important feature, or something in the UI was confusing, or there was an irritating bug, we'd hear about it, usually from more than one person. Bringing in new testers throughout the development process was especially valuable because it gave us the perspective of people using the product for the first time. That helped us to recognize parts of the UI that were confusing to new users.*

The browserless self-test

A surefire way to get some quick feedback on a website is to test it yourself using the **browserless self-test**. *Browserless* is my word for testing without the benefit of browser tools. All you need to do is hide the tools in your browser, so you can't rely on Back and Forward buttons, an address bar, a Refresh (or Reload) button, or bookmarks.

Each browser comes with a way to hide all its tools. The option to hide each of these tools is usually tucked away in the View menu. Simply select the appropriate menu option to disable each of the various toolbars and you're ready to go.

Once you've gone browserless, you can find out how good your navigation really is—you can gauge how well it tells users where things are and how to get things done (if your design is filled with implementation-model information architecture, this will be more difficult, as a system's logical groupings and associations are usually very different than a user's).

Lay out a series of tasks to perform, such as "Purchase a rubber duckie" and "Find a desk lamp." Then run through each task to see if you can get around easily. You'll quickly find that going browserless is a little like cutting off your right hand. You never realize how much you rely on the Back and Forward buttons until you lose them. Suddenly, you realize that in order to go back, you have to remember the name of the page you were on, be able to use a link to get it, and be confident that the link you click is the right one. Of course, you can cheat a little by using the backspace or delete key to go back, but try to keep yourself from doing this. Most people don't even know about this shortcut, and cheating won't help you make your site better.

Finding a page within the site is easier to do if it has a clear, relevant title that maps directly to a link on the page you're viewing now. If the link can't use the exact page title of the page it links to, it needs to instill at least enough confidence that users can tell they'll go right to it by clicking the link. If the page cannot be linked to directly from every other page, then users need to be able to *eventually* get to the page they're after by following a path through the site.

Browserless self-tests help support a user's mental model by forcing you to see how the site is really organized. If your site holds up against this test, odds are the organizational structure is pretty solid.

For example, an About the Company page will probably be linked to in the persistent navigation on your site. Almost every page will contain this link and users can always find it. But a product information page about the rubber duckie you want to buy, on a site that sells thousands of different products, isn't going to be so prevalent. To find the duckie, you need to be able to wade through the architecture of the entire site. You might start by doing a simple search using the site's search function. If the search results are good, you'll find the duckie in no time. If the results aren't good, because the underlying database isn't designed with the same conceptual groups and this design flaw made its way to the site's navigation, or if there is no Search box, or you're not sure what keywords to use in your search, you might click the Products link, choose the Rubber Toys category link on the landing page, and then choose a particular rubber duckie from the category's main catalog page.

What this means is that every page needs to not only provide access to the products catalog, but also be incredibly clear that the link leads to information about your products. Not information about the fact that you sell products, or how you sell them, or how you ship them, but a page that starts the process of drilling down into the site hierarchy to find the rubber duckie.

Here's Target.com without the aid of browser tools like back and forward buttons.

Using Target.com in a browserless test to locate a desk lamp, I landed on a page full of desk lamps in exactly *two clicks* by choosing Home Office from the Furniture drop-down menu in the persistent navigation, and then clicking Desk Lamps in the sidebar navigation on the landing page. Nice.

The five-second test

User Interface Engineering (www.uie.com) advocates the use of what they call the "five-second test." This type of usability testing involves gathering up some users, or going somewhere many people are likely to be gathered at once (they suggest the company's cafeteria). So it's slightly more complicated than a browserless self-test, but the focus is very different, as it is intended to yield insights about the clarity of a site.

To perform a five-second test, write a list of screens on your site or in your application that need to be particularly clear and concise, and either open them up in different browser windows (or tabs within a single window) or print them out and show them to the users. Show each user the screens, one at a time, for five seconds each, and ask them to write down notes about everything they saw. Alternatively, you can try **www.fivesecondtest.com**, a fantastic site whose sole purpose is to enable you to run five-second tests, with the added advantage of being able to run them remotely by sending a link to the test page (which only displays for five seconds) to anyone you wish.

A prime candidate for a five-second test is a page that has only one purpose and is critical to the success of the site. For example, a page on a domain-name registrar's site that lets users search for domain names—the key product for the company—should be crystal clear, because making the domain-search function and purchase path difficult to understand would seriously affect the company's sales. Ask each user to look at the screen for five seconds and locate the possible extensions (.com, .net, and so on) they can use with their new domain name. When the five seconds are up, have the users write down everything they remember about the page. Ask them what they think is the focus of the page. Ask them what the domain extension options were. Ask them what they'd click to choose a domain extension.

If you get the answers you want, you're doing well. If not, it's a sign you should redesign the page. Don't perform a major redesign on it, though, unless it's really off the mark—just apply incremental changes to it until it works. The goal is usually to incrementally reduce clutter in this design until the point of the screen becomes clear. We'll talk more about reducing clutter in Chapter 10.

For more information on five-second tests, see UIE's article at **www.uie.com/ articles/five_second_test**.

Interview testing

A more complicated but more in-depth approach to usability testing is to perform interview-style sessions. These are done by meeting with users in person, asking them to complete various tasks in an application, and having them think out loud about what they experience so you can determine how the application holds up to the user's mental model. Typically, interview sessions require three to eight users and last several days, but they can be reduced to two or three users with all the tests performed in a single morning.

These types of sessions involve more planning than other tests. Prior to performing a usability session like this, you need to plan a set of tasks that users will be asked to complete, prepare a lab of some kind—a room where you can perform the tests and record the sessions (preferably on video, using a video camera or a screen-recording tool like one of TechSmith's products, Camtasia Studio or Morae)—and schedule users to come to your company.

Preparing tasks to be tested can be time-consuming, because the ideal tasks are those that satisfy the key business objectives while also lining up with a user's goals. For example, a stock photography site might have a key business objective to establish a large base of repeat visitors, while the user's goal might be to find a quicker way to get through a site's thousands of images. To meet these goals, the application might enable a user to add any image she sees to a personal library so that on future visits she can go straight to a small set of images she already knows she likes. The tasks of creating and using the personal library are perfect for usability testing. If a user doesn't understand the core concept of the personal library or how to work with it, the goals of the application cannot be met. Through active listening and the use of surveys taken by users before and after the session about how they felt about the application while using it, you can extract quite a bit of insight about how understandable the application is, and you're likely to learn a few things you weren't even thinking about.

Recruiting testers

One thing to note here is that finding users to do the test is sometimes tricky. Some companies use marketing agencies to handle this, because they keep detailed profile information on hand and can simply pull up a list of people who fit the profile for the test session. Then the agencies handle calling all those people and scheduling as many people as the company needs. This has a cost, of course, but it can be a big time-saver. If you have a product support department within your company, however, you can try to leverage that fact by getting the support people to help you sign up and schedule testers. You might also add a link to your site that lets people know they can get involved in improving future versions of your product by volunteering for usability tests. This link should direct users to a screening survey on your site to help determine ahead of time who might be good for a particular testing session. You can leave this up all the time, in fact, provided you have a way to manage the pool of users that will be generated by it. Doing this, you can simply pull up a list anytime you want to run a new test, make a few calls, and you've got yourself a testing session.

By the way, don't forget to compensate the users somehow. Gift cards, free software, things like that. Give users a reason to get involved.

Contextual usability testing

Interview-style testing can have one major downside: users tend to open their critical eye while participating in usability testing sessions, which can obscure the truth about the test results. Despite telling them you're testing the software and not them, users tend to think they need to be thorough and mention every little thing they come across, and this isn't really how people work with applications in their own environments. Also, the fact that the testers are in lab settings means they won't know certain information about the computer they're using, such as bandwidth settings and what (fake) credit card number to use if they'll be making a purchase as part of the test. This can throw off the tester and interrupt the testing session.

To avoid all this, and potentially gain more honest feedback, you can try **contextual usability testing** (a.k.a. *reconnaissance testing*). This involves watching users interact with your product without telling them that you're taking mental notes about how they're using it. You can do this by asking people within your company to walk you through a certain task under the ruse that you don't already know how to complete it, or simply walk over and strike up a conversation with someone using the product and ask what they're up to.

Of course, you run the risk they'll stop working while you're talking to them, and that won't be any good at all. To prevent this, you could just eavesdrop from behind a nearby rubber tree plant. Pretend you're reading something and just listen to the user complain to her neighbor about how difficult it is to find a rubber duckie on your site. Bring the test to the user under the ruse that you need it double-checked for typos, broken links, and so on (a.k.a. *bulletproofing*). Watch for what confuses users and what irritates them. Do they gradually get more frustrated, for example, when asked the same question ("Are you sure?") every time they delete data within the application? If so, the implementation model is winning again, and you know what needs to be done.

Keep the "tests" informal and in context. Perform usability tests the same way you perform contextual inquiry. Then ask the users what they thought of the overall experience, and employ active listening to bear out the critical information they are dying to give you.

Eat your own dog food

Eating your own dog food is the act of using the products you create, as religiously as your customers. It's a very simple idea.

It is also the single most effective method I've found yet, not only to test an application, but also to get an up-close and personal look at the experience I'm forcing upon my users. It pays off in ways that cannot easily be described. You simply have to do it to understand just how great it is.

Consider this story.

My local library once changed its domain name. No big deal. But to avoid the incredible marketing and customer education campaign that would be needed to inform patrons of the change, they opted to redirect users to the new site automatically. Instead of redirecting users from every page of the old site, however, only the library's homepage was pointed to the new location. If every user went straight to the homepage, and all the bookmarks that patrons had ever created went only to the homepage, this would have worked. But this wasn't so.

On the day after the switch, librarians all over the district were inundated with phone calls—far more than normal—from customers saying said they couldn't log in. Others said they couldn't even access the log-in page.

All of these customers had bookmarked the log-in page. The rather obvious fact, which no one involved with the creation and maintenance of the site realized, is that the vast majority of library patrons go to the site to perform tasks involved with their accounts. The homepage offered no way to log in, so it wasn't the page they used. The log-in page, on the other hand, wasn't redirecting them to the new domain.

The logical thing to do when a site provides account access is to provide a log-in widget on the homepage. That's the obvious design. The library did not do this. Its understanding of how users worked with the site didn't match how users actually worked. The solution was based on the system. The system says the homepage is the major entry point to the site, so it's the page that was redirected. In other words, the library had a dysfunctional mental model of its users.

If the library's web team had been eating their own dog food, they would have known about the issue long before that fateful day when all those customers were suddenly stuck with no ability to log in to their accounts. They could have avoided the issue completely and improved the user experience for *all* of their customers in the meantime.

When you use an application yourself, it's very hard to trap yourself into theoretical, academic conversations about whether Solution A is more usable than Solution B. You get to see the problems firsthand. In addition to giving you an inside perspective on what it's like to be a user of your application, it's also incredibly motivating, because you're in a position to fix the issues.

Only by eating your own dog food can you really see what's great, what needs work, what needs to be added, and what needs to be removed. Sure, you can learn some of these things by simply doing quality assurance testing prior to release, but QA is not personal. When you use an application every single day, it becomes very personal. It's part of your life. You use it to complete the very same tasks your users do. And since it's your application, you can actually make it better.

All in all, there are a million ways to uncover how users think about an application and implement solutions that meet those needs. Sketches, wireframes, prototypes, and usability tests are all great ways to find those pesky implementation-model designs and replace them with something more in line with a user's mental model. Focusing on these things will make your applications better. And better applications make for happier users who keep coming back.

6

Turn Beginners into Intermediates, Immediately

- ▶ Use Up-to-Speed Aids
- ▶ Choose Good Defaults
- ▶ Design for Information
- ▶ Stop Getting Up to Speed and Speed Things Up
- ▶ Provide Help Documents, Because Help Is for Experts

When we, the more computer-savvy users of the world, dive into a new application, we tend to learn everything we can as quickly as possible, hunting through all the nooks and crannies to uncover features and find out how the application stands up to others we've used. We want to see how far we can push the application. We strive to become experts.

Other people don't do this. They get up to speed just enough to become productive with the application, and they stay at this level until there's a compelling reason to learn more. Usually, there is no compelling reason.

Alan Cooper points out in *The Inmates Are Running the Asylum* that the skill level of users doesn't break down quite as neatly as we usually think, into beginner, intermediate, and expert. First of all, most users are not experts. In fact, only a very small percentage of users ever extend their skills within an application beyond that of an intermediate user. Secondly, beginners tend to quickly learn what they need to know to use an application, stepping forward at great speed into the land of what Cooper calls "perpetual intermediates."

What this means is that when we design for beginners and/or experts, we're usually designing for the wrong crowd. The intermediate users are by far the largest group.

Even when an intermediate user does become an expert, it's often for a very short period of time, when the application being used is particularly important for a certain project or task where the user has to spend a substantial amount of time using it, and therefore learns to use it with greater proficiency.

Since beginners turn into intermediates quickly and intermediates rarely become experts, user skill levels, in chart form, actually take the shape of a bell curve.

Focusing on the features intermediate users want and need means improving usability all around by leaving out many of the more obscure features that take a long time to create and learn. Building less also translates to shorter time lines, so we can get applications to market sooner and spend less money doing it. (Isn't it nice, by the way, how well the concepts of improving usability and getting to market quickly work together? It's counterintuitive, but often the less time you spend building an application, the better it is.)

Along the way, however, we have to remember to teach our future intermediate users how to use our applications, or else they'll never become intermediates. We also have to remember that since we're designing for intermediates, continually shoving beginner-level tools in their way will annoy them in the long run.

To satisfy both goals, we need to offer up some sacrificial lambs, so to speak. That is, we need to implement some tools that stick around long enough to help users learn what they need to know, but then disappear once their purpose has been served. We also need to make smart decisions about which features to put up front and which ones to tuck away in the back. We need to inject instructive elements into interfaces that help new users and serve as reminders to intermediate users. Finally, we need to provide help documentation for the users who will eventually read it, and instructive hints throughout the application so everyone can be productive without a lot of hassle.

▶ Use Up-to-Speed Aids

Getting users up to speed in applications is something that needs to be handled on a case-by-case basis. There isn't one best way to do it. But there are plenty of ways we can get it done via the use of "up-to-speed" aids.

For example, we can provide a Getting Started guide to new users and display a link to it when a user logs in for the first time. We can offer a video tour or a set of screen shots that shows new users a quick overview of the product's main feature set. In an application where users collectively contribute to a large base of information, like a wiki, we can point users to examples of content created by other users so they can see the end result of the work they're being asked to perform.

Getting Started guides and video tours, however, are used out of context. Users can't read information about how an application works at the same time they're using the application because the two usually appear in different windows. In an application where examples of content can be shown to new users, the examples generally don't offer insight into how the content was created, so users still need information about how to get going and how to complete basic tasks. And this is a prime moment for us as application developers, because if a user is looking around for a way to get started, it means we've already convinced her that our application is worth trying out. Now is the time to pounce and show the user what we've got.

Many applications resort to walking new users through **setup wizards**, which are step-by-step sequences of screens designed to get a user to configure the initial settings for an application. The least objectionable of these offer insight into how to use the application along the way. The most objectionable have a few common bad habits.

First, setup wizards ask questions about how a user wishes to use the application right off the bat. The problem is that the user has never previously used the application, so answering such questions, while not impossible, is purely speculative on the user's part. The next problem is that wizards rarely assure users that they can change their decisions later on. But worse than this is that the presence of a wizard is a clear sign the application designers haven't made good decisions for users in the first place. Users may not catch on to this, but they will catch on to the fact that the wizard is keeping them from *playing around with the application.*

If we manage to convince a user to check out an application, the next logical step is to get them moving forward. Quickly.

The masterful designer Jason Putorti recognized this challenge when approaching the design of Mint.com. Mint is a personal-finance management tool that attempts to make bank and credit card records understandable and practical by consolidating information, highlighting finance charges and other important things that affect your income but could be difficult to spot through bank's website, and enabling you to set budgets and goals for your income.

He recently told me:

> *The most important part of designing the setup process was to motivate users to add that first account. To that end it had to be approachable, intuitive, and presented in a friendly, non-threatening manner. Users are entering bank credentials, after all. Security language (SSL, etc.) needed to be available*

> *to prevent abandonment, but trust is a gut feeling. The first
> version of add accounts had clickable cards like you'd find in
> your wallet. Clicking on a card would prompt for the required
> information, and once the add account process was kicked off
> on one card, we taught the user that others could be added at
> the same time. The first-time setup interface was the same as
> adding an account later.*

Mint does an excellent job of getting users up to speed, constantly providing
helpful hints about how to do things.

The first time you sign in, for example, Mint offers a three-step overview of
how to get started.

Mint explains the three steps for getting started.

The first screen in the process of tracking a bank account offers all kinds of
instructive elements. There's a list on the left side that explains what you're
doing and how it works, a list of examples of how to enter a bank's name, and
even a section of links for popular banks so you can skip the typing completely.

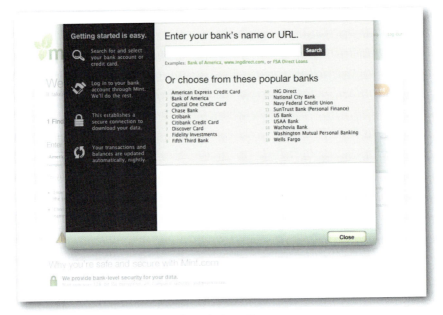

Mint's bank setup screen steps you through the entire process.

Even the email that is sent to new registrants contains a clear, useful list of numbered steps, followed by a link to the site.

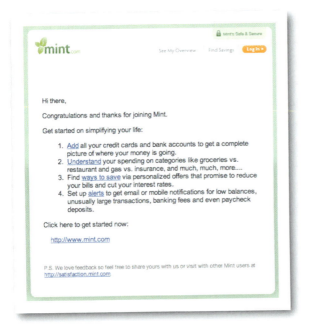

The Welcome email sent to new Mint users puts the most useful information into a numbered list.

Jason told me more about his approach:

> *My belief is that once a user figures out how something works, they'll remember it the second time. They do not need to be reminded every time they use the application. Hence, I like instruction to be self-discoverable, not visible all the time like a tooltip. Not every link on Mint is blue and underlined, for example, to enhance readability. Other examples are the spending pie charts—there's no text nearby to tell people to drill down to a subcategory by clicking, but the pie slice will light up on hover, indicating that a click will do something. In fact, there was never any help documentation created for Mint, the goal was not to need it.*

These and other elements like them help users get up to speed quickly and start taking advantage of the Mint.com service. And touches like this appear throughout Mint.com. The site is so good that potential clients regularly tell me they want their sites to be "the Mint.com of [*insert industry here*]."

Provide a welcome screen

Many desktop-installed applications—Adobe Dreamweaver and Flash, for example—provide welcome screens to new users. These screens often offer links to a quick tour of a tool's feature set and tutorials to get started, and that's awfully nice of them; but again, these types of aids are used out of context from the application and end up not being as helpful as they could be. Yes, people can learn in one window and apply new knowledge in other windows, but users can only focus on one window at a time. And a window containing a tutorial is not an application window, so users are focusing in the wrong place. It's better to train users by having them actually use the application.

To build a better welcome screen, we need to *Know the Best Ways to Implement It*. Instead of offering tours and tutorials out of context, a welcome screen should be integrated into the application screens themselves and remain contextual. For example, we can designate an area at the top of an application screen to display information about what to do on that page and perhaps what to do next. We can also reveal new information whenever a user switches screens. Keeping it contextual like this means each and every screen in the application can teach users how to perform tasks without preventing them from using it at the same time.

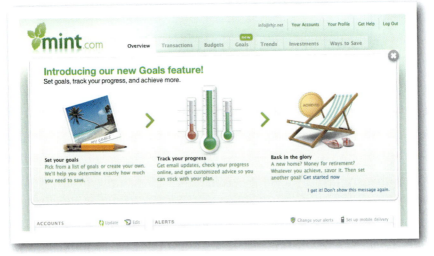

An integrated welcome screen informs users of what they can do on Mint.com's user homepage.

Welcome screens implemented like this should, of course, offer an obvious way for users to disable the screen so it doesn't appear on repeat visits. A simple check box lets users close the welcome screen.

Fill the blank slate with something useful

A blank slate can be a scary thing. It's a big empty space where there will eventually be content you create yourself. It's a blank sheet of sketch paper. In an application, it's often a page with no content that the user is supposed to fill.

Some people are inspired by spaces like these. I'm one of them. When I look at a blank slate, I see all the things I want to put in it. Many designers can do this. But for users just getting to know an application, a blank slate can be a barrier in the learning process. Instead of knowing exactly what to do first, users can become stalled when faced with the empty canvas.

To eliminate these moments of immobility, it's good to fill the blank slate with something instructive. In addition to helping users get up to speed, it can be a great way to compel users to jump in and start using your application, which can be the hardest thing to do. The first few moments users spend with a new application can be intimidating. Again, the goal is to get them moving forward quickly.

When asked how 37signals gets users going in new applications, Jason Fried told me:

> *Have them dive in. Experiment. Use them. Make mistakes, even. Don't throw a big manual on someone's desk and say "READ THIS!"—that will only set them up for an ugly experience. Software shouldn't be something you have to use, it should be something you want to use. When you have to train people to use something, or when you force them to read page after page, software becomes a chore. Not good. So make simple software that doesn't require a manual, and let people derive immediate value from your product by encouraging them to just dive in.*

37signals makes the act of jumping in very simple. In applications like Basecamp and Backpack, it's easy to know exactly what to do as soon as you log in for the first time, because there is no blank slate. Instead, there is a very noticeable block of text or an image that explains what to do, like a help document that appears exactly when and where you need it.

Basecamp's blank slate features large links that tell users how to start creating content and what kinds of content they can create.

The sketchbook app Penultimate for iPad offers something similar the first time it is launched. Rather than provide a blank sketchbook, it offers a *Welcome to Penultimate* sketchbook, eight pages long, featuring instructions on how to use the app and some of its major benefits. On the web, an instruction manual runs a high risk of going completely ignored, but in Penultimate's case, the very act of using the manual teaches users how to use the app. Each page contains a different instruction—about how to turn pages, draw, erase, undo an action, and so on.

First impressions are vital, and we often have only a few seconds to convince users that our applications are worth using (especially on the web). Showing users exactly what they're getting into and helping them get up to speed can make them comfortable, eager to dive in, and immediately knowledgeable.

These are all good things. Not only do users get to feel productive and smart, we get to keep another customer.

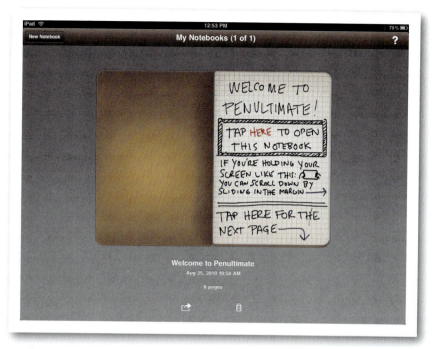

Penultimate fills its blank slate with a user manual that is itself a sketchbook, making the learning process very hands-on.

Give instructive hints

Another effective way to help users get moving, now *and* later, is to apply a little **instructive design.** Instructive text, for example, can be used in form elements and interfaces in general to guide the user within the context of her current task without being intrusive.

A text field that accepts only a numerical value can display a sample value of 0. The sample value is displayed so users can clearly see what type of information is required and enter the right type of data without having to think about it or guess. This small bit of instructive design helps guide users toward completing a task or through the use of an interaction without interfering with workflow. It simply eliminates questions in the user's mind before they come up.

Instructive text can also be used as an inline tip about how to perform a certain action or what happens as a result of performing an action.

When providing tips in an interface (for example, a line of instruction about what will happen when the user interacts with the page element), instructive text should be set to a small font size—smaller than the default font size for the text in the rest of the page—and simply positioned near enough to the interaction to which it applies that the connection is obvious. The goal, ultimately, is to get rid of the little thought bubbles that appear over users' heads that say things like, "Um, what's this button do?"

Instructive text can be used in these cases:

- When a form field requires a specific data type (such as a number) and it is potentially unclear to users what needs to be entered

- When users are expected to enter a value in a specific format (such as "123456-A")

- When it is unclear what the result of an action will be or how to perform an action (for example, "Click inside the text block to specify where the new text should be inserted")

When a default value is offered within a form field, the dummy text should be shown in a midtone gray font instead of the standard black so the user knows the text is only there as a guide. But for instructive text (as opposed to text used as a default value), it's not usually necessary to change the font color. And when the field gains focus—when a user clicks or tabs into the field—the instructive text should disappear immediately so the user can begin typing.

Pandora for iPhone offers instructive text on its Settings screen to help users understand how a change will affect the app. To explain the effect of enabling higher-quality audio, for example, Pandora uses inline tips.

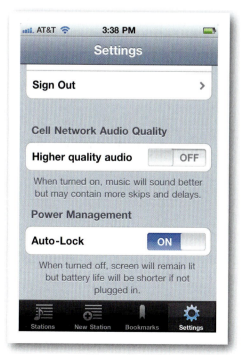

The iPhone version of Things, a to-do list app, offers instructive text inside form elements to let users know what new content needs to be entered.

Pandora offers inline tips to explain the effect of each setting.

Flipboard does a good job here as well. Flipboard is an iPad app that pulls the content linked to from whichever RSS feeds you've chosen, as well as your Facebook and Twitter streams, and dynamically converts them into a magazine.

The "Add a Section" statement positioned in the lower-right serves to tell new users exactly what needs to be done to add a new section to the highly personalized magazine. This text block also features a different background than others in the page to make it stand out. A quick glance at the page reveals exactly where to add the next magazine section.

Tapping one of the options adds the content as a new section to Flipboard and returns the user to the Contents screen.

Instructive hints come in many forms, but all of them show up just in time and keep users on track, alleviating confusion and frustration.

Interface Surgery: Applying instructive design

Users expect feedback when they interact with computers. In fact, they generally expect the same level of feedback from computers as they would get from real people in real situations. If a user is supposed to answer a set of questions, for example, she'll expect some feedback that the system can use the answers as she provided them and that she's moving forward in the process.

Forms don't usually supply this feedback. Instead, users often complete a form in its entirety without getting any feedback at all until the end, when users are told they've entered data in a way the system can't handle. When it comes to forms, typically users only get feedback if they mess something up.

This happens often when users enter email addresses and phone numbers, among other things. A user can get all the way through a page-long form and click the Submit button feeling pretty confident she's going to see a positive result. Instead, she sees a JavaScript alert message telling her the phone number she entered is in an incorrect format, or the page refreshes and displays a list of the errors that must be addressed before she can move on.

This is not a good way to reinforce positive behavior on the user's part. And it can be rather insulting to have a computer tell you that you're not conforming to its rules. Isn't the computer a tool that helps you instead of the other way around?

Lots of companies have heeded the call to make their applications more usable and have leapt into action, but sadly, many of them are just redesigning bad behavior. One of my longtime favorite (bad) examples is the registration form used on a former version of Odeo.com, a podcast aggregation and creation service.

Odeo's registration form was definitely simple. It didn't ask for any information it didn't actually need. It asked for only three pieces of information: name, email address, and password (though it did ask you to confirm your chosen password, requiring you to enter it twice). But the problem wasn't with the simplicity, it was with the size.

The image shown here may not do it justice—the important thing to notice is that the four form fields are *huge*. Maybe Odeo's designers thought they were improving the usability of the form by making it readable from across the room. Maybe they just wanted to fill up the space. Who knows. Whatever the case, they didn't do any of the things we can do as application designers and developers to make the form truly more effective, so their apparent intention to improve usability looked more like an insult. It's as though they're saying to all the less computer-savvy users out there, which they appeared to be rather tired of, "Go ahead. Just try to screw *this* up!"

Most users wouldn't have had problems seeing the form. Making your form fields big won't help. Let's take a look at what *will* help.

First take a look at this rather typical form used to store contact information.

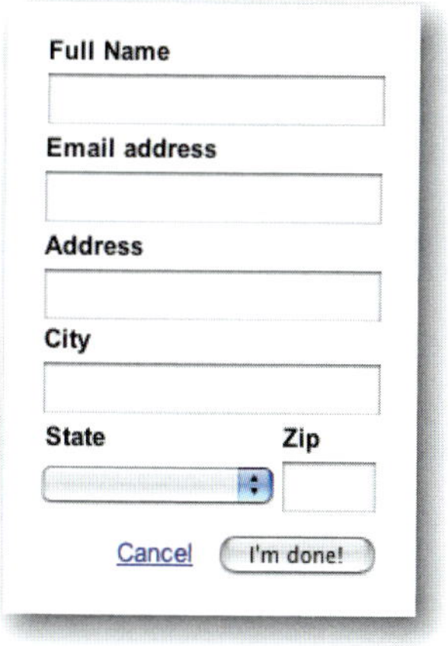

One generic form, served up fresh.

Nothing special here. Looks like 1,000 other forms we've all seen (and probably created).

The form is one of the most common interactions on the web, used for everything from purchasing airlines tickets to signing up for an Amazon account. And while they're usually simple enough to get through, they tend to exhibit some weaknesses.

The problems with the form above are as follows:

1. Many users don't know, don't understand, or don't remember the differences between an email address and a URL. ("I use AOL, so I guess they want me to enter *aol.com*.") This may not be true in your world, but believe me, it's true in the rest of the world. The people using your applications are not nearly as computer-savvy as you think (unless, of course, your target audience is composed of other developers).

2. Zip codes come in two forms in the United States: the short form of five digits, and the long form of nine digits. Some forms let you enter all nine digits. Some don't. Some of those forms require hyphens between the first five digits and last four. Some don't. It's not clear which version can be used in this form.

3. The I'm Done button is fairly personable, but it's also enabled by default, which means users can click it to submit the form data at any time—even when no field has been completed. This will produce errors. The goal is to avoid errors (more on this in Chapter 7).

4. Nothing indicates which fields are required. This can result in error messages if some fields are, in fact, required. At the very least, users have to wonder whether or not fields are required because so many other forms have required fields. The expectation is to find some sort of indicator.

5. No feedback is given as a result of completing form fields. The user must simply *guess* how to enter data in the correct way.

Time to apply some instructive design.

To fix the first issue—that many users are likely to enter something other than a valid email address—we can provide a default value in the text field. The most useful instructive text in this case is a fake email address because it shows users all the elements of an email address that must be entered. Again, the font color should be a midtone gray instead of the default black.

Another way to hint that the displayed data is instructive rather than already completed is to italicize it. We can do this in the Zip field as well, so users know exactly what version of a zip code can or should be entered. We can also add a simple disclaimer to the form to indicate that all fields are required. And just for good measure, we can add a default value to the State menu to prompt users to choose an item.

Applying instructive text to the form clears up a few questions.

Finally, to prevent users from attempting to submit an incomplete form, we can disable the I'm Done button until all required fields are complete.

A disabled button means users can't even attempt to submit form data until everything is just right. Believe it or not, this is a good thing.

This is a vast improvement to the original form, but we can take this much further. To provide real-time feedback to the user that the form is being completed correctly, or incorrectly, we can add visual cues to let him know what's going on by performing inline validation on each form element.

To do this, we can display icons when the user clicks or tabs to a new field to let him know the previous field has been correctly completed, and inline error messages to indicate when the field contains data the system can't use.

Inline validation and well-written error messages tell me I've messed up my email address. It also tells me how to enter it correctly.

Here, check-mark icons are shown to let the user know a field has been completed in a way that agrees with the system. As soon as the user leaves a field that is correctly completed, the check-mark icon appears. In the code for the page, JavaScript is used to verify that the Full Name field, for example, has had a string of characters entered into it. If not, an error message is displayed immediately.

Errors are shown in the right place and at the right time: the very second the user makes the mistake and tries to move on. When the user tabs away from the Email Address field, having entered an invalid email address, a red text message appears directly beneath the form field, so he knows not only that there has been an error, but also which field contains the error.

The key to an effective error message in a form like this is to avoid leaving the user wondering how to fix the problem. Many error messages simply inform the user an error exists. In the image above, however, the error message tells the user what needs to be entered in the field. This prompts him to fix the entry and tells him how to fix it.

Finally, once all required fields in the form have been completed correctly, the I'm Done button is enabled, letting the user know he has done all he needs to do and can move forward.

Check marks offer immediate feedback every time I complete a field correctly, motivating me to continue. When all is well, the I'm Done button lights up and I'm on my way. No mistakes. No mess. No questions.

Yes, this version of the form is more visually complex than before, and yes, the form is more difficult to build than the original (building a form this way requires a combination of HTML, Javascript, and CSS), but inline validation and instructive text help keep the user confident that he will complete the interaction correctly and continue being productive.

Incidentally, since the I'm Done button is disabled until the required fields are completed, it's actually now impossible to submit the form data until it's correct, so the user will never find himself in a situation where he feels false hope that the form is complete, and he will not see a refreshed page with error messages displayed.

Instructive design, applied in forms or otherwise, helps beginners learn how to complete an interaction and simply serves as a reminder to intermediate and expert users without getting in their way.

▶ Choose Good Defaults

Many web applications offer configuration options at every turn. This usually happens because developers like to offer every available option they can to users even if it makes little or no sense to do so. "If it can be done, it shall be offered as an option," they say. But the better way to go is to choose good defaults, because it improves a user's chances of learning an application quickly and allows her to dive in and start exploring without having to make a bunch of decisions all the time.

Users typically don't want to configure applications and customize them as much as developers would like to believe. In fact, most users stick to whatever defaults they are offered and avoid customizing at all. Choosing good defaults, then, is not only important, it means that the decisions we make while developing new applications are decisions we make for all of our users. Defaults have long-lasting effects, and we must be careful about what we put in front of users by default, as the user's first impression (and all the others after that) is greatly affected by what we decide to show them.

Jakob Nielsen, renowned guru of web usability, says in "The Power of Defaults" (one of his many revered Alertbox articles):

> *Users rely on defaults in many other areas of user interface design. For example, they rarely utilize fancy customization features, making it important to optimize the default user experience, since that's what most users stick to.*

Doesn't get much simpler than that. Yes, we could try to gather statistics so we'd have a hard and fast rule to live by, but users don't work that way. The best we can do is use our best judgment and choose good defaults whenever we can in the interest of providing a quality user experience.

Nielsen states in the same article:

> *System-provided default values constitute a shortcut since it is faster to recognize a default and accept it than to specify a value or an option. In many cases, users do not even need to see the default value, which can remain hidden on an optional screen that is only accessed in the rare case where it needs to be changed. Defaults also help novice users learn the system since they reduce the number of actions users need to make before using the system, and since the default values give an indication of the kind of values that can be legally specified.*

Fortunately, many good defaults are built into applications already and can be used as a lesson in how to choose them. Yahoo email doesn't ask if you want to use regular text or bold text every time you start a new message. Google doesn't ask if you'd like to run a Boolean search or a keyword search. And Amazon doesn't ask if you'd like to see its recommendations based on your previous purchases. These are default behaviors, and obviously they're quite helpful.

A good default is one that is most likely to benefit the most people. While there may be options that can be configured at every turn in many applications, the default options should be the ones users would most likely choose if they had to make the choice and the effects of the choice were clear.

Consider a help system that includes a search box designed to let users search either the help system or the web, with radio buttons that let them make the choice. Which option should be selected by default? Odds are, the user is there to read help articles, so let's show him help articles. My vote goes for searching the help system. Every design decision affects the user's experience—even things as small as this.

Consider, too, Google's old site-builder tool Google Page Creator (circa 2004, now part of Google Sites). First, it automatically selected a template for you so you could immediately start designing. Each template also had a default layout, so if you switched templates, you didn't have to make another choice at the same time. You could just start building a page. (If you wanted to change layouts later on, you could do so without damaging the work you'd done in the original.) Default fonts and font sizes were used for headings, subheadings, and body text. When you imported images, default dimensions were chosen (which you could immediately change via the inline toolbar). Filenames were also assigned by default based on the name you chose as a heading for a page.

Google Page Creator made one decision after another for its users, so they were free to be productive instead of being forced to make decisions at every step.

See how many times I used the word "default" in that description? Sure, you can change anything you want, but defaults get you moving. *Fast.*

Many developers latch onto the idea that users should have every option available to them. But people don't work like that. We'd rather get something done efficiently so we can move on to something else. Decisions get in the way. Options, settings, choices—they all get in the way. For software to be most effective, it needs to get *out* of the way. Choosing good defaults accomplishes this goal.

Integrate preferences

The real goal behind choosing good defaults is not to get rid of settings and options completely, but to show logical settings by default while still offering alternative settings when they're needed. When this is done well, we can make things even easier by integrating the settings users will likely want to change into the main application screens.

Settings are often best presented in the context of the application itself. Instead of relegating them to a settings screen full of options where users cannot readily see how a setting affects the application, settings can be integrated seamlessly into main application screens and handled inline. For example, default options that can be changed can be shown alongside a Change This link that reveals a way to change the setting without leaving the page via an inline form or other widget, thus enabling users to make their changes without losing context.

By all means, include settings and configurable options if you think people will want them, but don't force users to make decisions at every step. Make decisions for them—long before they ever see the application—that help them get up to speed. If they want to change things, they will. Just let them get their hands dirty first.

▶ Design for Information

The organization of an application's features can be determined in a lot of ways. In simpler tools, the answers usually present themselves. After all, an application with few features really can't hide much, so each feature is often equally as important as the next. But more complex solutions, like intranets and company-wide accounting systems and such, are a different story altogether. In cases like these, we can learn quite a bit from the world of information architecture.

Information architects have been spinning complicated globs of data into works of organizational art for years, and this expertise has carried over to the web, where it helps keep sites like CNN.com and NYTimes.com on the straight and narrow. From this world of expertise, we can gain incredible insight into how users would organize features if the choice were theirs, and learn how users search for things on the web.

The Boxes and Arrows article "Four Modes of Seeking Information and How to Design for Them" (**www.boxesandarrows.com/view/four_modes_ of_seeking_information_and_how_to_design_for_them**), written by Donna Spencer, discusses four principal ways that users search for content within information-based websites. The four methods Spencer talks about are:

- **Known item** In this search method, users know what they're looking for and know the words they need to look for to stay on the trail. Typical support methods for this type of information-seeking are navigation, indexes, and search features.

- **Exploratory** In exploratory searching, users may know what they're looking for, but may be unable to put it in words in a way that allows them to jump on a trail and start following it. In these cases, presenting related information can be of great help to users, as it increases the odds that they will stumble across the right words and go into known-item mode.

- **Don't know what you need to know** This mode of seeking is employed by users who may think they need to find one thing, when in fact they need to find something else. Or they may be scavenging the web for no particular reason, just browsing their way around to see what comes up. In this mode, short, concise answers that link to deeper explanations can be helpful so users don't waste a lot of time reading through the wrong information.

- **Re-finding** This mode becomes important when users are attempting to find something they already found before. One way to address this mode of seeking is to enable users to mark their favorite pages somehow or use the system to remember recent activity.

These four methods certainly encapsulate most of how I find information online. Although the article isn't specific to web applications, it does provide a useful clue into how users might try to locate operations within an application.

Addressing each of these modes is simple enough to achieve, especially now that you know about them. To put this in context of an application, pretend you're designing an application that lets users record podcasts, associate them with a feed users set up themselves, and list the individual shows on their own page within the site.

For known items, when a user knows what she's looking for, logical keywords are generally enough to get her on the right path. A quick way to head her toward recording a new podcast is to use words like *create* and *record* in the main navigation. To help her set information about her feeds so she can better market the podcasts to other people, words like *describe* and *settings* will catch her eye while scanning her account pages. These are **trigger words** that will make it easy for users to find what they need. (We'll talk more about trigger words later in this chapter.)

In another instance, the user might be looking for information on ID3 tags (metadata associated with an audio file), but may not know the term for such information. All he knows is that he wants to provide information about the author of his podcast, the publication date, duration, and other details. In this case, where the user is in exploratory mode, a button labeled Podcast Details could provide access to all these things on a single screen.

If the user is looking for information on how to apply a different theme to the podcast player that appears on her page, but doesn't know the word *theme* is typically how color palettes and font styles are categorized ("don't know what you need to know"), you might avoid using the word *theme* altogether. In this case, surfacing several words all associated with themes will be helpful to newer users who haven't yet made the association.

For example, a menu named Themes can be used as part of the main configuration screen for the podcast player, but a "quick tip" on the page that informs the user she can change the color of her player will lead her to the Themes screen, where she will then learn about themes. Even better, you might show the player on the same page where the user creates his podcast, and simply provide a couple of options to change its appearance, bypassing the Themes screen altogether and keeping the creation process in the context of what other users will see once the activity has been completed.

Finally, a list of recent activities the user has performed or a favorites list could be just the thing for helping the user remember the name of the podcast he listened to last week on another user's page so he can jump straight back to it and send the URL to his friend. This method of enabling the user to "re-find" information will make the information-seeking task effortless. And without even realizing what makes your application so great, the user will be on his way in seconds flat, happy as a clam that he found what he needed without a lot of trouble.

There are almost certainly more than four modes of seeking information (for example, knowing what you're looking for, but having no idea where to look), but these four provide an excellent base. Providing for these four modes alone should keep us all busy for a while.

Card sorting

Card-sorting exercises can be a great way to learn how users think things should be organized within an application. Typically used by information architects to help determine an understandable navigation scheme within an information space, like a website, card sorting can help us organize application features just as well by revealing to us what trigger words our users associate with the types of features we plan to include.

Card sorting for applications starts with a simple stack of index cards. The idea is to write down all the features you plan to build, hand the stack off to some appropriate users, and ask them to sort the cards into stacks according to how they think the features should be organized. The exercise is very simple to perform, produces results quickly, and is inexpensive, so it's a viable option for any company looking to solve an information design problem fast.

The first step in performing a card-sorting exercise is, obviously, to determine the list of things that need to be sorted. And while this may be a simple enough task, as it's a quick matter of writing down the names of each of the features on separate index cards, it's important to keep the stack of cards down to a reasonable size so participants in the card-sorting session don't get overwhelmed by the sheer volume of things to organize. If your application has a lot of features, try to organize some of them on your own, or split the work into two sessions so each group can take on a smaller set.

Also, while writing down features on the cards, avoid using keywords in the feature or operation names that imply an organization, like "Insert photo" coupled with "Insert video." It will be far too easy for participants to latch onto the term *insert* and name a menu by that name even if it's not the most appropriate. And avoid using terms that might end up being used as menu, panel, or toolbar names. The whole point of the exercise is to see how users group the features.

Participants in the session should be people who will actually use the application once it's built, as this will help ensure the right people are doing the organizing. This group should be kept small so it doesn't become too difficult for you to keep the session focused on moving forward.

During the session, the only real goal is to get the participants to organize the cards in whatever way they see fit. To facilitate this, the session should begin with a quick explanation of what they'll be doing. Hand them the stack of cards, set down a second stack of blank cards, and instruct the participants to sort the cards into stacks of related groups and write down a name for each group on one of the blank cards.

Your goal as mediator is to keep things moving forward. If the group gets stuck on a certain card or debates at length how to name a certain stack, encourage everyone to move the unnamed cards to a separate stack to be sorted later. Simply flip the proverbial coin to choose possible names for card stacks that don't immediately beg specific names, and write them down as title cards instead of fixating. It's not important that every last detail is worked out, only that some initial impressions are made so you can better determine how users in your target audience associate the different features and operations within the application.

It's important to take notes during the session. Try to record the suggestions and confusing points that emerge from discussion during the card sort. These, along with the final stacks of sorted cards, will help you determine how to name and group all kinds of things in your application. Menus and toolbars, for example, can easily be organized according to how users in the session think they go together.

When all the cards have been sorted, thank everyone for their time and take the stacks back to your desk to start sorting out the details.

Yeah. Bad pun. Sorry.

One thing to note here is that if your application has users that span multiple contexts or situations, each using the application in a different way, you should consider holding card-sorting sessions with groups of users from each context or situation. By doing this you can compare the differences and decide how to accommodate each of the groups in your design.

For more information about card sorting, check out James Robertson's very thorough article "Information Design Using Card Sorting" at **www.steptwo. com.au/papers/cardsorting**. It's aimed primarily at more typical information architectures, like that of a website focused on information rather than interaction, but the knowledge you gain from the article can certainly be applied to application design as well.

▶ Stop Getting Up to Speed and Speed Things Up

Once beginners become intermediates, they don't want to keep tripping over up-to-speed aids. Not all the tools that help get people moving forward need to stick around for the long haul. Beginner tools can actually interfere with intermediate users in the long run by making them feel disrespected. They're not beginners anymore, so it's time to stop getting users up to speed and start speeding things up.

First, we can get rid of the up-to-speed aids. Welcome screens, for example, in addition to providing an option to be hidden, can be designed with rules about how and when they appear. For a relatively simple application intended for frequent use, for example, a welcome screen can be set to disappear automatically after the user has logged in and used the application a few times. This is roughly equivalent to telling a friend you've taught him everything he needs to know and he should try to fly on his own for a while. (Of course, there should be an easy way to get the screen back should the user feel a little lost without it.) Once a user is comfortable with an application, the welcome screen becomes an obstacle that gets in the way of other, more important features, but strangely, odds are the user won't even notice it's gone.

Blank-slate filler help should also disappear. In most cases, a blank slate doesn't stay blank for long, so your filler might only show up for a few minutes, if even that long, as a user learns what to do in the application. But hey, if it helped a user get moving, it's done its job. Time to go.

Once some of these aids are out of the way, we can also do some small things to speed up task completion for users.

Making software adapt to users is not always the simplest thing to do, but it's well worth it. An application that seems to get smarter the more a user inter-acts with it stands a good chance of making her even more pleased with the tool as she goes along.

For example, continuing with the example of a stock photography site from earlier chapters, the image library the user builds up while browsing through thousands of images can feature a way to categorize the images he adds to the library. After he has created categories and he decides to add a new image to the library, a menu can be offered that enables him to assign the image to a category he's already created. This menu can be set to remain hidden until categories have been created. It can also assign images to a General category by default so the user doesn't have to make this decision every time he adds a new image.

Reuse the welcome screen as a notification system

Not all up-to-speed aids have to go away permanently once a user is comfort-able with an application. After users can move fluidly through your applica-tion, those old sacrificial lambs can come out to play once in a while with a new purpose.

A welcome screen, for example, can be set to reappear when a new and impor-tant feature is added to the interface, so users are guided toward its use and shown how to get started with it. In this way, welcome screens can be reused as a notification system for new features and anything else that comes up that might be really important.

Blank-slate fillers can also return any time a user's page is emptied out (hope-fully not as a result of some serious damage to a database on your part).

Basecamp (described earlier) does this whenever a user's page is void of con-tent. If the user has no messages under the Message tab, for example, the instructional blank slate is shown.

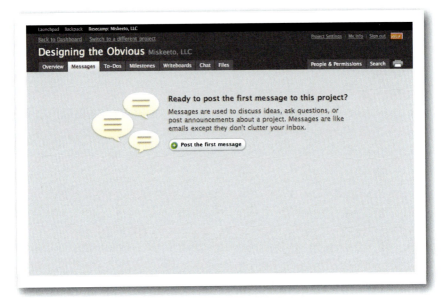

The blank-slate filler shows up any time the Messages section is empty.

Use one-click interfaces

Despite the fact that I'm probably not the only one who gets nervous every time I click Amazon's one-click purchase button, one-click interfaces can really help users get things done quickly. It provides a patented one-click system that enables users who have already stored their billing and shipping information with a way to make a purchase in a single click.

Amazon's mystical, magical one-click button. So easy it's crazy to switch to another online bookseller.

Clearly, this works to Amazon's advantage. First, it makes it really simple for repeat customers to buy more stuff. Second, it increases what is known as the "cost of switching." That is, the cost of switching to another online bookseller is slightly higher as a result of having such an easy way to purchase items. Users moving to a new bookseller have to create new accounts and enter all the billing and shipping info from scratch. Later on, users will likely have to continue entering the information with every purchase, because Amazon is the only one with the one-click system.

Amazon's system is patented, but nothing says we can't apply similar techniques to our own interfaces. We can at least get it down to two clicks—one to click through to the shipping cart, where the user is shown the billing information he currently has stored, and the second click to make the purchase.

Amazon even extends this functionality to email campaigns. Recently, I received an email advertisement from Amazon about a specific book—not a list of books, just one—that was related to a topic I searched through a couple of weeks or so ago. The email told me about the book and offered a button by which I could purchase it. I clicked the button. The purchase was so easy that I completely forgot about it until just a few minutes ago when I received another email to let me know the book has been shipped. Not only was the purchase process made faster, it was catered entirely to me because Amazon knows what I want based on my prior visits and adapts what it sends to my in-box to show me things I'll likely want to buy. Amazon really has this efficiency thing down pat. You can bet I won't be switching to another bookseller any time soon.

Use design patterns to make things familiar

A big part of what makes an obvious design is the element of familiarity. When we learn how one application works, we can quickly apply what we've learned when working with other applications.

Google, Yahoo, and MSN all handle pagination in search results pages with the same type of interaction. Each one features a series of links (in the form of page numbers) for jumping from one page to the next, and each includes a Next link for walking through the search results in a linear path. This is a design pattern.

To expand this definition, design patterns are common solutions to common problems. In the case of search engines, pagination is a common issue in the various applications. Each site chose to use the same pattern—the pagination pattern—but each chose to do it a little differently from the others.

Patterns are frameworks for designs, not specific rules, so they leave a lot of room for creativity and innovation (innovation, in fact, is often an extension of existing patterns). Each search engine uses page numbers as links, and each one includes a Next link, but each looks different from the others. They don't actually need to look the same. It's only important that each user who visits each site can quickly understand how it handles navigation through multiple pages of search results. Since the pagination functionality is so effective, many sites have implemented their own variations on the design, so it has risen to the status of design pattern.

In My Yahoo, the design patterns used to handle all of the editing within a page were unfamiliar to me at first, but since signing up, the patterns have appeared in a number of web applications, and I've been able to move from one to the other with little effort because each one is leveraging the experiences I've had with previous applications. This familiarity makes new applications easier to learn, explore, and master.

Design patterns tend to emerge when the pattern in question proves itself to be effective over time. When it works on one site, others emulate it, and when it succeeds across many sites, everyone else starts to use the design. Before you know it, the pattern can be seen all over the web.

Design patterns help users learn new applications quickly by allowing them to parlay their previous experience from other sites to the new application. For this reason, patterns can be immensely helpful when attempting to design the obvious.

The major lesson to learn here is that when you're designing a new application, you should pay attention to what patterns are used by similar or related applications and try to leverage them in your own. The growing use of these patterns will tear down many of the barriers users face when trying to learn a new application, allowing them to learn yours more quickly.

This book is not about design patterns—it's more about the conceptual, application-level patterns that make web and mobile software great—but there is a book all about design patterns called *Designing Interfaces* (O'Reilly, 2005), by Jenifer Tidwell, that can provide a wonderful base of information about patterns and serve as an ongoing reference for when you get stuck on a design problem and need a good standard to rely on. I highly recommend you check it out. You know, after you finish up *Designing the Obvious*.

Provide Help Documents, Because Help Is for Experts

Jensen Harris, who works on the Microsoft Office team, once talked on his blog about how infrequently users access help documentation (this post is available at http://blogs.msdn.com/jensenh/archive/2005/11/29/497861.aspx). Instead of jumping to the help files anytime a user needs to understand something new, he'll attempt to learn the procedure himself. As counterintuitive as it may be, expert users are actually the ones most likely to check help files.

My own usability testing experiences confirm this. It's extremely rare for a new or intermediate user to dig through or even seek out the provided help documentation. (It's actually pretty shocking how infrequently users rely on help documents. A recent usability session on a fairly complicated application, where users were in constant need of assistance, showed that not one of the five testers looked for help articles. One of them even said she wished help was available, but never looked for it, despite the fact that a link to it was prominently displayed in the main interface.)

Harris tries to explain this in the context of his own history. When he made the move to the Office team, he immediately went to a bookstore to buy a book on Excel to increase his skills instead of relying on help documentation.

He believes this lack of interest in help is the result of several factors. First, there is a language barrier in help documentation. Users may be in exploratory mode, but they likely won't know the terminology they need to locate the right information. Most help systems don't produce search results nearly as well as Google, and users are often limited to using exact terminology and feature names to find what they need. This doesn't work when you're new to an application, and often fails even if you're an intermediate user. Experts, on the other hand, know the lingo used by an application and can quickly find specific information within a help system.

Second, help documentation generally lacks the personality usually found in books and articles on the same subjects. Help files are meant to be technically accurate and concise, but authors of books and articles can loosen up and inject humor and liveliness into a piece to bring the material to life in a way help files usually cannot.

Finally, the web itself is one of the greatest help resources around, and many people latch onto it because the *voice* found there is more appealing. Online articles, forum posts, and blogs full of information on features and examples are as easy to find as a simple search through Google. These authors are not held back by the same constraints most tech writers face, so the information found there can be of greater use, as it's easier to digest information wrapped in a friendly package.

For these reasons, the more effective approach to teaching new users how to move around in your application is to apply the techniques outlined earlier in this chapter. But when you do get some expert users, help documentation can be the perfect thing to keep them happy and motivated to learn more. While applications should really be designed for intermediate users, experts are the people who have invested the most time and energy into learning and using our applications. To this end, a little well-designed and well-written help can go a long way.

7

Be Persuasive

- ▶ Draw a Finish Line
- ▶ Solve a Significant Problem
- ▶ Make It Explainable
- ▶ Know Your Psychology

Attention is valuable. Losing it is expensive.

From a business perspective, as designers, our job is to compel people to do what we want them to do. In the easiest cases, these are things people want to do on their own and all we have to do is facilitate. But when the case isn't so clear—when there are multiple competitors from which to choose, when the value proposition is something new and unfamiliar, when we're busy doing other things—persuasive design elements can be the difference between diving in and walking away, between holding a person's attention and losing it forever.

From a customer perspective, as users, we need to know if what we're doing is worth the attention required by it. And rather than fully consider every aspect of the potential answer to that question, we evaluate what's easy to spot and easy to know, and we stack up all these little slices of answers and see if they add up to a clear choice. Some decisions are tough and require a lot of thought, but not *most* decisions. All day long, we make small decisions in just a few seconds, if not quicker.

As users, we need to be persuaded. We want to be persuaded. And as long as it's done ethically, we are open to being persuaded. It helps us make choices without doing all the research, without knowing all the facts. It's how we get through our day without our heads exploding.

We need to know our effort is worth it. We take shortcuts to find out. We make guesses. Persuasive design informs our guesses.

This chapter is about how to be persuasive in the same ways in which users want to be persuaded.

▶ Draw a Finish Line

Often the easiest way to create a persuasive design is to simply draw a straight line from the beginning of a process to the end of it, telling the user at each step what you want her to do next. If the line you draw is dotted with things the user wants, she'll follow it. (We'll talk about this idea from a different perspective in Chapter 9.)

Apple's iBooks app for iPhone or iPad is a perfect example.

Knowing full well that providing a preview method for a book would be key to sales, Apple offered a way for users to download an excerpt. As a user, you simply locate a book you're interested in, download the sample, and read it. But Apple drew a finish line for this sequence by way of a button that encourages you to purchase the full edition.

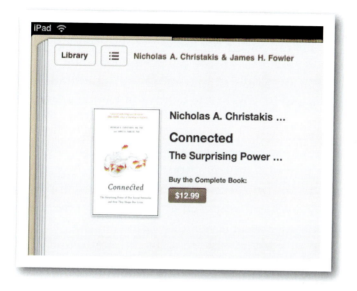

The third step in the iBooks previewing process offers a way to buy the book.

In three steps, the app walks the user straight to where Apple wants him: credit card on file, ready to click the proverbial Buy button.

A good task flow works by guiding the user, step by step, from finding what he wants to do and how to do it to completing the interaction. And the only trick to making it successful is drawing a finish line at the end. *Tell them what you want them to do.*

Ownership

Part of what's so effective about the iBooks previewing process is that the excerpt is downloaded to the user's iPad or iPhone, where it can be read in the iBooks e-reader interface as can any of her other books. This is effective because it encourages a sense of ownership, and if you've ever actually tried taking candy from a baby, you'll know why this is a good idea.

A sense of ownership is a powerful motivator. We humans tend to fight like hell to hold on to things we believe belong to us. Social psychology studies (such as those run by Dr. Robert Cialdini, author of *Influence: The Psychology of Persuasion*, discussed later in this chapter) have shown that we even perceive things that hold little or no value for us—for example, things we acquired for free—as *more* valuable when we're under threat of having them stolen away from us. Once that excerpt is on your iPad, you're more likely to want to keep it there. You're more likely to want to buy the book. You've gone through a multistep process to get it, after all—clearly, you wanted it for some reason. Now that it's yours, it's not only easy to convince yourself it's worth keeping, it's also quite easy to simply take one more step to complete the purchase.

In your own app, what you give the user doesn't have to be a download—in fact, in most cases a download would be an annoyance rather than a point of persuasion. It can be a record of the user's recent activity. It can be a promo code. It can be a connection to another user (MySpace used to do this by automatically creating your first friend connection after registering). It can be any number of things as long as it helps the user feel invested.

Give users something they can call their own and maybe you'll soon be able to call them customers. Threaten to take it away from them (politely, of course) and they may just be even more compelled to do what they need to do to keep it.

Solve a Significant Problem

Sometimes, a single feature is persuasive enough to compel people to start using an application, such as when it solves a problem so well that it literally changes a user's behavior for the better.

Chase Mobile is one such app. Like some other banks, Chase has created an iPhone app that enables its customers to make a deposit simply by taking a photo of the front and back of a check, entering the amount of the check, and choosing which account should receive the deposit. In other words, customers can make deposits *without going to the bank*.

Here, the most compelling Chase Mobile feature is highlighted via a set of screen shots on its Apple App Store page.

This is such a compelling solution to such a common problem that it makes the app persuasive all by itself. The marketers could say next to nothing about the app beyond "Deposit a check by taking a picture of it on your phone"—simply explaining how you can use it—and people would still install the app in droves. In this case, a single feature is the most persuasive thing about the app.

Being persuasive doesn't always mean crafting copy and images that convince people of an app's value. Sometimes the very purpose of the app is its most persuasive aspect. Sometimes you can solve a problem so well that all you have to do is describe the solution outright to earn major points.

▶ Make It Explainable

The most persuasive statement is the one that comes from a friend (more on this in the next section). When we seek out advice on which digital camera to buy, we ask friends what they think of theirs. When we want to know which movie to watch, we recall what our friends have said about their recent movie experiences.

"I've heard it's good," we say. Our friends, after all, are very often like us. If our friends liked it, it must be good.

Of course, to get people to recommend your app, they need to be able to explain it easily.

"Blinksale is a site for creating and managing invoices."

"GoodReads is a site for sharing what you're reading and getting book recommendations."

"Campaign Monitor is a service for creating and managing email newsletters."

People feel more confident about an app when they can explain it to themselves and others. And an app that is explainable can be recommended with a few words. But like every rule, there are exceptions to this one. Dropbox, for example— arguably one of the most useful services around—can be quite tricky to explain.

Dropbox is a cloud storage service that syncs files between the "cloud" (remote web servers—in this case, Dropbox's servers) and your computer. It also offers iPhone and iPad apps so you can access these files from anywhere. What's tricky about it is that, except for an icon that indicates the sync status of each file stored by Dropbox, the Dropbox folder on your computer is indistinguishable from any other folder on your computer. You create a folder. You put files in that folder. Those files live on your computer. Easy. But with Dropbox, files are automatically synced to Dropbox's servers every time you make a change to one. And you can access the newest version of theses files from an iPad, iPhone, or another computer anytime you want.

File systems are frustrating enough for many people to deal with that they just dump everything into a default folder and never bother trying to organize it. Trying to explain Dropbox to people just complicates that even more.

To explain Dropbox's success, then, see the previous section. Dropbox solves the significant problem of making sure your files are properly backed up by making backup an invisible process. For people to whom frequent and reliable backups matter and who understand how it works, it's a brilliant solution. You don't have to plug in a backup hard drive or remember to run your backups or configure any sync scheduling. All you do is keep the files you need backed up frequently in the Dropbox folder. Done. It's invisible. It does what it's supposed to do and stays out of the way.

Coincidentally, while I was writing this riff about Dropbox, I received the first interruptive email I've ever gotten from the Dropbox team. It's to inform me that I'm running out of storage space. It offers a link to upgrade my account.

A finish line.

▶ Know Your Psychology

There are several books in the Computers section of your favorite bookstore that expound on the following six principles of persuasion developed by the renowned psychologist Robert Cialdini—not to mention *Influence: The Psychology of Persuasion* (Harper Paperbacks, 2006), the one in the Psychology section written by Cialdini himself—so I won't go into great detail on them. What I will do is describe each principle and show you an example of it in action.

Reciprocity

The principle of reciprocity describes that tug we all feel to reciprocate a gesture. This gesture can come in the form of a concession (such as lowering a price to help close a sale), a loan, a gift, a favor, or something else. Perhaps the most common form is the giving away of information or insights for the benefit of others. A blogger, for example, who frequently writes posts on a specific topic that people care about, no matter how few or how many people, will build an appreciative audience. Those people, when the blogger needs assistance in some way—to raise money for a cause, find a job, answer a question, whatever— will naturally tend toward responding in kind when the blogger needs it.

In short: you scratch my back and I'll scratch yours.

	Stiff: The Curious Lives of Human Cadavers	Roach, Mary	☆☆☆☆☆	currently-reading [edit]	4.03	Apr 25	x edit view
	Nudge: Improving Decisions About Health, Wealth, and Happiness	Thaler, Richard H.	☆☆☆☆☆	currently-reading [edit]	3.54	Apr 25	x edit view
	A Whole New Mind: Why Right-Brainers Will Rule the Future	Pink, Daniel H.*	★★★★☆	read [edit]	3.86	Apr 25	x edit view
	The Checklist Manifesto: How to Get Things Right	Gawande, Atul	★★★★★	read [edit]	3.83	Apr 25	x edit view
	The Paradox of Choice: Why More Is Less	Schwartz, Barry	★★★★☆	read [edit]	3.65	Jan 18	x edit view

GoodReads, a social network centered on books—what you're reading right now, what you've read, what you thought of it, and what others are reading—taps into this urge by encouraging you to list your favorite books and what you're reading in exchange for learning about books you may like from others in your network. You get something from GoodReads, you put something back in. Simple.

Commitment and consistency

This principle comes in two parts. First, commitment: when we commit to something, we're more prone to honor our commitment even if the reason for the commitment is removed as a factor after we've done so. Second, consistency: we strongly prefer our actions to remain consistent with our own prior actions. If we made a decision once in the past, regardless of whether or not it was of our own free will, we are more prone to maintain that decision later. When we commit to an idea, we are more likely to stay committed to it.

As designers, then, we can persuade people to take action simply by reminding them of something they've done before and asking them to take another action that's in line with the first.

When President Barack Obama was still Senator Obama, his campaign funding approach was practically built on this principle alone. Rather than pursue and rely heavily on big donations, the fund-raising team used social media and email campaigns to encourage potential voters to contribute very small amounts of money. By responding, people made very small commitments. But these were *commitments*, and they were to a specific candidate. With that single commitment, the Obama campaign could continue to pull that psychological string for the rest of the presidential race.

Specifically, the campaign could remind people of their own prior commitments and actions in email correspondence and simply ask them to build on their commitment by taking another step. They constantly reiterated to donors that *they* built the campaign. *They* were the reason it was succeeding. *They* were the ones calling for action. From there, it was a simple matter of asking them to do again what they did before: donate.

The commitment of donating increased the chances that the donor would be consistent with his own actions by actually voting when the big day finally came. A person who has taken one action is more likely to follow it up with another action. Donate to a political fund and you're much more likely to *vote* for that person and ideology come election day.

There's also a lot to be learned about persuasion via commitment and consistency through gaming techniques.

The professional networking site LinkedIn, for example, displays a progress meter (like one you'd see in a game to measure your advancement through levels) designed to encourage you to complete your profile. The basic idea is that by reminding you of your prior behavior of beginning to fill out your profile, LinkedIn can encourage you to continue doing so.

(I'll point out more gaming techniques throughout this section.)

Social proof

Social proof describes our tendency to look to the actions of other people for cues on what to do. Every day, this version of peer pressure helps us make decisions. When other people start crossing a street, we go with them, even when the signal still says not to. When others slow down in traffic, we do as well, even if there is no obvious reason to do so or when the reason for an earlier slowdown has long since cleared up. When lots of other people do something, we tend to think that it must be a good thing to do.

Amazon capitalizes on this notion by telling us outright what other people who have done the thing we're now doing did next. And they do it in just a few words.

When Amazon tells us that "Customers who bought this item also bought" these other items, they're tapping our sense to do what others do. We think, If the people who like the item I like also like these other items, then I may like those other items as well.

They don't stop there. They offer a full range of social influence tools—reviews, ratings, recommendations, and referrals—so that customers have not only a way to talk about their product experiences, but also the important social proof they need to make decisions.

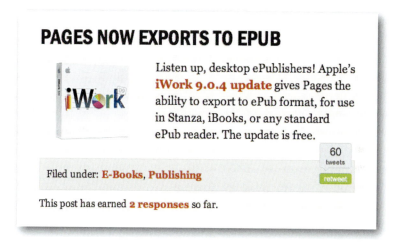

Another example is this one from Jeffrey Zeldman's blog. Here, he simply offers a Retweet button (available for free at http://tweetmeme.com/about/retweet_button) to indicate that other people have shared the post via Twitter, and the number of people that have done so. The number is both a barometer for the popularity of the post and an influence tool for convincing more people to tweet about the post.

Authority

The principle of authority describes the fact that we tend to trust those we consider experts, or people in charge. The pull to do this is so strong that we'll continue to trust those in charge even when they've made decisions that are questionable, or even downright objectionable.

A typical example of this is the page at the beginning of this very book that offers quotes from industry experts who have said positive things about *Designing the Obvious*. I didn't add this page to the book to boast of my expertise, but to persuade you by helping you make a quick decision about whether or not this book would be worth your time and money. If you recognized one or more of the names on that list, but perhaps weren't familiar with my name or the book itself, your willingness to trust people you see as authorities may have kicked in to do some of your vetting work for you.

On your own projects, a quote or two from a known expert can be all it takes to establish credibility for someone who otherwise doesn't yet have enough reasons to become a customer.

Liking

We also tend to trust people we like, and people we think are like us. This is why, again, the most persuasive statement is the one that comes from a friend. It's also why customer reviews are such a powerful motivator when it comes to purchasing decisions. People we like and people who are like us, we believe, are good sources for reliable opinions.

Amazon's "Customers who bought this also bought" feature also applies here. People who bought *this* book, which we like, also bought *that* book. Since those people are like us, at least enough that we're buying the same book, maybe we can trust their opinion on other books as well.

Twitter does this by showing whose streams a member is following. *If you like this person, and this person likes those people, you may like those other people as well.*

Scarcity

The last of Cialdini's principles of persuasion is that of *scarcity*. It goes like this:

We believe that things that are scarce are somehow more valuable. When there are a limited number of openings to a club, for example, the openings feel more valuable, even if they're not.

When Google's Gmail launched years ago, it did so as a private beta. To use the service, you had to be invited to create an account by someone who already had one. This played into the idea of scarcity in two ways. First, it made Gmail appear exclusive to outsiders, convincing them that they were being deprived of something great and making the service more desirable. Second, it involved those who already had accounts in the game—periodically, Google dished out a few invites at a time to current users who could then gift the invites to whomever they wanted. The company never said when these invites would be made available or how many would be offered. One day, you'd simply sign into your Gmail account and see that you now had a few invites to give away. (Countless sites have taken a similar approach since then.)

The idea of scarcity as a persuasion tool can also be applied by offering a lower subscription rate to a service for a limited time, a limited number of seats for a conference registration, a discount code with an expiration date, and countless other ways. If you can make something exclusive, you can make users perceive it as more valuable.

RECENT ACTIVITY

Gene A. in Park City, UT:
became the mayor of **No Name Saloon and Grill**.

Khal W. in North Augusta, South Carolina:
unlocked the **'Newbie'** badge.

Tetsuya S. in 福岡県北九州市八幡西区, Japan:
became the mayor of **黒崎駅**.

Vicky in Cambridge, MA:
unlocked the **'Photogenic'** badge.

Murdani W. in Depok, Indonesia:
became the mayor of **Stasiun Pondok Cina**.

You can also see the scarcity principle in action on sites that dole out badges to indicate achievements, much as video games reward players. For example, Foursquare users are given profile badges for achieving a specific status, such as becoming the mayor of a restaurant after visiting and "checking in" more than other members. These badges are scarce—only one user can be the mayor of any given place. The exclusivity of this status symbol can have a lot of persuasive power as earning it becomes a goal for users when they visit their favorite places.

Ethical persuasion

There are endless possibilities for how to nudge a visitor to become a customer, or a customer to become a repeat customer, or a beginning user to become an intermediate user. And indeed, every aspect of a design is persuasive in one way or another. Every design element either encourages users, dissuades them, or leaves them ambivalent. It's your choice what message you deliver. Make it intentionally.

No matter what your solution, make it an ethical one. Never use dishonesty or deception as a method of persuasion. If you've got a good, strong brand, you'll damage it. If you've got a weak brand, you'll kill it. Persuasion is not about tricking people into doing things they don't want to do. It's about making a connection between what your users want and what you want, through design elements, that make the connection clear. It's about creating designs that facilitate the mental shortcuts we all take when making decisions. If we assume that a higher price is indicative of a better product (and we do), then price accordingly. But make sure your product is in fact better. If it's not, your customers will notice. Believe me, the Internet always finds out the truth. Be deceptive and you will be found out. Be honest and persuasive, and you'll be revered.

8

Handle Errors Wisely

▶ **Prevent and Catch Errors with Poka-yoke Devices**

▶ **Ditch Anything Modal**

▶ **Write Error Messages That Help Instead of Hurt**

▶ **Create Forgiving Software**

We like for things to go smoothly. When we use applications, we don't want intrusive errors popping up to tell us how dumb we are for having tried to do something that the system can't handle. We don't want to be interrupted. We don't want to know the system doesn't work. And we definitely don't want to be blamed for its shortcomings by an error message that tells us we did something wrong.

Our users don't want these things either.

When we perform a task in an application that results in an error message, we blame ourselves. After all, we're the ones not smart enough to use the application correctly. We don't understand what it is we're supposed to do, and that's why we're doing it wrong.

But somehow, because we're computer-savvy, when we find out that *other* people using an application *we* built are having problems, we think those people are just too dumb to use it. We blame them. After all, they're the ones not smart enough to use the application correctly. They don't understand what they're supposed to do, and that's why they're doing it wrong.

Clearly, there's a problem with our logic.

Because I don't want to perpetuate these obnoxious error messages and make the users of *my* designs feel stupid, I've spent quite a bit of time considering how errors are displayed, what causes them, and when they are shown. Through this, I've come to a fairly obvious conclusion:

The best way to handle errors is to prevent them from ever occurring.

When an application is bad, it's bad for a thousand different reasons. When it's good, it's good because the user is able to glide through each and every interaction effortlessly, without hassle, and without being forced to learn how the underlying system works to accomplish his goals.

To rise to this seemingly unreachable level of quality, we need to handle errors before and after they occur. The goal is not to tell the user something has gone wrong. The goal is to design the system in such a way that the user never has a chance to make a mistake. And if a mistake does occur, we need to make it as painless as possible to get back on track quickly.

There are plenty of mistakes to be made. Good design can cure most of them.

▶ Prevent and Catch Errors with Poka-yoke Devices

Poka-yoke devices are all around us.

Poka-yoke (pronounced *POH-kah YOH-kay*) is the Japanese term for "mistake-proofing." A poka-yoke device is whatever is used to prevent an error. It's what makes something foolproof.

The Popcorn button on a microwave oven is a poka-yoke device. Stick the popcorn in, push the button, and watch the microwave turn a bag full of little seeds into a night in front of a good movie. No thought required.

The remote for my car locks all the doors at once so I don't have to wonder if I left any unlocked. My car has a little plastic strap that tethers the gas cap to the car so I won't accidentally leave it on my trunk and drive off without it properly attached. The keys can't be removed from the ignition unless the engine has been turned off. And I can't put the transmission in reverse unless I'm at a complete stop.

Dryers stop running when the door is opened so no one gets hurt. Irons shut off automatically after sitting idle for a while to help prevent fires. The bathroom sink has a small hole toward the top of the rim that prevents the sink from overflowing.

Poka-yoke devices are *everywhere*.

Sadly, even in this age when *user-friendliness* has become a household term, they still don't show up in our applications nearly as often as they should. When they do, though, it's fantastic. Users can get things done without incident. Things go smoothly. You know, the way things *should* go.

Poka-yoke on the web

A webmail application I used to use a lot had a built-in memory of what I did with specific kinds of email messages.

For example, every time I got an email from my task-management system that said "Status changed" in the subject line (the email was sent whenever I changed the details of a task), I would throw it away by selecting the check box next to the subject line, choosing the Trash option from a drop-down menu, and then clicking the Move button. After the first time I did this, however, I noticed that I no longer had to choose Trash from the drop-down menu. After checkmarking a message I wanted to throw away, the Trash option was being automatically selected for me. All I had to do was click Move to throw the email away.

The people who built the application did this on purpose. They figured that since it's statistically probable I will move a message to the same place I moved all the other ones that were just like it (which all had "Status changed" in the subject line and were sent from the same email address), the application, very politely, remembered that I have thrown all the other messages into the Trash and selects that option *for* me in the drop-down menu.

It's the tiniest detail, but it prevented me from making the common mistake of moving items to the wrong folder. (It also made me feel as if the application was reading my mind, which was a little creepy, but that's a different story.)

Let's face it. Most of what's really bad about an application is how many times we mess something up while trying to use it. The more mistakes, the worse the application. Good design can cure this. Implementing poka-yoke devices is probably the number one thing you can do to improve a poor design. Even the worst designs can be improved by eliminating the possibility of errors.

Prevention devices

There are two types of poka-yoke devices: prevention devices and detection devices.

Prevention devices are those that prevent errors from ever occurring. The hole in the rim of the sink that keeps it from overflowing is a prevention device. The user can leave the water running all he wants to—the sink will never overflow.

Keeping users from making mistakes is no small task, but there are plenty of things that can be done to minimize most of the potential errors and keep users feeling productive.

Problems are big, fixes are small

Several years ago, I designed a web app called Dashboard HQ with a friend of mine—a very simple bookmarking and note-taking tool that resembled a start page such as My Yahoo or iGoogle, but with very limited scope. And it makes for a nice example to illustrate this point: it's easier and cheaper to prevent problems than to create them.

The initial design went through several small iterations. At one time, the panel used to add content, called Add Content, was designed so that the user had to choose which column a new module would go into once it was created. It was easy to forget to choose a column number from the menu prior to creating the module, so we considered what type of error message would best handle the situation. A red text message that appeared in the pane? A little box at the top of the page that faded in to catch the user's eye and tell him what went wrong?

Dashboard HQ made it impossible to mess up when adding new content.

We quickly realized the best way to take care of the issue was to make it impossible to make the mistake. In true poka-yoke fashion, we simply set "1st column" as the default value, making it impossible to produce the situation that required the error message. Not only was this method foolproof, it also meant we could improve the application substantially without writing a single new line of code. In this case, the poka-yoke prevention device was a single attribute inside of a single HTML element. Five seconds later, it was done.

Next, we removed the code that checked for values in the fields the user should fill out to create a new module. In truth, it wasn't necessary for a module to have something in it to exist. It could simply exist. It could just sit somewhere on the page with a default title ("Enter a title...") and no content whatsoever. Users could always edit the module after it was created—in fact, that was the whole point of the application—so why stop them from creating it?

In just a few minutes of modifying and testing, we completely erased the potential to make a mistake when creating a new module. Users didn't need to name the module, add content to it, or choose where it should appear: they could simply open the Add Content pane and click Create. There was no way for them to go wrong.

Not only did we avoid having to write more code, we actually *removed* code. In doing this, we also kept ourselves from having to debug the error code (which is always an exercise in irony). One less thing to maintain later on. One less potential problem for users. Win-win.

Remove the possibility of error

Another thing we did for Dashboard HQ was to write a tiny bit of JavaScript that ensures URLs entered into bookmark lists function correctly after being saved. Upon saving a new bookmark, the entered URL is checked to see if *http://* was entered at the beginning of the address. If it wasn't, it was added automatically before the bookmark was saved. If a user entered *amazon.com*, for example, the bookmark address was converted to *http://amazon.com/*.

This script ensured that links work properly in all browsers and that the user was far less likely to see an error after clicking the link later. This poka-yoke device required only a couple of lines of code, but saved users from many potential errors.

Traditionally, poka-yoke devices are simple and cheap. If it takes a lot of work to implement one, you should review the source of the issue to see how you can simplify. Sure, it may mean admitting you were wrong about how your application should work to begin with, but after solving the issue, the application will be leaner and less problematic. (Incidentally, when you accomplish this, it's suddenly easy to admit you were wrong, because it's the precursor to boasting about how gracefully you fixed the problem.)

Many problems can be solved without a lot of extra work. Tiny modifications, like choosing a good default value instead of writing error code to tell users they've done something wrong, are quite often all it takes to improve an application, or even a single interaction, tenfold.

The only downside to using poka-yoke devices is that no one will ever realize how clever we were by coming up with them. The user will never see the error that could have happened. He'll point to his own common sense as the reason he can use the application effectively.

But nothing says we can't smile knowingly from the back row.

Detection devices

In our original design for Dashboard HQ, we were going to write code to show the error to the user immediately so he could fix it and move on. This would have been a *detection device*. In the case above, we chose the more optimal prevention device, but it's not always possible to prevent every error. When things go wrong—and they will—it's time to rely on the other form of poka-yoke devices: *detection devices*.

When poka-yoke can't be used to prevent an error, it can still be used to detect the error and notify the user so it can be remedied immediately. In web terms, this usually comes in the form of an error message.

We've all come across a billion error messages (give or take) in the time we've spent using computers, and we've been trained over time to ignore them (unless they look unusual in some way and happen to catch our attention). Just click OK, we think, and move on. Oh, wait. Was that something important?

Most of the error messages we see are useless. They are written in cryptic developer-speak, tell us something we already know, don't tell us what to do to remedy the error, and don't offer any choices. If clicking OK is the only thing that can be done, we click OK. Then we're back at square one. Gee, thanks for the helping hand.

Quality error pages

Most server setups allow the configuration of custom error pages, but many designers neglect this part of an application. That's a drag, because error pages can do so much to help users that we're really missing an opportunity by ignoring them. Instead of simply telling users a page cannot be found, we can create error pages that guide users straight to other content so they can get moving again without even thinking about the fact that they just saw an error message.

One of my favorite examples of a bad error page is from an old version of the Federal Emergency Management Agency (FEMA) website. FEMA, as you may know, has a disaster assistance program for people who have been the victims of a natural disaster. I came across the error message shortly after Hurricane Katrina devastated the Gulf Coast. At the time, the online application process for this program contained several key problems.

The process began with an image verification system that displayed highly illegible images of words, the kind users are meant to type in a text field to verify they are human beings and not automated systems. Users were given three chances to enter the correct word. Upon failing the third time, the resulting error message read:

"We are sorry for not being able to proceed your requests because you have failed our tests."

Not only was this message poorly written (for starters, the word *proceed* should have been the word *process*), making it more difficult to understand than it needed to be, but it also offered no way out. There was no link back to the home page, no suggestions about what to do next, nothing. Just a meaningless error message.

And if you were unlucky enough to have had your home wiped out and unlucky enough to have had access only to a Macintosh (and this is one of the few times you would have been unlucky to have access to a Mac), you would have come across another error message informing you that Microsoft Internet Explorer 6 was required to complete the form.

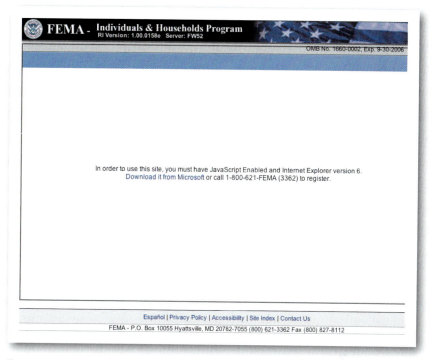

In order to use this site, you must have JavaScript Enabled and Internet Explorer version 6. Download it from Microsoft or call 1-800-621-FEMA (3362) to register.

I'm sorry—you want me to download *what* now?

Internet Explorer 6 didn't, and still doesn't, exist on Mac. And according to Microsoft at the time, it never would. Users who didn't know this fact were likely to wander off to try to download and install the software equivalent of a purple squirrel.

The worst part is that the browser incompatibility message didn't appear until after the user managed to get past the image verification system. This message did suggest to users that they call FEMA directly or download the appropriate version of Internet Explorer, but the application should have worked in any browser, on any operating system.

What's so hard, after all, about a simple HTML-based form? Forms are all over the web. Macintosh users use online forms on a daily basis to purchase books and music, register for new applications, install software, check email, and so on, with as little effort as any Windows user. How is it that FEMA managed to make something so simple so complex? How is it that they managed to break something that works so well on a million other sites?

Many error pages lack the elements that can help users get moving again, and this is where they fail. Many just explain that the page cannot be found and that the user should hit the Back button or head back to the home page and try to find the information another way. This information often comes in the form of bulleted lists that are heavy on text and light on links, and nothing really useful stands out on the page except for the large error message. But the error message is the least helpful part of the page.

Error pages should help users get back on track by offering up links to other pages that do, in fact, exist. Beyond that, they can offer search boxes so users can try to find the missing content another way, continue displaying persistent navigation items so users can jump to the main pages within an application, and even serve up a log-in screen in cases where users have accounts.

All of these things turn what would otherwise be a useless error page into a poka-yoke detection device. They show users that something has gone wrong and immediately offer them a way out. They enable us to create error pages that offer solutions instead of more problems.

Inline validation

Inline validation scripts are one of the best forms of poka-yoke detection devices on the web, because they catch errors immediately.

Inline validation, handled by JavaScript within a page, is the act of performing real-time checking to verify that an interaction has been completed correctly. In a registration form, for example, inline validation can be used to verify that the user's chosen user name has not already been taken, the email address has been written in the correct format, and the first and last names have been entered. Upon determining that a field value has been incorrectly entered or has been skipped, error messages can be shown *within the form*, before the user ever has the opportunity to click the button that submits the form data.

TypePad (www.typepad.com), a site that offers a blogging service, features an example of well-designed inline validation.

The checkmarks tell me I'm smart enough to use this application.

Upon entering correct values (or at least the correct type of value), a green checkmark icon displays next to the completed field. When the email address is entered, a loading animation plays while it's validated to ensure the email address is real.

I skipped a required field, but the application told me immediately so I could recover gracefully.

And when a field is skipped, a red error message appears to indicate the field was not completed correctly.

These simple interface elements guide users toward a successful interaction. The only thing I would suggest to improve the interaction is to disable the Create Account button until the required fields are complete.

It's important that inline validation be carefully designed so it comes across well. Remember the Milk (www.rememberthemilk.com), a to-do-list management application, uses inline validation on its registration form, and does a great job of validating that a user name has not already been taken. But error messages are displayed every time a field gains focus, even when the user hasn't yet had time to enter anything into the field. The result is that users are shown error messages almost constantly while completing the form.

Remember the Milk showed me an error message before I even had a
chance to make a mistake.

Validation should only be performed when a user leaves or passes over a field that is required without correctly completing it. When a text field that accepts required information, for example, loses focus, an error should be shown. An error should not be shown if the user has not yet had a chance to enter the correct information.

Turn errors into opportunities

Poka-yoke detection devices usually result in the error messages we're all used to seeing—JavaScript alerts and such—but some companies try to improve on this idiom by putting a positive spin on an otherwise negative situation. This is by far one of the best ways to deal with errors that can't be prevented.

For example, when a user's search on Squidoo produces no results, Squidoo turns the error into an opportunity by displaying a message that prompts the user to create a lens on the searched topic.

I'm one of the first to search for this topic? Fantastic! I'll build a page and be a Squidoo pioneer!

Squidoo developers recognized that it takes a lot of time to build up a knowledge base of every subject for which users could possibly search, and attempted to find a way to compel users to create more content pages. Smart move. The poka-yoke device in this case is the search engine itself, detecting that no results are available for a topic and displaying a call to action instead of an error message. The result doesn't even look like an error. It's way too friendly to make a user feel like he's messed up. Instead, the user takes a moment to decide whether or not to create a content page on the subject, which is exactly what Squidoo wants to happen.

Blurring the line

Google puts this technique to work as well. When a user runs a search that appears to contain a misspelled word, the first item in the type-ahead list of possible matches is an attempt to clarify what the user was trying to search. (Of course, what actually happens on the Google side to detect misspelled words and suggest alternate spellings is much more complicated, I'm sure, but my mental model is that it *just knows* I misspelled a word.)

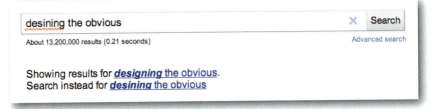

Yes, actually—that's exactly what I meant. Thanks!

Google, in fact, blurs the line between the two types of poka-yoke devices by putting both to good use. It *detects* what the user is attempting to search so it can keep potential mistakes from occurring, and then *prevents* them by helping the user enter the correct search terms before the search is run. When the user begins entering search terms, a list of words and terms that are likely to match what the user is looking for appears, so the user can choose the desired search term and avoid common misspellings.

Google helps me spell correctly, type faster, find common search terms, and even shows results for what I meant as opposed to what I typed. Nice.

The Phone app on the iPhone, like many other iPhone apps, does this as well. Rather than require a full search term, it begins to list possible matches as quickly as it can.

Feeling smart

Detecting errors and guiding users to deal with them immediately is much less aggravating than waiting until they click a Submit button or make a mistake. At that point, it's far too late because the user already has an expectation that the next thing she sees will be whatever comes next in the process. If she is shown a registration form a second time, this time with errors, her expectation will be broken and she may lose confidence in her ability to complete the form correctly the second time. If she searches for something that has no results and sees an error, she can lose confidence in her ability to search well within that particular search engine. If she loses confidence in herself, she's much more prone to stop using your application. Inline validation and other methods of implementing poka-yoke help ensure errors are dealt with before the user's confidence is diminished. Our goal is to make her feel smart. Smart enough to use our application. Because if we help *her* feel smart, she'll like *us* a whole lot more.

Whenever possible, errors should be prevented instead of detected. The code required to perform inline validation is not always easy to create, but it's far better for the user than tossing up JavaScript alerts and the like after the user has been given hope that things will go smoothly. Displaying errors after this point is, well, too little too late. If the errors cannot be prevented from ever occurring, applications should at least be courteous enough to detect them as they occur so the user always knows exactly what's going on and can remain productive. The application should also make a decent attempt to get the user back on track by spinning the error message as an opportunity rather than an error.

▶ Ditch Anything Modal

Error messages in desktop-installed applications are most often displayed in some sort of modal dialog box. Paraphrasing the Apple Human Interface Guidelines, there are three types of dialog boxes:

- **Modeless** Enables users to change settings in a dialog while still interacting with document windows; the Find window in many word processors is an example of a modeless dialog. Modeless dialogs have title bar controls (close, minimize, and zoom buttons).

- **Document-modal** Prevents the user from doing anything else within a particular document. The user can switch to other documents in the application and to other applications.

- **Application-modal** Prevents the user from doing anything else within the owner application; the user can switch to another application. Most application-modal dialogs do not have the standard title bar controls (close, minimize, zoom); the user dismisses these dialogs by clicking a button, such as OK or Cancel.

Modality exists on the web as well, but it comes in a slightly different form. Pop-up windows, for example, are modeless. They are often used in applications to configure settings and change preferences (for example, to add or remove a user from a webmail program), but they don't interfere with a user's ability to work with the parent window. Sure, clicking the parent window usually means losing track of the pop-up window, whether intentionally or not, but at least you can still interact with the main part of the application.

JavaScript alerts, however, are application-modal. Not only do they prevent the user from interacting with other parts of a web application, they also hijack the browser itself by making it impossible to switch pages or tabs or close the browser until the user clicks a button in the alert to close it. The user is left with no choice but to deal with the alert. She is unable to move on until the magical OK button is clicked.

This behavior is just plain rude. It's not the user's job to jump through every little hoop an application comes up with. It's the job of the software to do what the user wants.

Redesigning rude behavior

Getting rid of application-modal messages in favor of document-modal messages has become an interesting, albeit disturbing, trend on the web.

Instead of relying on JavaScript alert messages, for example, designers have been creating floating inline dialog boxes that serve the same purpose. It's as though everyone heard that users hate JavaScript alerts and decided they'd cure the issue by moving the confirmation messages and such into the page instead.

In one recent example, a message appeared that looked similar to a JavaScript alert, but it was displayed in the page itself as a floating box. I couldn't move past it without clicking Okay. This was a document-modal message. I could still interact with the browser itself, but not the application.

This modal alert is disappointing. All it does is a nice job of redesigning rude behavior.

In another case, the entire page was dimmed out and all its interactions were disabled while a modal dialog box displayed in the center of the page. Also document-modal.

Listen up, fellow designers. The issue isn't that the errors come in the form of separate controls, like JavaScript alerts. The issue is that the messages are modal. Making the messages document-modal isn't any better. Yes, document-modal messages still allow the users to interact with the browser or leave the page, but these messages still interrupt workflow, prevent users from working with the rest of an application while dealing with the message, and do so unnecessarily. A new spin on the same old trick is not the answer.

A new design for modal errors doesn't cure the problem. *It just moves it.* These designers are just finding more interesting ways to make the same mistake. They're redesigning rude behavior.

Replace it with modeless assistants

Instead of redesigning rude modal alert messages, we need to devise better solutions that help users maintain forward momentum while using our applications. We can do this by going modeless.

For example, we can implement undo functions instead of relying on implementation-model, application-modal JavaScript alerts or document-modal errors and confirmation messages (especially ones that act like faux JavaScript alerts). Undo functions have been around for a long time in desktop applications, but somehow this behavior wasn't translated for the web—that is, until Google decided to create undo functions for its popular webmail application, Gmail.

When messages are deleted in Gmail, a notification appears toward the top of the page that tells the user the conversation has been moved to the Trash and offers an Undo link. As expected, clicking the Undo link reinserts the deleted messages back into the list of messages.

I can undo my last operation? Brilliant! Bravo, Google. Bravo.

Google does three things right with this feature.

First, it eliminates the need to show confirmation messages that ask the user if she's sure she wants to throw the messages away.

Second, it offers a way to get the deleted messages back.

Finally, *it shows the user how to do it* via the inline text message at the top of the page.

The final feature is exposed right when it needs to be, and the yellow background used to display the message draws the eye right to it, so users are much more likely to see the message and know the feature exists. This message remains visible until the user performs a new action, like creating a new message or deleting another conversation. In other words, it stays active just long enough for users to backtrack and undo the delete action.

What Google did was brilliant, but not because implementing an undo feature was an original idea. It was brilliant because no one else was doing it on the web.

Now that Google has proven undo functions can be created on the web, and has shown us a great way to do it, we're all out of excuses. Any application that allows users to perform what are normally irreversible actions should include an undo function.

I know, I know, building this functionality isn't always going to be easy, but it's definitely worth it. And hey, someone's bound to release a JavaScript framework one of these days that makes implementing undo features really simple. (Someone, steal this idea and run with it. Please.)

▶ Write Error Messages That Help Instead of Hurt

Jillions of error messages on the web are written in cryptic developer-speak. *Jillions.* If you're responsible for writing even one error message in an application, now's the time to pay close attention.

Error messages need to be written by someone who knows how to write.

If this is not you, step away from the keyboard and consider taking a writing class. If you do write well enough that other people can read your email messages to them without crossing their eyes, then stick around. You might be a good person to write error messages. It's not glamorous, but it's necessary.

So what's so hard about writing an error message? Well, it's hard because it needs to be done in a way that avoids demeaning people. Developers tend to write error messages during the development phase of any application so it can be debugged more efficiently. But these types of error messages, unfortunately, often make their way into the released product where they confuse and alienate users on a daily basis.

Instead of writing an error that says "[*object*] is null" (as though that means anything to a non-developer), for example, explain what's happened in plain

English and how to deal with it. Say something that makes sense. Say, "Unfortunately, your request could not be handled. Please try again. If the problem persists, please restart your browser."

Yes, this message has a lot more words, but it also means a lot more to a user. It tells him something has gone wrong and explains what can be done to move forward.

Error messages that do not provide useful information do not help users. They hurt users.

A poorly written error message is one that explains what is wrong in terms not likely to be understood by the user. Here's an example from a fictitious calendar application, in which a user is trying to schedule an event:

"**Operation failed.**"

Users cannot be expected to understand what this means. They will understand that something went wrong, but many users will not know from a message like this how to react, nor will they understand that they were performing an "operation." Some will try the "operation" again. Some will just give up.

Improving the message is a simple matter of using language more likely to be understood.

"**We're sorry, but we could not schedule this event. Please try again.**"

This version of the message tells the user what to do to get back on track, but still doesn't explain what went wrong in a way that prevents the user from repeating the same mistake.

An effective error message might look like this:

"**We're sorry, but this event cannot be saved without a date. Please select a date and save it again.**"

In this version, the error tells the user what went wrong in plain English and offers instructions about how to remedy the error.

Simple changes like these convert error messages from rude bits of useless information into helpful, explanatory bits of *useful* information.

Interface Surgery

This episode of Interface Surgery is a simple one, but it covers a little trick that can be used in any application in about a billion ways. I frequently use it to display error messages in web applications.

The *inline-expand* design pattern is made possible by a simple <div> in an HTML page that is displayed and/or hidden on demand, via JavaScript, based on user interaction. The first time I ever saw this in action was in Macromedia's weblog aggregator, prior to Adobe Systems' acquisition of Macromedia. The FAQ (Frequently Asked Questions) section of the site contained the usual, long list of questions. But each one was a simple link; no answers appeared on the page. Wondering what would happen when I clicked, I was happy to see the answer presented inline, right where I needed it. No waiting for a page refresh. No pop-up windows.

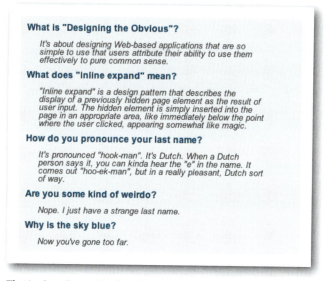

That's a lot of text. I don't really want to read all that.

A typical FAQ page looks rather crowded. It contains a ton of questions, each separated by an answer. All the blocks of text for the answers make the questions harder to pick out. Sure, the questions are somehow visually distinct from the answers, with either a bold font or a different font color, but this isn't usually enough to make the page as clear as it needs to be. Users are forced to scan long pages full of text to find the particular question they need answered.

To clean up this page, the answers must be stripped out of it.

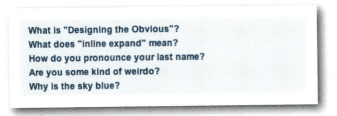

A short list of links. Much easier to read.

A single JavaScript function (which toggles the answer between visible and hidden), the conversion of each question into a link, and the addition of an ID attribute to each link in the HTML are all it takes to turn the list of remaining questions into links that display answers "automagically."

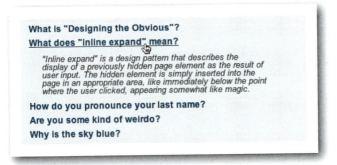

One chunk of information at a time, please. Thank you.

The much shorter list of questions is significantly easier for users to scan. Spotting the right question is a simple matter of a quick glance down the page. Upon finding the question the user needs answered, he clicks the link and is shown the answer.

I started using the inline-expand pattern to avoid the use of application-modal error messages and document-modal faux JavaScript alerts, like the one described earlier. Using inline expand, when something goes wrong that I can't otherwise prevent with a poka-yoke device, I show the error message like anyone else, but I do it nicely: I show it in a prominent location on the page, but in a modeless fashion so users can deal with it when they want, not when I want.

There is usually no compelling reason to prevent a user from interacting with other parts of an interface while displaying an error message. That is, nothing about the error is so important that the application thinks, *You absolutely must handle this right now or I'll just die!* There's certainly no reason to stop a user from interacting with the *browser* until he's been notified of the error. That's just crazy.

Instead of relying on rude, implementation-model error notifications, we can be polite. We can go modeless and show users something that lets them continue working, and incidentally maintain their self-esteem. The inline-expand pattern lets us do just that.

▶ Create Forgiving Software

At a deeper level than the need to prevent and detect errors is the need to create software that is forgiving to users as errors occur. Applications should allow users to play around and see what they can do without serious consequences.

A site-builder tool I used once featured the ability to create forms, such as contact or reservation forms, for a website. It wasn't easy to do this, however; it took several minutes just to figure out how to create a new form, add the appropriate form elements (such as text fields and check boxes with labels), and set properties for them (such as their default values and whether or not the fields were required).

After a while of muddling through this grueling process, I attempted to select a text field and delete it. Instead of deleting the single form element, the entire form was removed from the screen. My hard work disappeared forever.

I would have stopped using the application immediately and never looked back, but it was my job at the moment to do an expert review of the application to tell the people who built it how I thought it could be improved. You can probably guess what I reported as my number one recommendation.

An application should never allow users to mess things up so badly that they lose lots of work. Not without some sort of warning. And if a warning cannot be provided in an appealing, nonmodal fashion, an undo feature should be provided so that users can quickly backtrack and get moving again.

This bit from Apple's Human Interface Guidelines really says it all:

> *Encourage people to explore your application by building in forgiveness—that is, making most actions easily reversible. People need to feel that they can try things without damaging the system or jeopardizing their data. Create safety nets, such as the Undo and Revert to Saved commands, so that people will feel comfortable learning and using your product.*

The iPad version of Kayak, a travel-booking app, offers a handy option for people who want to examine multiple options. Rather than requiring users to start over with a new search every time, Kayak keeps a list of the flights you look up so you can easily review them or jump back and forth to compare.

Kayak keeps track of your previous searches so you can review multiple options.

Writeboard, another application from 37signals, enables groups of people to collaboratively contribute to a single piece of copy (such as that for the About Us page of a website, or a research paper). This application has a rather unique way of allowing users to undo changes: it offers version tracking and comparison. Each time a Writeboard is edited, it can be saved as a new version.

Color key

Green is new text
Strike is removed text
The rest is the same in both versions

You're comparing

28	☑	< 1 min ago	Robert Hoekman, Jr
27	☑	1 min	Robert Hoekman, Jr
26	☐	08 Oct 09	Robert Hoekman, Jr.

Writeboard's version tracking makes it easy for users to see what has been done.

Users can at any time compare two versions of the same document by checkmarking the two versions they'd like to see from the list in the sidebar and clicking the Compare button (which, incidentally, remains disabled until two document versions are checkmarked—another nice example of a poka-yoke device).

Good software promotes good practices

This topic is a bit fuzzy. It's quite subjective and can only be dealt with on a case-by-case basis, so it requires regular reexamination as we develop new applications.

Promoting good practices, in a nutshell, means that our applications need to make it difficult to produce bad work, and easy to produce good work.

Remember the web-based site-creation tool? Aside from the disappearing form issue, I found it quite taxing to do anything really well with that tool. The simple act of creating navigation took many steps and involved at least one pop-up window. It was difficult to format text and links, and the end result was a navigation bar that looked almost nothing like I intended. Continuing, I replaced the default background image for the page's title area with my own, and somehow ended up with two copies of my image, one on top of the other. After a while, I figured out how to get rid of the second one, but the title text itself didn't look quite right. So I accessed the pop-up window required to format text and was very surprised to find none of the text tools applied to the title text. (It turns out the title text wasn't text at all. It was an image, which is why I couldn't edit it. It *looked* like text. How was I to know?) Ultimately, I left the title text the way it was and gave up.

The whole experience was pretty frustrating and left me with a web page I didn't like that took a lot of time to create. For all the work I had done, I wasn't at all satisfied with the results.

I blamed myself for this, as most users do. I assumed I just didn't get it. I didn't understand some crucial piece of information that would make the whole process make sense. I had missed the basic workflow, out of sheer stupidity, and thereby created a page I wouldn't show to my dog.

I realized I was blaming myself and stopped, because how could I, an experienced designer, have messed this up so badly if it hadn't been for poor interaction design and weak task flow? And if *I* was messing things up, how much harder was this application to use for people without design experience?

This tool made it really easy to produce bad work. I don't ever want to use it again.

Here's the flip side:

Google Page Creator, as previously described, had quite a few good defaults in place. First, it offered a default page template for the user. Second, it offered a default page layout. And when the user entered text into a page she was creating, it relied on default font sizes and colors for body text, headings, and subheadings. This was all very nice and groovy of Google, because it helped users get moving right out of the gate so they could become intermediate users as quickly as possible. But the real key to success for users was that the defaults offered by Google Page Creator promoted good practices.

The default template contained an area at the top of the page for a page title, another area in the center for the main content of the page, a space at the bottom for footer information such as a contact link and a copyright disclaimer, and usually some sort of sidebar to be used for persistent navigation. These are all elements typically found in a well-designed web page.

The default template was also void of annoying tiled background images. It didn't contain superfluous animations, ad banners, blinking text, or anything else that is known to annoy users.

The default fonts styles were appropriate for the template as well. A page with a dark background used a light-colored font. Body text was a standard size and font (10-point Arial). Headings were noticeably larger so visual hierarchy is established. The fonts used for headings and body text complement each other so they looked good on the same page.

All of these settings could be changed by the user, but Google Page Creator, by default, guided her toward a page that looked good and adhered to typical design standards for the web. Since most users stick to the default settings in web applications, Google Page Creator made it likely that the user would create a decent page every time. It increased the chances users would produce good work. Users, again, would probably have never noticed this fact and would have attributed their own common sense and design savvy to their success. But once again, this was *exactly* the right thing to do. Google didn't need the credit. Google only needed users to really like Google applications so that they would keep coming back to use them.

It pays to create applications that help users do good work themselves. If your application is meant to help users produce things that will be seen by other people, follow Google's lead and help *your* users look good to *their* users. If you can meet this goal, your users will love your application and will keep coming back.

9

Design for Uniformity, Consistency, and Meaning

- ▶ Design for Uniformity
- ▶ Be Consistent Across Applications
- ▶ Leverage Irregularity to Create Meaning and Importance

Design is the difference between this and a form that is easy to analyze and understand.

Nature.com's article "Web Users Judge Sites in the Blink of an Eye" (January 13, 2006), by Michael Hopkin, reports that users can make judgments about a website in just 50 milliseconds. (You can read this article at **www.nature.com/news/2006/060109/full/060109-13.html** .)

The article states:

> We all know that first impressions count, but this study shows that the brain can make flash judgments almost as fast as the eye can take in the information. The discovery came as a surprise to some experts. 'My colleagues believed it would be impossible to really see anything in less than 500 milliseconds,' says Gitte Lindgaard of Carleton University in Ottawa, who has published the research in the journal **Behaviour and Information Technology**. Instead they found that impressions were made in the first 50 milliseconds of viewing.
>
> Lindgaard and her team presented volunteers with the briefest glimpses of web pages previously rated as being either easy on the eye or particularly jarring, and asked them to rate the websites on a sliding scale of visual appeal. Even though the images flashed up for just 50 milliseconds, roughly the duration of a single frame of standard television footage, their verdicts tallied well with judgments made after a longer period of scrutiny.

Pay close attention to that last sentence. It says, basically, that users maintain similar impressions about the visual appeal of a site in the long term as those made within the first 50 milliseconds. The first impression is solid and incredibly important.

Does this mean that users actually judge a site this quickly? Do the first 50 milliseconds make so much of an impression that users actually decide if the site is appealing?

In a word: yes.

The first 50 milliseconds is not necessarily enough time to determine whether the information on a site is useful, see where on the landing page to find information, or learn anything about the site. It's a super-fast first impression. But it is enough time to cast an impression.

All I could absorb in a 50-millisecond test was the background color, the fact that there was an image on the page, and that content appeared to be laid out in columns. I couldn't discern the subject of the photo, the content of the columns, the company name or logo, or anything meaningful. This hyper-speed glance did not show me whether the site was going to be meaningful for me or not, but it *did* give me enough time to know it wasn't one of those obnoxious, brightly colored sites generated by Microsoft Word about someone's cat. This is useful information, since it's highly unlikely I'll ever need information from such a site, so it turns out that 50 milliseconds was indeed enough to tell me the site might contain something useful and was at least well-designed enough that I might be able to find what I needed.

At 500 milliseconds, elements were much more discernible. I had enough time to recognize that the photo was of a woman with a baby, there were three columns on the page, there was a text field on the left (probably a Search box), and that there were some icons on the right. It was still not enough for me to decide if I was going to leave the site or stay and try to find the information I needed, but it was definitely enough to ascertain I was staring at a well-designed site that I could probably trust to contain valuable information.

Uniformity, visual hierarchy, structure, flow, meaning, and consistency are vital tools in the job of making a great first impression, because these things allow a user to analyze pages quickly and make sense of them. Consistent and uniform design also allows users to rely on what's known as "spatial memory" (more on this later in this chapter).

All these things contribute to a simple, obvious design. One that helps users form a mental model that enables them to be productive without having to think about how an application works.

For example, users shouldn't need to determine (even subconsciously) whether one large object on a page is more important than another. Even tiny inconsistencies cause small blips in the brain that are enough to throw off a user's workflow and interrupt an otherwise calm and productive state of mind. Anytime we can maintain consistency to eliminate these interruptions, we give the user another reason to trust our applications, and we create a way to leverage *irregularities* to create meaning and importance (more on this later in this chapter).

The ability to design these qualities is both the result of everything talked about in this book so far and a necessary ingredient for an obvious design.

Design for Uniformity

When a builder puts together a staircase, uniformity is about making sure each step is the same height and depth so that people don't trip all over themselves while heading up or down. (Can you imagine a staircase where one step is 4 inches high and 6 inches deep, the next 12 inches high and 3 inches deep, and so on? You'd have to examine every step to decide how to proceed.)

When designing an interface, things are not all that different. Elements such as visual hierarchy, proportion, alignment, and typography play major parts in the uniformity of a design, and each must be designed so that users can quickly extract meaning from each screen and form a mental model with which to work.

Visual hierarchy

When markup code is written properly, titles are titles and paragraphs are paragraphs. Semantic code is written so that content is organized similarly to a term paper—with headings, subheadings, body text, and so on. When this is done, pages are more organized by default, because browsers render headings larger than other elements, each heading type defaults to gradually descending font sizes, and body text is shown smallest so it's clearly separated from the headings.

All this adds up to a page that can be analyzed at a glance, because the user can immediately see what's most important on a page and what on the page lends support to the first element. This allows him to make a snap judgment about whether or not to stay because the page contains useful information, or to leave because it does not. It also allows him to quickly find a link that might lead him to other useful information.

HTML organizes content into a visual hierarchy on its own. No wheel-reinventing needed.

When creating the user interface for a web application with semantic code, these elements can be created easily and maintained across multiple screens to provide a sort of built-in meaning for users. Users can quickly recognize the relationships between headings and content because each has its own default display settings that make the organization clear.

Sticking to the basics and letting HTML do what it does best—define structure for written content—is a clean and simple way to ensure visual hierarchy in a web application. Yes, page elements should be styled to create the look and feel you want for your application, but the CSS used to style the elements should support what HTML is designed to do on its own. Headings should be big and obvious, and body text should be small while remaining clearly legible. Supporting the natural tendencies of HTML keeps things clear.

Proportion

Proportion is defined by the size or quantity of certain elements as compared with others.

Many application screens (and website homepages in particular) use less than half of their available space for actual content. The rest is made up of header graphics, navigational elements, footer content, ad banners, white space, and other things that don't directly support the content. This figure may vary wildly depending on the design, but most of what appears on a given application screen is there to orient users to the app itself, not the content.

Designers tend to focus their screen designs around making sure the user knows where he is, how to get to other sections, and so on. (Of course, they do this because countless usability studies have told us it's a good idea, so they're right to do so.) And graphical elements meant to give an application its look and feel (referred to by many designers as the "chrome") often take up as much as one-third of the visible space on a screen. Add a little white space and advertising to that, along with even the simplest of navigational elements, and it's a wonder we have any room left at all. This proportion of pixels to data means applications often suffer from long, scrolling pages and a lack of **scanability** (the ability to easily scan a page for a particular element).

Sadly, content often takes a backseat to navigation and other design elements.

However, the content is the most important part of the application. Minimizing chrome to leave plenty of room for the interaction elements is crucial to helping users be productive. Just as much as error and confirmation messages get in a user's way, excess chrome can be a big annoyance when trying to move around within an application. Having a large proportion of non-essential elements is a sure way to detract from those things that are most important in a screen.

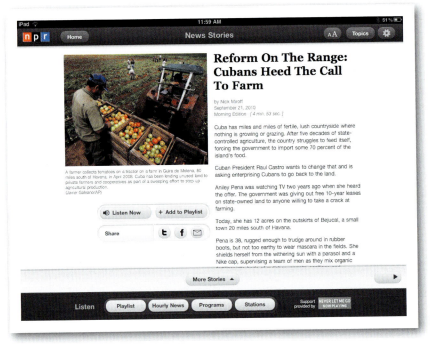

Room to breathe.

NPR for iPad is a nice example of how to minimize chrome and leave plenty of breathing room for content. The principal purpose of this application is to disseminate the news. Chrome would get in the way. The designers at NPR decided to focus the interface on the content instead of the tool. The graphical elements that make up the interface have been minimized to allow a wide-open view of the stories. Even within this layout, there is room to minimize chrome further by tightening up the space used for the sliding navigation panel, indicated by the More Stories button, and perhaps converting it to a small button elsewhere in the interface. But this interface, especially when compared with the BBC News iPad app, is nice and open.

BBC News for iPad wastes a lot of space by devoting half of its entire screen space to the navigation interface. Making this a collapsible element, or a menu, would really open up the area used to display the content.

NPR, on the other hand, leaves a good chunk of the available screen real estate open for content. The design creates a better environment for reading and watching the related video. It keeps the interface out of the way.

Content in BBC News for iPad gets less room than the rest of the interface.

Alignment

Many of us played the classic "one of these things is not like the other" games when we were children, designed to enhance our innate ability to discern one thing from another. We'd stare at pictures containing three rubber ducks and a fire hydrant and scream with delight, "*That* one is not the same!" We prided ourselves on our ability to pick out the thing that didn't match.

As we age, these lessons stay with us (in addition to our intrinsic, human ability to notice differences). When we see something that doesn't match up, we wonder why, even if only subconsciously. When fields in a registration form all line up to the left edge except for one field that's 12 pixels to the right, we think about it. Does it mean something? Why is this one out of place? We're hardwired to see the *differences*.

Alignment is about avoiding difference. Newspapers, books, Word documents, floor plans, and millions of other things are designed so that various elements are aligned to each other: groups of elements are aligned to one side, others to another side, everything is aligned to a common top edge, and so on. Without uniform alignment, books and sites are much more difficult to read because we have to constantly evaluate whether the positioning is meaningful.

There isn't necessarily anything wrong with a non-aligned design. Sometimes it's used intentionally. But the goal of a web application is usually to enable a user to get something specific done in an efficient manner, and messiness detracts from this goal. Uniform alignment is key to streamlining the process, because it ensures that nothing distracts the user while she is trying to complete the task at hand.

Form elements, for example, should be justified to each other's left edge, span the same width (when possible), be distributed evenly and consistently from each other (for example, if two fields are 15 pixels apart vertically, all others should be as well), and generally form a large rectangle when the page is looked at in terms of geometrical shapes so that no individual element stands out and makes users think it means something more than the others.

Tumblr's registration form is designed uniformly—the fields form a straight line on both the left and right edges.

With everything flowing in a straight line down the page, the screen is easy to read at a glance and minimizes the effort required to understand what the page is about and how to deal with it.

Typography

Much like misaligned objects on a screen, users notice differences in fonts, font sizes, colors, and so on, and attribute meaning to them. Consistent typography, like uniform alignment, enables users to stay focused on the task instead of wondering what to infer about each difference in font.

Fortunately, there are a few hard and fast rules that have become standard on the web when it comes to typography.

First, never use different fonts from screen to screen. Make a decision and stick with it. This is the simplest way to ensure consistency from page to page within an application.

Second, choose one typeface for the big, pop-off-the-page elements like headings, and choose a second typeface for the rest of the content. These two typefaces should differ enough from each other that the difference appears intentional. If the typefaces are too similar, headings and such can blend too easily into the rest of the page, and the meaning otherwise implied by clearly distinct typefaces can be lost.

Third, never use more than two or three different fonts. In fact, three is often too many. Multiple typefaces on a single screen can be disorienting, making it harder for the user to easily find what she is looking for.

Finally, limit the sizes and colors used for fonts. Of course, headings should be larger than body text, and body text should be larger than footer content, but avoid using different font sizes within body text. Also, use as few colors as possible. Choose colors for headings, body text, footers, links, visited links, active links, and so on, and use those choices for every page.

When it comes to typography, the less you do, the better.

Spatial memory

Spatial memory is the ability to recall where physical objects are in relation to other objects. It's what allows us to move around in a dark, but familiar, room. As we step into the room and fumble for the light switch, we can find it because we remember where it is located on the wall. If we continue into the room without turning on the light, perhaps to grab something off a desk, we can usually safely move around without bumping into objects and potentially injuring ourselves. Using spatial memory, our brains can recall the locations of the desk, the chair, the item on the desk, and other furniture.

Our users navigate pages using spatial memory. After a user has interacted with a page a few times, he forms a subconscious knowledge of the relative locations of elements on the page. He moves his mouse pointer without looking and without thinking. When every page contains the same navigational elements, in the same location as all the others, this is easy to do. Users can reliably jump to the point on a screen where they know a button is located and click or tap without having to really think about it.

It takes very little time for users to form these mental maps. The first couple of times a person uses an app, he learns where the navigation is located and what some of the main options are. From then on, he can move around the space more easily because spatial memory goes to work and he no longer has to evaluate the page in its entirety every single time to figure it out.

Consistent layout supports this behavior. So does proper alignment, because it's much simpler to move to something that appears in a straight line with everything else than it is to move the mouse to a somewhat arbitrary spot in the middle of a bunch of content.

▶ Be Consistent Across Applications

Companies frequently have more than one application. And a company that bases its business on the sale of applications or subscriptions wants to convey a consistent brand, consistent level of quality, and consistent user experience. When this is the case, it's important to look at all the applications put out by the company to see how they mesh.

Without consistency, a company's brand can end up on shaky ground. When customers are forced to learn a dramatically different interface with each application, the company itself can look as though it lacks focus and a clear purpose. Using different sign-on screens for every application, an inconsistent appearance, different approaches for similar task flows, and distinct design patterns for otherwise identical interactions forces users to work to learn new information all the time. Users don't like that.

Learning to use one application should make learning all the others easier. Not only is this better for users, it's better for us. Consistency allows us to more easily convert customers already happy with one application into customers who will be happy with new ones. Consistency in design allows one success to be built upon another.

Consistency in design also means new applications can be put together in less time and with less energy. Reusing interface paradigms already proven effective in current applications means new solutions will be easier to learn for users, easier to develop, easier to design, and more effective right out of the gate.

Consistent messaging

In addition to everything else you can do to maintain consistency, it's important to make sure system messages remain consistent as well. In fact, it's actually easier to do this than to create different types of message displays for different scenarios. Once a system is in place for the display of messages, it can be reused over and over via a simple function in the code. I highly recommend implementing such a system in each application you create so that messages are always as simple to display as a function call, and users know what is happening every time a message is displayed and never have to wonder why the differences exist.

Consistent messaging allows users to trust they know what to expect from an application. No surprises, no thought.

Understanding design patterns

Design patterns are a powerful tool when trying to maintain consistent user experiences across multiple interactions within a single application and across multiple applications (for example, when several applications by the same company are integrated to work together). The patterns are the glue that holds everything together.

Design patterns are used all over the web because they allow software designers to leverage the experience users have from other sites in their own applications to make them easier to learn.

The pagination design used by Google is used by many other search engines as well, so no one has to struggle with understanding a new design.

The design used for pagination in most search engines, for example, looks very similar in almost every case, and is used so widely because it works in such a way that users no longer have to think about how pagination works (or even that it's called "pagination"). Users can simply glance at the series of numbered links, wrapped with **Previous** and **Next** links, and know what to do.

For more information on design patterns, I highly recommend checking out Jenifer Tidwell's book *Designing Interfaces*. It's a tremendous resource on the subject, and anyone designing web applications for a living would be wise to read every page. It's the kind of book that should take up permanent residence on an application designer's bookshelf, much like Strunk and White's *The Elements of Style* is kept on a writer's bookshelf. That said, you can check out most of the design patterns themselves via the book's support site, www.designinginterfaces.com.

Design pattern libraries

Possibly the greatest thing a designer can do to help ensure consistency across applications (and even throughout a single application) is to create a design pattern library.

As previously described, design patterns are the glue that holds everything together in an interface. They help users learn new applications based on experience with others (for example, the pagination element used at the bottom of many search results pages) and can be used across multiple applications to support a consistent user experience.

A design pattern library is a collection of design patterns that have been documented so designers and developers can reuse the paradigms that have been proven to work and that maintain consistency across applications. A pattern library can come in the form of a wiki for multi-user collaboration or even a simple Microsoft PowerPoint document with just a few slides. The important thing is that each pattern has a name, a description of when and how to use it, and preferably a screen shot or wireframe of a possible implementation of the pattern so others can easily put the descriptions into context.

Jenifer Tidwell's www.designinginterfaces.com site is a pattern library, but one that serves a broad range of applications instead of a focused set of solutions provided by a single company. The patterns found there can be abstracted and used in any company's internal library, or can simply be used as a reference encyclopedia whenever you get stuck on a design problem.

In the case of a company-specific library, the patterns usually pertain to the solutions the company has devised for its own applications. If all of the company's tools, for example, are meant to use the same basic layout and pagination structure, its design pattern library contains patterns that explain the details.

Patterns can be as broad as a general framework for a design solution or as specific as describing exact details about how each solution should work (for example, "If more than five options are to be presented, a drop-down menu should be used instead of radio buttons, and the menu should be set to an appropriate default value."). Whatever the case, a pattern library is a great tool for a company to have in its toolbox. Disparate teams building applications for the same company can rely on the library to determine how to handle almost any design problem and end up with a solution consistent with the company's other tools. This benefits the company, its users, and the internal design staff, who can spend less time answering questions about how interfaces should work and more time evolving the company's products to support a long-term vision.

The Yahoo Design Pattern Library is one of the best resources on the web for a glimpse into how pattern libraries should be created.

To see another example of a design pattern library, swing by http://developer.yahoo.com/ypatterns, where Yahoo shares its own patterns with the public. This library features patterns as generalized as grid-based page layouts and as specific as the Drag and Drop Modules pattern used by My Yahoo, Google Personalized, and even Dashboard HQ to handle the reorganization of content modules on a customizable page.

Yahoo also offers a code base that can be used to implement many of the patterns in web applications. It's available through the Yahoo User Interface (YUI) Library at http://developer.yahoo.com/yui.

You can learn more about design patterns, and about the concept of **interaction design frameworks**—collections of patterns that guide the design of complete task flows or contexts—in my book *Web Anatomy: Interaction Design Frameworks That Work* (New Riders Press, 2009), coauthored by Jared Spool.

Intelligent inconsistency

Sometimes it's better to be inconsistent than to maintain consistency at all costs. For example, a purchase path (the sequence of screens shown to a user when she is making a purchase on a site) might show different add-on offers based on what the user is purchasing. In this case, it makes more sense to show appropriate add-on offers than to offer the same ones regardless of the user's interests (intelligent add-ons are much more profitable). Likewise, it makes sense to show a Cancel button only when canceling is a likely and necessary choice, whereas most interactions don't really need this option. (In most cases, a Cancel option is just plain unnecessary, despite the fact that it's provided in the vast majority of online forms.)

Knowing when to be inconsistent is the mark of experience. If you don't feel comfortable enough yet with your ability to decide when and where to be inconsistent, err on the side of consistency.

▶ Leverage Irregularity to Create Meaning and Importance

This is the part where I pull a bait-and-switch on you. After all this talk about consistent design and uniformity, telling you to leverage irregularity may seem a little insane. But this concept comes straight from the basics of design knowledge, and is vital to the representation of data and interface elements in an application.

Uniform and consistent design, as we've discussed, is key to helping users extract meaning from the design of an application and keeping them focused on tasks. But sometimes we need to make something stand out a bit on purpose so users realize it actually *is* more important than other elements, or at least different somehow, and requires additional attention. When this is the case, we need to stray from the rules of uniformity.

The best way to make something stand out is to present it differently than everything else. Much like the notion of creating applications that stand out by taking a completely new approach to the completion of a common activity, irregularity is a great way to make individual elements on a single page stand out from others. And the same tools used to design uniformity and consistency can be used to make page elements unique. In fact, consistent and uniform interfaces make it *possible* for things to stand out. Uniqueness is the product of *difference*, and difference can only occur in an environment of sameness.

Yelp uses color and dimension to make its Search box stand out from other page elements.

For example, Yelp features an omnipresent Search box on its homepage (and every other page, for that matter) because the primary purpose of the site is to allow users to search content. To make the Search box stand out, the designers wrapped it in a nice, bright banner that includes the site's logo. The Search box is easy to spot on every page and, as a bonus, reinforces the Yelp brand every time it appears.

Google's Search box, also readily available throughout the application, is set apart by always being displayed next to the Google logo.

Making something stand out is not complicated. It's usually a simple matter of *making it stand out*. (I love it when things are obvious.)

That said, there is one small thing to keep in mind. If something is meant to stand out, the element should be inconsistent enough from the rest of the interface that it appears to have been done intentionally. Small differences in alignment, coloring, and dimension may appear accidental and decrease a user's confidence. Big differences, on the other hand, make it clear that whatever was done was intentional.

Color

Color is a great way to make something stand out. It's also the simplest. When everything in an interface is blue and white, for example, a red error message sticks out like a sore thumb.

When deciding which colors to use throughout an application, reserve one or two additional colors for things that need to stand out from everything else. Just make sure the contrasting colors play well with the color palette you choose for the rest of the site. Making something stand out shouldn't mean completely disrupting your design.

Simple as that.

Since the predominant colors here are white and orange, the eye is drawn right to the green Buy the Book button, which is green.

Color differences can also be very subtle. If the predominant color of a page is light blue, a page element using a slightly darker shade of blue easily distinguishes itself from the rest of the page. Subtle differences like this can be just enough to draw the user's eye to the element without being disruptive to the flow of the page. Sharper differences, however, are more effective when a page element is particularly important and *must* be noticed. In this case, use strong, contrasting colors.

Dimension

Elements that take up a lot of room are viewed as more important, mainly *because* they take up more room. Because of the contrast, smaller elements convey less importance. Dimension can define what's most important on each page by simply making an individual element stand out from the others by its size.

If you use dimension to make a page element stand out from the others, be sure to make the proportional increase in dimension consistent from page to page as well. The consistency will, again, help a user reliably know that a large element equates to an important one as she moves around the application.

If elements are sized differently each time, she may find herself wondering why, and the whole goal is to avoid this.

Interface Surgery: Surfacing the bananas in a process

In his book *The Big Red Fez* (Free Press, 2002), which came out in the early days of the web but still contains plenty of truth, Seth Godin posited that users follow trails of clear, distinct signposts much in the same way that monkeys follow trails of bananas. In other words, if you add a button to a page that tells users exactly what you want them to do, and it meshes with what they want to do, they'll click it. It's a strange metaphor, but it does do a great job of illustrating yet another way to design the obvious. And designing page elements to stand out is exactly how we can achieve this effect.

I can't tell you whether or not the designers at VaultPress ever read *The Big Red Fez*, but they do seem to have gotten the point.

VaultPress used the banana approach to help you get started.

At the center of the VaultPress homepage is a very obvious block of text that tells you explicitly what VaultPress wants you to do: *sign up*.

This is a banana. It tells the user how to get started. It tells her what VaultPress hopes she will do, and how to do what *she* wants to do.

Bananas are incredibly useful when you want the user to do something specific, like complete a task. For example, a user wishing to purchase a new desk chair needs to locate the chair she wants, add it to her shopping cart, enter her billing information, and confirm the purchase. This process is much easier to follow when each screen in the process uses a banana to guide her toward completion of the task.

Surfacing the bananas in a web page is a matter of understanding what is most important on the page and then making it stand out somehow. Sometimes, there may be more than one important element on a page, but in most cases, there should not be more than three or four. If there are more bananas than this, odds are the design is not as focused as it should be, and users are being given too many options.

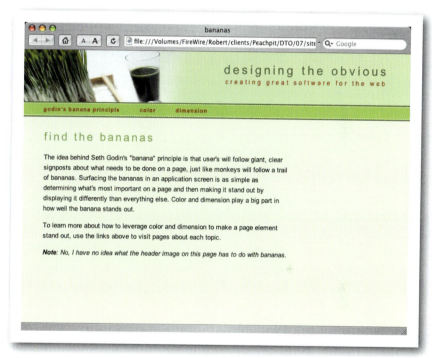

No bananas here.

Pages containing a lot of text do not always do a great job of surfacing the bananas in a process. The intent of the screen shown here is to compel the user to learn about Godin's banana principle by reading the three pages that explain the concept and how to achieve it. But ironically, although the text explains how to do this, there is no clear and obvious path toward the completion of the task. Sure, there is a navigation element toward the top of the screen, but the goal is to get the user moving quickly and in the right direction.

The first thing we can do is convert the terms within the text that point to the appropriate pages, into links.

Links are easy to spot within large blocks of text, but this page still lacks a banana.

This minor change can certainly help anyone who bothers to read the text on this page, but odds are, not many people will stick around long enough to find the links. We need to put up some big signs that explain what to do.

Bananas for everyone!

In this version, the graphical buttons indicate the actions the user should take. The new design points the user to the three pages and offers an obvious way to access each one. It also takes focus off the text.

These buttons use the same colors as the rest of the page, but since the main content area does not contain the dark green and red colors, the buttons stand out. They also stand out by appearing larger than everything else on the page. The buttons use a larger font than even the page title and logo areas of the page.

The final version of the page leverages color and dimension to make the bananas stand out.

And since the buttons now tell the user exactly what to do, we can remove the text telling the user to "use the links above to visit pages about each topic." The new, shortened version makes the block of text look even less important when compared with the buttons.

Godin's banana principle doesn't apply to everything. Portal pages and the like are not good candidates for large, clear signposts, because they are generally aimed at offering users a wide variety of options instead of just a couple. But when the mission for the company and the user is to move the user through a particular set of screens toward completion of a goal, bananas can be very effective.

Consistency and uniformity help users understand applications, derive meaning from screens, and stay on track without a lot of effort. But when it's particularly important for the user to focus on a certain page element, changes in color and dimension can be just the thing to make it pop off the page and communicate to the user what needs to be done.

10

Reduce and Refine

- ▶ Clean Up the Mess
- ▶ Practice Kaizen
- ▶ Eliminate Waste
- ▶ Put Just-in-Time Design and Review to Work

Every element on a page fights for the attention of the user. Text sits next to form elements, which sit next to ad banners, which sit next to logos, taglines, copyright information, and persistent navigation. How is a user supposed to know which things *really* need attention and which things can safely be ignored?

Interfaces full of unnecessary graphical elements, text that's longer than it needs to be, and features that don't really help anyone risk creating an environment of visual overload. Every time a user accesses a page, his brain must take a moment to process everything on the screen to see what's there and analyze the importance of each element. This moment can be disorienting when a page is jammed full of content and graphics.

Clutter diminishes a user's ability to form a workable mental model by crowding the important pieces of a screen in with unimportant ones. Clutter makes it more difficult for new users to become intermediate users by putting things in the way of the learning process. Clutter makes it hard to see the *design* in the design.

Clutter makes a mess of things.

Cluttered interfaces result in comments like:

"It's as though the marketing department threw up on this page."

Ouch.

Cluttered task flows

But clutter doesn't apply only to individual screens. It also applies to interactions and task flows.

The task-management system I use, for example, displays the Task Detail page every time I finish editing a task. This fact, in and of itself, is fine, and it makes sense. I do usually want to see the final version of the task details once I've completed editing the page. But there's no ability to add a new task to the project I'm currently working with from the Task Detail screen, so I have to click a rather insignificant text link, displayed amongst loads of other text, to return to the Project screen and then click again to create a new task. This would be no big deal if I only used the application once a week, and only edited or added a couple of tasks at a time, but I often need to set up a new project and define a series of tasks all at once.

Every time I finish creating one task, I have to click back over to the Project screen to add the next new task. Since projects generally involve many individual tasks, I have to do this upwards of 10 or 15 times within a half hour. One little link on the Task Details screen (something like Create New Task) would cure this completely. Without the link, the process of setting up a new project involves reloading the Project page over and over again when I have no need to view the Project screen in the first place. This clutters up the workflow unnecessarily, because it means I have to constantly revisit screens I *don't* want to see to get to the ones I *do* want to see.

Drives me nuts.

The path to simplicity

It's not always possible to keep a web-based application simple. There are some incredibly complicated applications out there, for good reason. Despite this, designing the obvious means striving for simplicity.

In the book *Designing Visual Interfaces* (Prentice Hall, 1994), authors Kevin Mullet and Darrell Sano state:

> *Reduction through successive refinement is the only path to simplicity.*

Every word in this sentence speaks volumes. "Reduction" tells us to reduce the scope of our software, stripping it down to what's really needed. "Successive refinement" tells us to iterate; don't stop at a single design and call it a day. Keep iterating, re-evaluating, challenging yourself to make the design cleaner, simpler, and more elegant (and thusly, more purposeful). And "simplicity" clearly references the principal goal of application design.

Making a complicated application clear requires making each piece of it as simple as possible. Designing the obvious means reducing and refining each screen, each task flow, and each interaction so that the purpose and function is as simple as possible.

When each piece of an application is reduced to its simplest form, the application as a whole achieves clarity.

NPR for iPad limits the number of graphical elements used so as to maximize the space allowed for the display of stored files. Backpack leverages inline editing features to reduce the complexity of tasks so users avoid round-trip interactions where editing is done on administrative pages. VaultPress shows only the bare essential graphic elements on a given page to lessen the visual load of each page and focus completely on the ability to create and review notes. Blinksale and Ballpark include only the essential elements needed by most people to create and manage invoices quickly.

All of these applications have a narrow scope, include only what's absolutely essential, rely on clean and simple interfaces, feature screens that are light on text, and focus entirely on the task at hand.

All of these qualities contribute to a simplified user experience, and help to reduce the complexity of their respective applications by avoiding clutter, both mental and physical.

Clean Up the Mess

For people to use our software, they need to be able to find the features they need. We need to unbury the things that make our applications great and put a giant spotlight on them. The best way to do this is to reduce clutter in the screens that make up our application interfaces.

As discussed in Chapter 9, contrast (often created through color and dimension) is an effective tool for making a particular part of a screen stand out. This is true because some things are *seen* before a user even begins paying real attention to particular elements. A bright red box on a page comprised of only shades of blue, for example, is seen first because it sharply contrasts with everything else on the screen. Before our brains ever register what's going on, we see the red box. But although contrast is one of the most effective ways to make something stand out from the crowd, it's not the only solution.

Another rather obvious way to ensure that an interface element is seen is to remove anything that takes a user's attention *away* from it.

Reducing the pixel-to-data ratio

The very same artwork that provides the look and feel for an application is also one of the biggest culprits of clutter in interfaces. The space that graphics take up, the colors used, the proportion of graphics to information, and the overall tone of graphical elements can all detract from the content of an application and take focus away from what matters. Reducing the volume of graphical elements is one of the best ways to eliminate clutter.

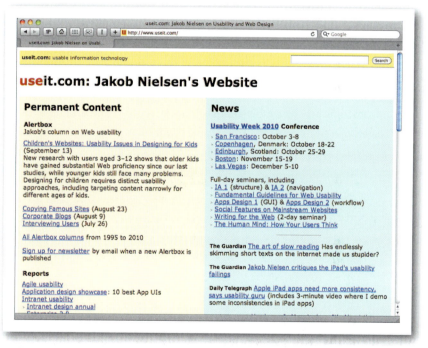

Usable, yes. Personable, no.

This is not to say we should all design our applications to emulate the *un-design* of Jakob Nielsen's website at www.useit.com. Nielsen may be a major guru of web usability, but it's more than possible to design an application that is both clean and aesthetically appealing.

Logos, for example, don't need to take up a lot of room, but they often do. Product names, product logos, and corporate logos often are displayed at rather large sizes near the top of application screens despite being probably the least important elements on a page.

I understand the urge to spotlight these elements. Marketing departments want to create brand recognition. It's a reasonable request. What they often forget is that by the time the user sees the giant product name and company logo, she's already decided to use the product. Using screen real estate to repeatedly tell her the name of the product is only going to limit how much space can be used for more important content.

The best marketing tool you can have is a well-designed application.

Users appreciate your well-designed application far more than they appreciate having the company name shoved in their faces every time they load a new screen. Feel free to add a logo to the application, but keep it small and bury it in a corner of the page so it's out of the way. Don't focus on logos. Focus on benefits.

Also, try to keep layers of organizational graphics to a minimum. Far too often, web applications organize individual sections into boxes and end up with so many levels of nested boxes that the simple divider-line graphics used to make such divisions take up dozens of pixels for no reason at all.

If sections of the design can be segregated without the use of boxes, do it. If page elements can be grouped into fewer individual areas and take up less space, do that, too. Whatever can be done to reduce the space used and the ratio of pixels to data will help the application's functionality and benefits shine through.

Minimizing copy

A lot has been said about minimizing copy online. (Isn't irony fun?) But some of the wisest words have shown up in, of all places, books.

Strunk and White's *The Elements of Style*, for example, is always a great source for learning to write more concisely and effectively, and the standards defined by this book apply every bit as much to the web as they do to print.

One of the guidelines offered in the book is "Omit needless words." Steve Krug had a little fun with this axiom in his book *Don't Make Me Think*, by titling a chapter "Omit Needless Words" and crossing out the word *needless*.

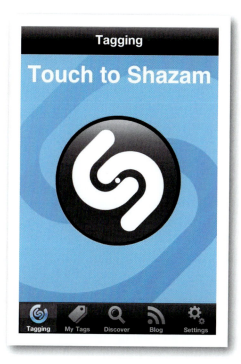

Shazam for iPhone keeps instructive copy to a minimum.

Removing words is a surefire way to reduce clutter in an interface, but it can be difficult to decide what to cut and how to revise what's left. Here are some guidelines:

- Move instructive copy into What's This? Help documentation.

  Much of the text that clutters up interfaces is instructive. Developers often assume that users will thoroughly read the instructions. They don't.

  Users typically skip right over anything textual and go straight to guessing. They click the first thing that looks like it might help them do what they need to do. So instead of cluttering up an interface with instructions, convert them to inline Help documents. Replace the text in the application screen with a **What's This?** link that either opens a pop-up window that contains the text or displays the text inline using the inline-expand design pattern discussed in Chapter 8.

- Write vigorously.

  In an application, you have very little chance of grabbing a user's attention with text (applications are about *doing*, not reading). So when text absolutely must be included, keep it concise. Omit needless words, limit the text to its core message, and try to break up paragraphs into shorter, more succinct bullet lists using as few words as possible.

- Avoid happy talk.

  "Happy talk" is what Steve Krug calls the text on a web page that aims only to tell the user how great the company or the application is, without backing it up with any real substance. It doesn't tell the user what to do, how to get started, how to complete a task, or even how an application might benefit the user. Instead, it uses buzzwords and self-congratulatory statements like "We were the first development team to land on the moon while simultaneously eating breakfast, standing on one foot, and patting our heads."

  Happy talk is most likely to be found on the introductory, pre-registration screens for an application, such as the homepage (you know, the page that's supposed to be one of the most important marketing tools you have).

  Get rid of the happy talk. Show screen shots, a giant Try It Now button, a tagline that summarizes the application's purpose, and a link to a (well-compressed) video about how the application works and what it does.

- Use trigger words, not a lot of words.

  A modicum of trigger words is better than a lot of really informative words. Informative text is informative only if anyone reads it. And no one will. If you must include text in your interface, be sure that text includes words the user might actually look for (according to *their* mental model and experience level, not yours) or that will jump out and grab the user's attention. And if the text is *really* important, refer back to Chapter 9 to see how to make it stand out.

Designing white space

Wichita State University's Software Usability Research Laboratory (SURL) posted an article in October 2003 (available at http://surl.org/usabilitynews/62/whitespace.htm) on the merits of white space and how it affects the usability and aesthetic appeal of a web page. White space is any area that appears blank on a screen. It describes the buffer of empty pixels provided between areas of a page to separate them, as well as the surrounding empty spaces provided to create page margins.

SURL performed usability tests to assess the differences in performance and visual appeal of varying amounts of white space. The testing was done in response to a 1997 report from Jared Spool, a web usability researcher, that sites using more white space are inferior to denser sites with regard to a user's ability to find information. Three versions of the same web page were created using varying amounts of white space (low, medium, and high amounts). Each version of the page was shown to 5 of 15 testers, so each person saw only one version.

What SURL discovered in its own tests is that there was no significant difference in the time it took users to find information relevant to the proposed tasks (such as "A friend of yours is interested in hiking the backwoods of Alaska or the jungles of the Amazon basin of South America. Find the site that mentions both of these areas."), but there were differences in the aesthetic appeal of the three different versions of the page.

Users were more satisfied with the version of the page that used a medium level of white space. They felt that a high amount of white space made the page slower because it required more scrolling to access content, but also felt that too dense a layout made the page less readable than the others.

The tests, basically, were the white space equivalent of the story of "Goldilocks and the Three Bears" (without the part where the user runs out of the lab, never to be seen again). One version of the page had too much white space, while another had too little. The third, however, was "just right."

So, while white space had no apparent effect on a user's ability to complete a task, it had a great effect on how much the user *enjoyed* the page.

This, as you can see, makes the act of designing white space a bit dicey, because "medium" is a relative term, so a designer's ability to allow a medium amount of white space is contingent on his own definition of the term and his analysis of individual screens.

Incidentally, the part of the report that indicates that the amount of white space had no effect on the time it took users to find information should probably be ignored. The tasks users were asked to perform during SURL's usability tests all involved searching for an appropriate link within the page, which contained nothing but three columns of black text on a white background, and section headings and a page title displayed in dark red text. Links appeared as default HTML hyperlinks, which means they displayed as underlined blue text.

Blue links stick out like a sore thumb on a page that contains nothing but text on a white background.

As you know from reading Chapter 9, color is one of the best ways to make something stand out on a page, and underlined blue text links stand out extremely well on a page full of black text. A user asked to look for a link on a web page like this needs only to glance at the page, regardless of how much white space is used, to quickly spot all the instances of underlined blue text. Because the links are so high-contrast, a user actually sees these links before they even begin to pay attention to specific elements. As a result, this test isn't the best gauge of whether white space affects the time it takes to complete a task.

A more realistic test might require users to add a comment to a blog post, using a button graphic (one that blends in with the page's primary color palette) as the trigger to add the comment. In this case, white space would likely have a bigger effect on the time it takes to complete the task, because a denser layout would make the button harder to find.

Filling in the gaps

White space is an effective alternative to using graphics to divvy up a page into clear sections because of how the human brain works to fill in gaps. When we watch a movie, the individual frames on a reel of film whiz by us at roughly 30 frames per second. Our brains fill in the rest and fool us into thinking we are seeing real, uninterrupted motion. When we look at half of a broken, ceramic mask, we "see" the whole face. Our brains fill in the gaps.

When we look at a web page, the same thing happens.

Two elements spread far apart appear to have little or no relationship to each other, while two elements positioned more closely together appear directly related. This is why OK and Cancel buttons are often next to each other, while a Save As button in the same dialog box, which provides a very different function, might appear farther to the left, separated from the OK and Cancel buttons.

In both of these examples, we *see the separation*. We don't need graphics to tell us there's a division between one section and another—we can see it just fine. Just as we see the close relationship of two elements positioned next to each other and the lack of meaning between two elements positioned far apart, we can see that there is a difference between *this* column and *that* column even without a vertical line to separate them.

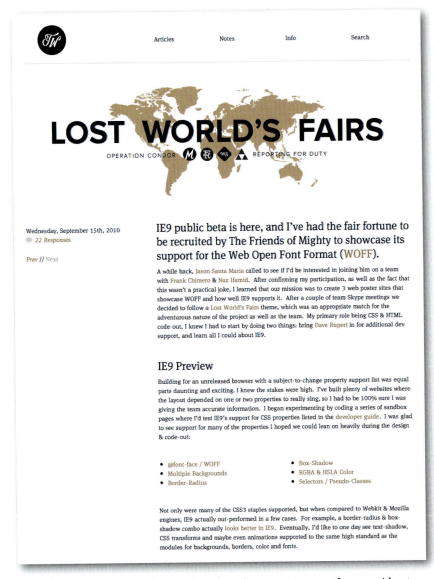

Here, white space does a good enough job of clearly separating areas of a page without relying on the use of graphics (which must be processed by the user's brain).

Instead of relying on graphical dividers to segregate sections of application screens, we can usually rely on white space. White space gives us the same separation between elements without the extra visual load of the graphical lines the user would need to process when glancing at the page.

White space also weighs less, in terms of file size, than graphics, so pages can load more quickly.

Cleaning up task flows

Task flows are a prime area for reduction and refinement. Unnecessarily complicated screen sequences go from mildly tedious to flat-out annoying in a very short time, especially when the task is performed regularly. Decreasing the number of screens a user must visit to complete a task improves workflow and makes application more obvious.

In the aforementioned task-management application, a simple **Create New Task** link would make the process of setting up a new project much quicker. Yes, the addition of such a link on the Task Details screen would add clutter to that page, but the cost is minimal compared with the reward of an improved workflow.

In many web-based email applications, users have two options for how to view messages. They can either display the Inbox in one screen and open individual messages in a new window or a separate screen, or they can show a Preview pane on the Index page and read email messages without switching to another screen or opening a new window. The latter of these two options consolidates the workflow, decreases the number of page loads, makes window management simpler (in cases where messages are displayed in a new window), and makes the Inbox screen significantly more useful.

Entire conversations display on a single page in Gmail. Please ignore the fact that I was talking to myself.

Google's Gmail does a great job of managing the primary task flow for checking email. There is no option to show message previews on the Inbox screen—you must click through to a different screen to read a message—but each message is displayed in a thread. All messages from the same conversation are displayed on a single page, so users can get an at-a-glance view of the entire thread, and simply select any individual message in the thread to display it inline, according to its chronological position within the thread. If a message is the third reply in a thread of messages, it is displayed beneath the first two messages and above any messages received later on. This not only consolidates the workflow for users, but also maintains context.

Cleaning up task flows is often as simple as going through various tasks in an application and justifying everything that is encountered while trying to complete it. It can be time-consuming and tedious, but it's not complicated.

On every screen you come across in a task, write a list of everything that exists on the screen and give yourself a 60-second deadline (as discussed in Chapter 4). Scratch out anything you think you can get rid of, move those things to a new list, and save that list for later. Then go through the code and rip out everything you crossed off. If the page still works and the task can still be completed successfully, you're done. If not, you may have crossed off too many items.

Once this is done, write a list of the screens required to complete a task, and see if any of them can be consolidated. Can the part of the registration process where you collect a user's address information be moved into the same screen where you collect her preferred user name and password? If so, go for it.

In my task-management system, clients are listed on one screen, while projects are listed on another. If these two screens were consolidated, so that each client listing displayed underneath it a list of projects associated with that client, I could access both the Client Details and Project Details from the same place instead of drilling down.

Next, see if you can create shortcuts from one screen to another. If users commonly access two or three particular screens in the same session, provide links to all of them from each screen to make the jumps easier.

Finally, on screens where editing is allowed (or required), modify the design so the editing can be done inline instead of sending the user to an Edit screen and back to the read-only screen upon completion (known as a *round-trip* interaction). Through inline editing, you can eliminate the need for entire screens in task flows, make the application simpler to understand, help maintain context for users (which contributes to a solid mental model), and make common operations more enjoyable.

The process of cleaning up task flows can be done at any point in your development process, including after the product has been released (in fact, this is a great excuse for releasing a new version, regardless of whether or not new features have been added). That said, it's far cheaper to do it before any code has been written. If code has already been written, money was spent to create the things that are now being cleaned up. It also means the tasks must now be retested to ensure nothing fails as a result of the improvements. Overhauling task flows while your application is still in its wireframe state, however, means you can fix things quickly and easily, and make major improvements when it's most cost-effective to do so.

Avoiding Interface Surgery

You may have noticed there is no Interface Surgery section in this chapter. There's a good reason for that.

Many of the topics in this book are related. This chapter applies to each of them, and each contributes to this chapter.

It's all related and it's all important. It's also all been said.

You've already seen examples of how to reduce clutter in an interface. The section about writing use cases in Chapter 3 described how to simplify an interaction. Chapter 4 was all about building only what's absolutely necessary. This reduces clutter by default. I've also talked about inline editing and inline validation, both of which add up to a faster and less cluttered task flow with fewer screens and fewer clicks. And designing screens in a consistent and uniform fashion contributes directly to a refined experience.

No need to say it all again.

▶ Practice Kaizen

Kaizen was first mentioned way back in Chapter 3 when I talked about how to write use cases, and again when discussing wireframes, but kaizen can continue to be applied long after an application is built and released.

Although kaizen was originally developed as a management approach aimed at improving quality and reducing defects in manufacturing, the underlying philosophy is central to my approach to application design. Kaizen is about doing the work of improving things constantly, in little tiny ways that add up to gigantic results.

Kaizen can be applied to the way you write code in the programming language of your choice, design task flows, or refine the visual design of an interface.

One of the major benefits of kaizen is that it keeps you from worrying about making things perfect on the first try. To the contrary, it enables you to focus only on getting something done so you can start improving it incrementally. You can start with a grayscale HTML page if you like. As long as you keep improving things as you go, you're in good shape.

Kaizen means iteration

Another major benefit of kaizen is that it enables us to get products in the hands of testers more quickly. The sooner a user starts using real screens to deal with real interactions and complete real tasks, the better. Wireframes, use cases, and mockups are great for planning a design and getting the ideas worked out, but things inevitably change once our designs go from paper to screen. It's at this point that we see how an application *really* works. Putting our designs in front of beta testers is what allows the truth about our work to come out into the light.

There's always a way to improve an application (and no, I don't mean by adding things to it). And every time you make a small improvement to an interface, doors open up for improving the new version. But none of the changes cause any major disruption in your work, because tiny changes take almost no time at all, so you can keep plugging away at the activity of building sites and software without becoming buried in documentation and conversation about all the improvements you've made.

Kaizen means iteration. To genuinely improve our applications in the long run, we need to repeatedly go over them, see where things can be improved, make changes, and put new versions in the hands of real users to prove the changes are better. Wash, rinse, repeat.

The 5S approach

5S is another Japanese improvement process originally developed for the manufacturing industry. And just like kaizen, 5S translates well to interface design and application-development processes.

In fact, this book has discussed every aspect of 5S without ever mentioning it specifically (until now, anyway). But while the whole concept of designing the obvious can be wrapped up by these five points, it's most appropriate to describe 5S in context of the topics of reduction and refinement, because each point of the 5S system contributes directly to both topics.

The rest of this section is a summary of each piece of the 5S system and how it relates to designing the obvious.

Seiri (sort)

Seiri is about sorting through tools and other materials to determine what must be retained and what can be thrown out or stored. In manufacturing, seiri produces a safer environment by keeping unnecessary items out of the way of workers, so they can be more steadily productive.

In web terms, seiri can be thought of as sorting through features, interface elements, and screens to minimize an application—or a single screen—to its most essential parts.

To sort through these things properly, you have to Know What to Build, which includes knowing what *not* to build. Even after a product is developed, however, we can go through an application repeatedly in an ongoing effort to clean it up and get unnecessary elements out of it.

Seiton (straighten)

Seiton refers to arranging things into their most efficient and accessible arrangements. In other words, order should be maintained relentlessly so resources are easy to access.

In web applications, this is about designing for uniformity so that users can derive meaning from a page's content based on how it is laid out.

Seiso (shine)

Seiso is about keeping clean, tidy workplaces. Cleaning should be a frequent activity and should always be aimed at polishing up anything losing its shine.

On the web, seiso can relate to improving or updating the look of graphical elements, devoting attention to more perfect alignment and distribution among page elements, and devising color palettes that contribute to the overall mood and personality of the application.

Seiketsu (standardize)

Seiketsu is about leveraging standards to enable consistency. Online, adhering to standards means using proper semantic markup in web pages and keeping the code used for presentation and content clearly separated.

HTML is designed to identify the structure of content. Headings are marked as headings, paragraphs as paragraphs, and so on. CSS, on the other hand, is used strictly for the presentation of the marked-up content. The standard use of these two technologies together improves the accessibility, maintainability, changeability, and sustainability of web content. But seiketsu goes far beyond markup.

Seiketsu also means establishing a set style for an application to which all screens can conform, so each screen enables a user to maintain her mental model, and makes it easier for her to learn and orient herself to new screens.

Standardization can go a long way. Many companies maintain style guidelines that detail when and how radio buttons, check boxes, and other elements should be used and how they should look and work. This can even be extended into a design pattern library, as discussed in Chapter 9. In this case, the library as a whole can be refined one pattern at a time and applied to multiple applications successively, so that a suite of tools can all be improved based on a single standard.

Shitsuke (sustain)

Shitsuke is about sustaining the work of each of the elements in the 5S system for the long haul.

Improvement (kaizen) should not come in small waves and then fade away. It should be kept up on a permanent basis. The repeated process of reduction to retain only what's needed in a screen or application (seiri), the arrangement of elements into their most effective forms (seiton), the polishing of what's left (seiso), and the standardization of screens and interactions throughout multiple applications (seiketsu) are all processes that should be maintained.

The long-term effort to refine the applications we construct is how we create solutions that are effective and desirable, both now and later.

▶ Eliminate Waste

Another way to reduce and refine is not in the application itself, but rather in the *process* of creating web applications.

Many companies step through a lengthy and complicated process each time a new application is designed and built. This process often begins with the creation of a **Vision Document**, which outlines the business goals and desires for a new application. This can be followed by a **Software Requirements Specification** (SRS), which details the features the application must offer. And this, in turn, can be followed by a functional specification, which describes how features should behave, look, and work, complete with both high- and low-level use cases. The creation of all these documents can lead to the design of wireframes (iterated repeatedly until approved), the conversion of the wireframes into final artwork, and finally, the construction, testing, release, and marketing of the application.

Even when an application is extraordinarily simple, this process can be slow-moving. It's a highly wasteful process that often results in an application no better (and often worse) than if the first three documents had been skipped and the developers went straight from use cases to code, with graphics created Just in Time.

In many cases, in fact, the people doing the strategy work for a new product—evaluation, situation research, vision definition, and so on—are not the same people who must create the wireframes and artwork for the application. This can create a large disconnect when the people with all the knowledge are on one side of a cubicle divider and the designers are on the other. And this disconnect can mean that those who did the strategy work must dump a ton of information on the designer, who must then translate the information into a design. And this can result in hours of design review meetings between the designer and the strategist to clarify requirements and discuss iterations. Quite wasteful.

Cleaning up your process

Cleaning up this whole mess can be highly beneficial—to the company and its users. In addition to cleaning up the interface for an application, we need to clean up the process used to build them.

Specifications

First, stop relying on specifications.

It's perfectly understandable that in many companies, specifications (aka *specs*) must be written. Typically, they're required to get buy-in from management and development teams and such to build the application in the first place. Beyond this, however, they have very little effect on reality. Applications almost never adhere to them, and they're almost never updated to reflect changes made to an application's design once development has started.

Furthermore, specs are usually about a million pages long, and no one really has the time to read them. Designers want to know about the activity so they can create a design that supports it. Developers want to know how the application will function. And marketers want to know how they can market the thing. Because specs are so long (and usually extremely boring), they fail to meet any of these needs effectively.

Once the development project has been approved and is in motion, put the spec away and stop worrying about it. At this point, your goal should be to Know What to Build.

Design now, not later

I also strongly recommend turning the application designer and the strategist into a two-person team that works collaboratively rather than independently (the two are rarely the same person—they do very different jobs with very different engagement models and focuses, and it can be difficult to focus on the big picture and the little details at the same time). When a knowledgeable designer is involved from the beginning, he can help decide what features are absolutely essential, study the activity the application is meant to support to gain a thorough understanding of it, and begin creating wireframes *right away* instead of struggling through a researcher-to-designer brain-dump later on and guessing his way through the design.

The designer is the one who needs to understand the application's scope and purpose and goals the most, so that he can effectively design an application that supports them. If research is to be done, the designer should be there, doing it. Sketches can be created the moment an epiphany strikes, and wireframes and use cases can be created and revised all along the way.

When the designer has *all* the information and knowledge he needs to design an effective application, the application will, indeed, become more effective. The designer should work hand in hand with the strategist.

▶ Put Just-in-Time Design and Review to Work

Sadly, many companies still skip the design process completely, leaving it up to programmers to "design" software themselves, making spur-of-the-moment decisions that greatly, and often adversely, affect the experience of using the application. When design is left up to programmers, applications often become complicated, extremely difficult to use, and bloated with features that, while giving marketers a hefty list of bells and whistles to cite in marketing collateral, actually inhibit the ability of most users to use the software effectively to accomplish their goals.

As long as this remains true, **Just-in-Time Design** and **Just-in-Time Review** are viable and necessary alternatives.

Just in Time (JIT) is the process of acquiring and delivering materials right when they're needed, as opposed to maintaining a surplus. In application design terms, this translates to JIT Design, which involves doing design work right at the spur of the moment—the moment right after someone has decided to add something to the interface and right before the programmer starts producing code.

JIT Review, on the other hand, is used as a final opportunity to reduce and refine a solution once it's been built.

JIT is especially appropriate when a development team practices **Agile development**, which creates a constant state of in-flux prioritization, but it can be used in any company to improve the state of an application before the latest version is released to users.

JIT Design

JIT Design generally entails holding a quick meeting before the coding starts for a new feature (or some other change to an application) to brainstorm and decide how a new piece of the software will behave, how it will be accessed or invoked, and how it will look and flow. This meeting can take five minutes or three hours, but it must be done, and it should always include someone with user-interaction know-how. If you don't have any experts around, grab the person with the most earnest level of interest in the subject and give him or her ownership (people tend to step up to even extreme responsibility when given ownership of the result).

During a JIT Design meeting, one programmer, one designer, one user, and one whiteboard should be present. Other people can come, too, but the fewer the better. More voices only make more debate. The meeting requires exactly what is needed for the purpose: a representative user (usually an internal employee) to talk about what he or she needs and wants, a designer to interpret those needs and make suggestions about possible solutions, a programmer to determine the feasibility of the suggestions and begin devising a coding plan, and a whiteboard on which to sketch interface ideas and list requirements.

A digital camera is handy also, so you can photograph the whiteboard sketches to keep a record of the meeting and either keep the interface ideas fresh in the developer's mind or give the designer a reference point from which to create a wireframe.

To begin the meeting, simply present the problem that must be solved. Everyone should then try to justify the change to the software—it needs to be determined whether the problem is really a problem by trying to talk yourselves out of it (for example, is there already a way for the user to do this? Is it the right solution? Does this change help 80 percent of our users?). If not, the meeting is over. One of the best ways to reduce an application's complexity is to avoid adding anything new to it in the first place.

If the problem really is a problem and must be solved, attendees should brainstorm possible solutions based on the representative user's needs and desires. Everyone can contribute ideas, but the resident user-experience expert should be the one who leads the conversation. JIT Design requires fast thinking, so be sure the person leading this conversation is able to produce design ideas quickly and consistently.

The meeting should not end until everyone has a clear idea about what to build and why.

The result of such a meeting may or may not involve assigning the task of creating wireframes for the new interaction. Wireframes are preferable, but when there's no time, at least the programmers will have a good idea of what to build and how it should behave prior to making impulsive decisions that lead to a weak design.

JIT Review

The other time JIT comes into play—the time most relevant to this chapter—is when the coding has been completed, as a bookend to the design meeting that took place prior to coding. JIT Review, as the name implies, is about reviewing what was built to make sure it adheres to what was previously agreed upon and to see how it can be improved prior to release.

In the fast-paced world of app design, there is usually very little time to review, let alone *refine*, an interface before it goes out the door, especially if you don't write the code yourself. Performing a JIT Review, however, is infinitely better than doing nothing at all, so try as hard as you can to incorporate JIT Review at the end of every iteration cycle prior to release.

In most cases, a meeting is not necessary for JIT Review (though you can certainly review the solution as a group and decide collectively how to refine it). Once the proposed solution is built and is available for testing by those who developed the solution in the first place, each person involved can simply review the implementation from his or her own desk. This is true anytime— even if ample time was allowed for design work earlier in the process.

Each person should try to interact with the solution with the same goals in mind that users will have when using the final product. Go through the interaction once and make mental notes about anything that isn't completely obvious, and then go through it again with the goal of discovering ways to improve it. Make notes about how to refine the solution—how to make it better adhere to a user's mental model, take less time, and become less complicated and more error-proof.

Stick all the notes into an email or, more preferably, a bug report, and send it off to the group. When everyone has made their notes, a quick conversation is usually enough to decide how to proceed. Make the changes, test the new version, and release it to the world.

One of the best things about the web is that it's conducive to constant change. An application doesn't have to be perfect the first time. You should certainly aim to present a good solution the first time out, but don't be afraid of imperfect solutions. The second you're done with one version, you can start iterating through the next one. Eventually, each and every part of the application will have gone through several iterations and the application will develop, almost by its own momentum, into a solid application that keeps users feeling confident and productive.

JIT as a solution

With complicated applications, JIT is the bare minimum of what can or should be done.

In simpler applications, however, JIT may be all that's really needed. An application built by only two or three people working in a room together can hold whiteboard sessions freely and often, so design decisions can be made and changed on a dime. (In fact, this can be quite fun and effective, as it creates a fast-paced environment of designing and coding that can produce amazing results in a very short time.)

Whenever possible, a resident expert on interaction or interface design (preferably a good, authoritative designer who's willing to *own* the interface) should be present so he or she can make educated suggestions about how to make the particular piece of software more usable, more flowing and intuitive, and more likely to help users achieve their goals. In a worst-case scenario, where no interaction gurus are available, you should at least have a graphic designer in the conversation, so that a high aesthetic standard, guided by someone with a design background, can help improve the interactions. Whenever possible, though, your company should have someone on-site who has a firm grasp on the user experience vision for the company or product, and a deep knowledge of how people actually use computers so he or she can make educated suggestions about how to improve the experience, preferably before *and* after the coding process.

A user whose goals are ignored is a user who will never be a true fan of your software, and a true fan is the best thing a company can possibly acquire. If you cannot allow time for quality design work, you should, at the very minimum, allow JIT Design and Review to run interference between programmers and users. It may be the best chance you have to design, reduce, and refine an application before your company banks its future on something that doesn't meet the needs of its customer base.

11

Don't Innovate When You Can Elevate

- ▶ Innovation
- ▶ Elevate the User Experience
- ▶ Seek Out and Learn from Great Examples
- ▶ Take Out All the Good Lines
- ▶ Get in the Game

I used to work for a small e-learning company that designed courseware for large companies. One of the problems that we commonly faced, as is true with most e-learning companies, is that the types of people for whom we designed content varied to incredible extremes.

Employees who handled baggage for an airline might be required by their employer to take some of the same administrative-type courses required by human resources staff, sales staff, and those people who wave the electric wands over you as you pass through the security gates.

Different people learn different ways. We couldn't possibly expect all these different types of people to learn the same information the same way. When it comes to education, one size does not fit all.

▶ Innovation

We decided to create an e-learning application that allowed non-linear education. Instead of forcing every user to go through the same set of screens in the same order, we would give users choices and direct different users through different paths of content based on their responses. Each person would get a version of a course adapted specifically to his or her particular learning style.

The innovation was a good idea. The concept worked well, it satisfied the need to address different learning styles, and the application was well received by clients.

Good for us. This is where innovation makes sense. There was a deep and persistent problem to be solved, and we conjured up a way to solve it that made sense and could be easily explained. This was the right kind of innovation. Soon, we ran into the wrong kind.

The problem with innovative thinking

We discovered a problem with how users navigated our courses.

Typically, the Next button in an e-learning application advances a user to the next screen in the course—a screen the user has not yet seen—like a slide show. But we had added *history* to our application. Instead of forcing a user to start a section over again each time he wanted to go back to a particular screen, we tracked the pages he went to so that the Back button enabled him to traverse through the pages he had already seen, one by one, just like a browser.

Here's a typical Next and Back button setup for an e-learning course.

The problem was that when a user began using the Back button to return to pages she'd already visited, the Next button did exactly what you'd think it would do—it advanced her through the same set of screens.

She eventually reached a point where the Next button advanced her past the last screen she'd already visited and began showing screens she had *not* visited. This is, after all, the purpose of the Next button.

So, we suddenly had a Next button with *two* purposes. This broke the single most basic rule about how users navigate courseware. And it was confusing users to no end.

Users needed to know when they stopped seeing *visited* screens and started seeing *new* ones, but the application did not indicate this in any way.

At the time this issue was being discovered, I was head down, fingers flying, writing code. Other people in the company, however, were meeting about the problem. Over the course of about a week, several people met several times to discuss ways to remedy the situation.

How could we make it clear to users that they had stopped going forward through the course history and had started seeing new screens? Should we show them some sort of message? That would affect the design for every course. Should we remove the ability to go backwards? That meant users would have to start over every time, or at least start a particular section over again. Should we simply explain it really well in our elaborate Help documentation? Sorry. No one reads Help documentation.

On and on the discussions went. We were innovators, after all. All we needed was some time to think it through and we'd come up with something amazing. But it just wasn't coming together.

Elevation

One day, I caught wind of the problem and suggested we create an animated button to replace the existing Next button.

When users went through the course normally, they would see the Next button, as expected. When users went backwards through screens, however, the Next button would convert into a Forward button via a simple animation. It would also change color, so users would have an extra little indication that the button now meant something new. Once a user reached the last visited screen, the button would animate again and convert back into a Next button, to indicate the next screen would be a new one.

Converting the Next button into a Forward button with a simple animation eliminated the confusion without innovative interface wizardry.

Twenty minutes later, we had a working version on a testing server. It worked extremely well. Everyone understood it immediately. The confusion was gone.

Innovation can be great thing when it's needed, but what's needed in most cases is not innovation. It's *elevation*.

▶ Elevate the User Experience

The company I worked with spent a week trying to come up with an innovative way to let a user know when the Next button was going to take her to a screen she hadn't yet seen. But any solution that required an innovative, new interface gadget wouldn't really solve the problem, but rather complicate it—and our code—even more.

Innovation at the conceptual level is often exactly what is needed to solve a problem. But at the interface level, innovation is expensive. Even *little* inventions can take a substantial amount of time to implement, require loads of trial-and-error experimentation, and are just as likely to fail as they are to succeed. Most importantly, inventions can create a learning curve for users where there may not have otherwise been one.

Besides that, most people are simply incapable of coming up with brilliant, innovative ideas *all the time*. Big ideas are few and far between. Most of the time, ideas are small.

Small enough to work.

Most of the time, companies and applications don't need big ideas. They need little ones that make small improvements *right now*.

The *kaizen* approach is about making frequent, incremental changes that improve things steadily and constantly.

These advances make for ongoing, positive changes that can be planned, designed, implemented, and tested very easily and quickly. They're also cost-effective, because it hardly takes any time at all to make small changes (at least, in comparison to expensive innovations), and the result often has such a high return that the investments are extremely easy to justify.

Elevation is about being more polite

One simple way to incrementally improve an application is to make it more polite.

If your application is any less polite than a really attentive and caring store clerk, iterate over the design until it becomes that polite. Your application may be the best source of customer service your company can provide. Make sure it does its job well.

What makes a polite application? Generally speaking, the absence of rudeness is all it takes. The applications that demonstrate the traits outlined in this book are more polite by default. Here are some other ways to be polite:

Don't interrupt the user's workflow. JavaScript alerts, errors that could have been prevented, confirmation messages, unnecessarily complicated interactions, and confusing task flows are all things that show off an application's rude nature. Get rid of the errors. Write meaningful error messages when they are needed.

Make it easy for the user to get her job done. Pages with elements strewn all over the place without any sense of uniformity are rude because users have a harder time determining the flow of the interaction. Screens that lack visual structure are rude because users are forced to guess what's important and what isn't. Help users get up to speed quickly.

Don't force the user to understand anything that's not relevant to the job she's doing. Applications that require understanding of the underlying system to be productive are rude because they force users to bend to the whims of developers instead of relying on their own mental models. Hide the system, so that users can rely on their mental models to work with an application and be productive without having to learn too much. Following these rules is a giant step toward a more polite solution.

Elevation means giving your software a better personality

One of the most difficult character traits to design in an application is its personality, but a "winning" personality can be one of the best ways to elevate the user experience.

Being polite is essential to creating a good user experience, but beyond this are more subjective factors, like the *tone* of an application, that enable users to connect with our applications in a more positive way.

People connect emotionally to the things they use. If a coffeemaker is difficult to use, the user's primary connection to it is one of frustration and resentment. But if the appliance makes it easy to brew great coffee, looks nice, maintains well, and does its job consistently, users feel at ease while using it.

The coffeemaker doesn't even have to match other appliances. Usually, in fact, quirky and fun designs make items more appealing. They appeal to the user's personality, not just the user's goal for the product.

For example, Woot (www.woot.com)—a retail site that lists for sale just one item per day—is filled with upbeat graphics and text written in a friendly, conversational tone that tells users it's okay to have fun. The overall vibe of the site is such that it invites users to poke around and explore. Check things out. Goof off.

Woot uses a lively and fun design style to add personality to shopping online.

Using the same level of humor they might use to talk to their own friends, Woot designers add personality to the site that contributes to the overall product experience and helps get users up to speed.

No one ever said the web had to be boring. Let's liven it up a little.

Elevation means understanding good design

It's important to look not only at the details of an application, but also what character traits the controls represent. We need to understand not just how a particular interaction works, but why it's effective.

In Twitter for iPad, for example, we can tap on a tweet with a link in it to pull up the linked web page. We can use a spread gesture on a tweet to display profile information about the person who posted it. We can tap a tweet that mentions us to display the entire conversation that led up to it, even if multiple people were involved in the conversation.

Twitter for iPad provides access to related posts and profile information faster than any other Twitter app.

So what is it about these interactions that make Twitter for iPad so nice to use? Part of it is the implementation, because the design of an interaction is vital to helping users understand how it works. But it's also the character trait it represents. Twitter for iPad is *responsive*. It delivers information via a single tap or other gesture that is more difficult to get in other applications. It offers an **on-demand interface**, and this results in an application that is easy to understand, reacts and adapts to user input in a smooth and appealing way, and generally *just works*.

A well-designed app offers users the features they need where they need them and when they need them. Twitter offers constant access to the left-hand toolbar for toggling between the stream, mentions, and direct messages. It allows us to review whole conversations anytime we want without taking a round-trip to another screen. It lets us view profile information without leaving the main screen.

Well-designed apps reduce both the number of steps involved in a task and the complexity of each one. Functionality is provided when and where the user needs it, exposing features in an on-demand fashion. Well-designed apps allow users to interact in a way that facilitates productivity. They appear to adapt to the user. As a result, the user experience is improved dramatically, and user satisfaction is taken to much higher levels.

These character traits—responsiveness, speed, a streamlined mental model, and so on—are what make an application great. The implementation of the design is a huge part of its effectiveness, but only because it means the implementation effectively supports the underlying principle.

In other words, when we Know What Makes It Great and Know the Best Ways to Implement It, we can design applications that not only live up to a user's expectations, but also stand out from the crowd by providing an elevated user experience.

▶ Seek Out and Learn from Great Examples

Throughout this book, we've looked at applications like VaultPress, Blinksale, and Mint, among others. These are all great applications, but this is not an exhaustive list, by any means. There are many other great applications out there, and while finding them isn't always easy, studying them is an effective way to gain more insight into how to design the obvious.

Inspiration

Studying great web applications is also an effective way to get some inspiration.

Backpack offers us a new approach to organization for small projects. Mint helps us manage our finances. Blinksale offers us a graceful solution to the difficult task of managing invoices to multiple clients.

All of the design problems these applications solve have been solved in myriad other ways over the years, but these simple web applications have taken a new look at the problems and presented interesting and engaging new solutions.

We can find inspiration in existing applications, common problems (like keeping track of bookmarks on multiple computers), and even installed solutions like word processors and spreadsheet applications. These are all things that can be looked at from a new perspective and redesigned for use on the web.

When asked how 37signals comes up with new application ideas, Jason Fried even suggests the outside world can be a good place for inspiration:

> *We're inspired by everyday simple problems. We're not interested in solving the huge problems. We're interested in solving the simple ones. Those are the ones people have to deal with every day. So it's those simple problems that inspire us to build simple tools to help people solve them. Nature is always a good place to look for really refined solutions too. There's lots of inspiration in nature. There's very little in nature that doesn't work. If it doesn't work it's been phased out a long time ago. So looking closely at the natural world really opens your eyes to wonderful and creative solutions.*

Elevate the standards

Standards are a wonderful thing, because they give us a solid ground to stand on when designing applications. But for the web to progress, we need to find ways to elevate the standards and drive the possibilities of the web further and further.

Many designers resist standards, saying that standards leave no room for innovation. But there's definitely a middle ground here. Between standards and innovation is *elevation*.

Web and mobile design would have never reached the point it's at now without a constant push toward new solutions and technologies that give us more power and more sophisticated possibilities for interaction. These technologies do this by improving what's already possible.

We don't need to innovate to make things better. Most often, we can elevate the standards and achieve very effective results that incrementally push the envelope.

In fact, it can be especially helpful to *avoid* innovation when introducing new interaction paradigms, because users expect things to work the way they always have, and often have a difficult time adapting to new paradigms. It's far more effective to leverage existing paradigms and try to improve upon and build on them in smaller, less dramatic ways so that users feel more comfortable getting started with them.

Be smart about it. If you can prove that a new way is better, then you're onto something. If you can't, rely on the standards until you come up with something that *is* better.

▶ Take Out All the Good Lines

Ernest Hemingway once said, "Write the story, take out all the good lines, and see if the story still works."

It's counterintuitive, but removing the good lines from an application truly is the right way to achieve great design. The good lines are the features that are flashy and cool, that don't really contribute directly to an effective application, that exist only because of their sex appeal (as sexy as applications can get, anyway). The good lines are the features that the marketing department might absolutely love, but most users will find cumbersome because they get in the way of the 20 percent of features that really matter.

When you take out all the *good* lines, what are left are the *best* lines. When there is nothing cool or sexy in the way, the features that matter are allowed to shine, and the whole user experience becomes significantly better.

When you take out everything that makes an application "competitive," what is left are the parts that make it better than the competition. What's left are the parts that let people get what they need and get out.

Elevating the user experience is not about adding features to make an application stand out from the crowd. It's about taking things away until the heart of the application is allowed to shine through. Elevation is about reduction. It's about focus. It's about kaizen.

The best software is less software.

▶ Get in the Game

Interaction designers and usability experts have a specific role to fill: to Know What To Build, Know What Makes It Great, and Know The Best Ways To Implement It.

When you work to meet these goals in the real world, you have to be able to make decisions in the interest of producing tangible results. Real applications have real design problems with real design solutions. Decisions must be made constantly in an effort to create these solutions and get things done.

Decisions are not always easy. Sometimes they're snap decisions based on very little information. Sometimes they're well-informed decisions based on long hours of usability testing and research. Whatever the case, the decisions need to be made.

Even though the most accurate answer to a design problem is usually, "It depends," the only way to move forward and get things done is to say, with great authority, *"This is how it must be done."*

When no one is willing to step up and say this, software is designed by accident, according to the whims and snap decisions of developers, managers, marketers, and anyone else who has an opinion. History has proven this is the wrong way to go. It's why we end up with so many bad applications and so few great ones.

No one really has all the answers—not even me. Every project will contain at least one design problem that lies outside the scope of this book, rendering it useless as an aid to help you make a decision right when you need it the most—when you need a little truth about the best way to design your application. But I offer you one simple fact:

Truth is a moving target.

What's true right now will very likely not be true forever. What's true for one solution will not be true for another. Design patterns will change. The capabilities of the web and of mobile devices will change. The way people interact with these technologies will change. So you may not be able to be right 100% of the time, but your ability to make decisions and get things done will get you through every project. Use that.

Don't be afraid to make decisions. It will hurt you in the long run.

Next time you find yourself saying "It depends," pretend you have no options but one. When you determine, and you will, which option you are most afraid to lose, choose that one. *Make the decision.*

And please, make it based on a long-term user experience vision. *What follows Why.*

Final note

The only way to really know if your design is working is to put it out there and see what happens. Great designs fail. Terrible designs succeed. Almost nothing goes as expected. But sometimes, a great design sneaks through and gets noticed.

When that happens, it's because someone was unafraid to make the tough decisions and design the obvious.

That person can be you.

I leave you with this note:

Visual design, content, and functionality are inseparable, and they're all designed. Design is a symphony, not a solo act. Application designers are not screen designers, usability experts, researchers, or visionaries. They are *all* of these things. Great applications require a great understanding of every aspect of application design. Only then can designers be in a position to say, with great authority, "This is how it must be done." And only then will they be right to do so.

Now, go forth … and design the obvious.

*   *   *   *   *   *   *   *   *   *

To learn more about me, visit www.rhjr.net. You can use the contact form there to email me directly. You can also find me on Twitter at www.twitter.com/rhjr.

Index

5S approach, 259–261
5-second test, 133–134
30 Days, 53
37signals
    and Backpack, 107, 108
    and feature lists, 88
    and self-design, 51–52
    sources of inspiration for, 278
    up-to-speed aids, 147
    and Writeboard, 213
60-Second Deadline exercise, 90–92
80-20 rule, 92–93

A

ACD, 45–48, 74
ActionScript, 130
active users, 33
activity, designing for the, 44–47
Activity-Centered Design, 45–48, 74
add-on offers, 233
Adobe
    Dreamweaver, 129, 145
    Flash (*See* Flash)
    Illustrator, 38
    Photoshop, 38
Agile development, 265
airline app, 85–87
alert messages, 110–111, 153, 204, 205
alignment, 225–227
Amazon
    customer recommendations, 186
    email campaigns, 171
    one-click purchase button, 170–171
    social influence tools, 184–185
Anderson, Tom, 22
Android, 84
animated buttons, 272
Apple
    human-interface design team, 46, 49
    Human Interface Guidelines, 203, 212
    iBooks app, 176–178
    iPad (*See* iPad)
    Keynote, 120, 125, 129
    mobile platform, 84
    Photos app, 115–116
    word processing app, 102
application design. *See also* design;
        obvious design
    and card sorting, 168
    good *vs.* great, 4
    and Just-in-Time Design, 265
    and kaizen, 258
    main goal of, 245
    and mobile devices, 85
    and Pareto principle, 92
    process of, 13
    role of users in, 37
    simplicity in, 245
    situation-centered nature of, 50
    and vision, 19, 34
application designers. *See also* designers
    and demographics, 42
    and forms, 155
    and mobile devices, 85
    recommended book for, 231
    role of, 264
    and setup wizards, 142
    vs. strategists, 264
application elements, 15
application errors. *See* error messages;
        errors
application form, 93–98
application-modal dialog boxes, 204
applications. *See also* software; web
        applications
    adding to *vs.* improving, 19, 259
    applying 80-20 rule to, 92–93
    being consistent across, 229–233
    card sorting for, 166–168
    characteristics of well-designed, 277
    choosing colors for, 235–236
    competitive analysis of, 26–28
    detailing features of, 262
    detecting errors in, 195–203
    eliminating implementation models in,
        119–127
    establishing set style for, 261
    getting user feedback on, 99–100, 128
    getting users up to speed on, 141–152,
        242
    how different people approach, 140–141
    importance of simplicity in, 89, 147,
        245–246
    knowing motivation for, 34
    learning from great, 277–279
    measuring effectiveness of, 32–33
    minimizing users' frustration with,
        78–80
    mistake-proofing, 191 (*See also* poka-
        yoke devices)
    outlining goals for, 262

applications (continued)
  preventing errors in, 193–195
  reducing complexity of, 266
  removing good lines from, 279–280
  reviewing/refining, 267–268
  taking inventory of, 25
  testing, 130–138 (*See also* usability
    testing)
  writing design criteria for, 30–31
application settings, 142, 163
application strategy, 24
attention, getting users', 176
attribution error, fundamental, 48
audits, user experience, 24–28
authority, 185–186
Axure RP Pro, 120

B

Back button, 271
Backpack, 107–111
  creators of, 107
  as example of metaphor that works,
    107, 111
  getting inspiration from, 278
  inline editing features, 246
  inspiration for, 108
  JavaScript alert message, 110–111
  purpose of, 107
  sample pages, 107, 109
  up-to-speed aids, 147
backup application, 181
badges, 188
Ballpark, 87, 246
banana principle, 237–242
banking app, 178–179
Basecamp
  blank-slate filler, 169–170
  purpose of, 51
  and self-design, 51–52
  up-to-speed aids, 147–148
BBC News app, 224–225
beginners
  designing for, 140–141
  and instructive design, 159
  and up-to-speed aids, 168
beta sites, 187
Big Red Fez, The, 237
billing software, 83. *See also* Blinksale
blank-slate fillers, 147–149, 168–169
Blink, 48
Blinksale
  creators of, 80–81, 83
  design process for, 123
  getting inspiration from, 277, 278
  how it works, 81–83

  main invoice-editing screen, 81
  mobile version of, 87
  payment options, 83
  purpose of, 80
  sample invoice, 82
  simplicity of, 82–84, 246
blogging service, 198
blogs, 105, 174, 181, 253
bookmarking tool, 193
book-preview feature, iBooks, 177
boxes, 248
Boxes and Arrows, 164
brainstorming, 31, 265, 266
brands, 22, 229, 248
Brin, Sergey, 23
browser incompatibility, 197
browserless self-tests, 131–133
browsers, hiding tools in, 131
bug reports, 104, 267
bulleted lists, 250
bulletproofing, 136
buzzwords, 250

C

Camtasia Studio, 135
Cancel button, 233
card-sorting exercises, 166–168
Chase Mobile, 178–179
chrome, 222, 223, 224
Cialdini, Dr. Robert, 178, 181
Cisco Systems, 66
Citrix Systems, 66
cleaning up
  application-development process,
    263–264
  task flows, 255–258
click-through mockups, 129
cloud storage service, 180–181
clutter
  interface, 122, 246
  task flow, 244–245, 255–258
CNN.com, 163
Cocoa Box Design, 66
code base, 233
cognitive walkthroughs, 25
color, 235–236, 241, 246, 252–253
commitment, 182–184
company brands, 22, 229, 248
company strategy, 20
company vision, 19, 21, 23
competitive analysis, 26–28
conceptual elements, 14
configuration options, 160, 163
confirmation messages, 110–111
consistency. *See also* uniformity

across applications, 229–233
and design patterns, 230–233
and first impressions, 219
leveraging standards to enable, 261
persuasion via, 182–184
vs. intelligent inconsistency, 233
when creating wireframes, 122
consistent design, 122, 234. *See also*
consistency
consistent layout, 228
consistent messaging, 229–230
consistent typography, 227
contact information, 155
content. *See also* information
adopting conversational tone for, 275
allowing sufficient space for, 222–225
defining structure for, 222
how users search for, 164
identifying structure of, 261
importance of, 223, 281
reducing clutter in, 248–250
separating presentation from, 261
contextual inquiry, 63–65, 137
contextual usability testing, 136–137
contrast, 237, 246
conversion rate, 33
Cooper, Alan, 37, 79, 140
corporate logos, 247–248. *See also* brands
correspondence bias, 48
courseware, 270
CSS, 15, 72, 159, 222, 261
customer reviews, 186
customer satisfaction rates, 33

D

Dashboard HQ, 193–196
Add Content panel, 193
Drag and Drop Modules pattern, 233
poka-yoke detection devices, 195–203
poka-yoke prevention devices, 193–195
purpose of, 193
data layer, 5
deception, 188
defaults
choosing good, 160–163
in form fields, 150
for Google Page Creator, 214–215
design. *See also* application design
consistent, 122, 234 (*See also*
consistency)
getting second opinion on, 126–127
improving, 33
instructive, 149, 153–159
Just-in-Time, 265–268
leveraging irregularities in, 220, 234–242

measuring effectiveness of, 32–33
obvious (*See* obvious design)
persuasive, 176, 179
prototyping, 127–130 (*See also*
prototypes)
situation-centered, 50
success/failure of, 281–282
symptoms of weak, 19–20
user-centered, 40–41
design criteria, 30–31
designers. *See also* application designers
and competitive analysis, 28
and demographics, 42
and error pages, 196 (*See also* errors)
essential book for, 231
and mobile devices, 85
and modal errors, 205
role of, 176, 182, 264
and self-design, 50
and user-centered design, 40, 46
and wizards, 142
design implementation, 32
designing
for the activity, 44–47
for information, 163–168
for intermediate users, 140–141
for mental models, 104–119
for mobile platforms, 84–87
for touchscreen devices, 111
for uniformity, 220–228
for the user, 37–44
white space, 251–255
Designing Interfaces, 173, 231
designinginterfaces.com, 231
Designing Visual Interfaces, 245
design pattern libraries, 231–233, 261
Design Pattern Library, Yahoo, 232–233
design patterns
collections of, 231–233
defined, 172
for displaying/hiding HTML page,
209–211
for editing within pages, 172
making things familiar with, 171–173
for pagination, 171–172, 230
purpose of, 172, 231
recommended book on, 173, 231
understanding, 230–233
design thinking, 31
desktop computers, 87, 102
detection devices, error, 195–203
DeWolfe, Chris, 23
dialog boxes, 203–204
digital cameras, 266
dimension, 237, 242
discount codes, 187

displaying/hiding HTML page, 209–211
document-modal dialog boxes, 203
document-modal errors, 205
dog food, eating your own, 137–138
domain name, changing, 137
Don't Make Me Think, 88, 248
Doublewide Labs, 81, 83
drag-and-drop interactions, 14–15
Drag and Drop Modules pattern, 233
Dreamweaver, 129, 145
Dropbox, 180–181
dry-erase boards, 124. *See also* whiteboards
dummy text, 150

E

ease of use, 46, 83, 105
eating your own dog food, 137–138
e-books, 49, 176–178
Einstein's rule, 122
e-learning application, 270–272
e-learning companies, 270
Elements of Style, The, 88, 231, 248
elevation
    and good design, 276–277
    and polite applications, 273–274
    and software personality, 274–275
    of standards, 278–279
    of user experience, 272–277, 280
    vs. innovation, 272, 279
elevator pitch, 14
email addresses, 156
email applications, 187, 192, 206, 255–256
email campaigns, 171
emotional connections, 274
e-reader interface, 177. *See also* e-books
error-detection devices, 195–203
error messages
    as bug reports, 104
    in desktop-installed applications,
        203–204
    examples of good and bad, 208
    for forms, 156, 158
    how users react to, 190, 195–196
    and implementation-model designs, 104
    writing effective, 195–196, 207–208
error pages, 196–198
error-prevention devices, 193–195
errors, 190–215
    converting to opportunities, 200–201
    detecting, 195–203
    how users react to, 190
    preventing, 193–195, 203
ethical persuasion, 188
ethnographic research, 63
Excel, Microsoft, 59–60

exceptions, 70–72
exclusivity, 187
expert users
    designing for, 140
    and help documents, 173
exploratory searching, 164

F

Facebook, 152
failure, product, 36–37
FAQs, 209–211
features
    dropping nice-to-have, 88–98, 121, 279
    reevaluating, 98–99
    sorting through, 260
featuritis, 78
feedback
    for forms, 153
    soliciting, 99–100
    via prototyping, 128
FEMA website, 196–197
Fettig, Abe, 130
file backups, 181
filing systems, 102, 180
Firewheel Design, 80, 83, 123
five-second test, 133–134
fivesecondtest.com, 134
Flash
    and mobile devices, 31
    prototypes, 130
    UI Component Set, 130
    welcome screen, 145
Flipboard, 152–153
flowcharts, 74–75
focused applications, 78, 92–93
fonts, 122, 227
forgiving software, 211–215
forms
    alignment of fields in, 225–227
    applying instructive design to, 153–159
    inline validation of, 157–158, 198–200, 203
    providing instructive text in, 150
    typical problems in, 156
    ways of using, 197–198
form *vs.* function, 22
forums, 99, 174
Forward button, 272
"Four Modes of Seeking Information..."
    article, 164
Foursquare, 188
Framework for Obvious Design, 12–16
frameworks, interaction design, 233
Frequently Asked Questions, 209–211
Fried, Jason, 108, 147, 278
frustration levels, user, 78–80

functionality, 281
functional specifications, 262. *See also*
    specifications
function *vs.* form, 22
fundamental attribution error, 48

G

Gadgets, 15
gaming techniques, 183–184
gestural interfaces, 84, 112, 115–116
Getting Real, 88
Getting Started guides, 141–142
Gladwell, Malcolm, 48
Gmail, 187, 206, 256
goals
    application, 262
    obvious design, 10–12
Godin, Seth, 237, 239, 242
good practices, promoting, 213–215
GoodReads, 182
Google
    Drag and Drop Modules pattern, 233
    founders, 23
    and JotSpot, 130
    and misspelled words, 201–202
    mobile platform, 84
    pagination in search results pages, 171, 230
    and scarcity principle, 187
    Search box, 235
    site-builder tool, 161, 214–215
    as source of help information, 173–174
Google Gmail, 187, 206, 256
Google Page Creator, 161–162, 214–215
Google Personalized, 233
Google Sites, 130, 161
GoToMeeting, 66
graphical dividers, 255
graphical elements, 223, 244, 246, 247, 260
graphic designers, 71, 127

H

happy talk, 250
Harris, Jensen, 173
help documents, 173–174, 249
help systems, 161, 173
Hemingway, Ernest, 279
hiding/displaying HTML page, 209–211
homepages
    defining vision for, 28–31
    design considerations, 222
    typical problems with, 26
    use of happy talk on, 250
Hopkin, Michael, 218

HTML
    headings, 221, 222, 261
    prototypes, 129
    purpose of, 222, 261
human-centered design, 45
Human Interface Guidelines, Apple, 203, 212
humor, 275
hyperlinks, 252–253

I

iBooks app, 176–178
ID3 tags, 165
iGoogle, 15
Illustrator, 38
image libraries, 135, 169
immersion, situational, 52–54
implementation, design, 32
implementation models
    converting into mental models, 111–119
    and ease of use, 105–106
    eliminating, 119–127
    and error messages, 104, 110
    and Netflix, 115, 119
    and user frustration, 106
    vs. mental models, 103–104
importance, leveraging irregularity to
    create, 234–242
inconsistency, intelligent, 233
Influence: The Psychology of Persuasion, 178, 181
information. *See also* content
    architecture, 163–164, 166
    designing for, 163–168
    helping users find, 251
    how people learn, 270
information-based websites, 164
"Information Design Using Card Sorting"
    article, 168
informative text, 250
inline-expand design pattern, 209–211
inline tips, 150, 151
inline validation, 157–158, 159, 198–200, 203
Inmates Are Running the Asylum, The, 37, 140
innovation, 19, 270–272, 279
inspiration, 278
instructional designers, 64
instructive copy, 249
instructive design, 149, 153–159
instructive hints, 149–153
intelligent inconsistency, 233
interaction design, 34
interaction designers, 280
interaction design frameworks, 233
interaction element, 15

interactions
  drag-and-drop, 14–15
  round-trip, 257
interface layer, 5–6
interfaces
  designing visual, 245
  one-click, 170–171
  providing tips in, 150
  reducing clutter in, 122
  reusing, 229
  reviewing/refining, 267–268
  testing, 130 (*See also* usability testing)
  uniformity in, 221
  using color in, 235–236, 241, 246
  using wireframes to design, 121
interface surgery
  applying instructive design, 153–159
  designing page elements to stand out, 237–242
  for displaying/hiding HTML page, 209–211
  implementation- to mental-model conversion, 111–119
  on job application form, 93–98
intermediate users
  designing for, 140–141
  and help documents, 173
interview testing, 134–135, 136
Intuit QuickBooks, 83
inventory, application, 25
invoicing applications, 80, 87, 246. *See also* Ballpark; Blinksale
iOS, 84
iPad
  BBC News app, 224–225
  Flipboard app, 152–153
  iBooks app, 176–178
  Kayak app, 212
  most popular uses of, 85
  Netflix app, 112–119
  notes app, 66
  NPR app, 224, 246
  Photos app, 115–116
  prototyping apps for, 129
  sketchbook app, 148
  Twitter app, 276–277
  word processing app, 102
iPhone
  Chase Mobile app, 178–179
  iBooks app, 176–178
  Pandora app, 150, 151
  Phone app, 202
  popularity of, 84–85
  prototyping apps for, 129
  Shazam app, 249

Southwest Airlines app, 86–87
Things app, 151
to-do list app, 151
iPod, 49
irregularities, leveraging, 220, 234–242
iteration, 259
Ive, Jonathan, 47
iWork, 102, 120

J

Japanese improvement processes, 72, 259–261. *See also* kaizen
JavaScript
  alert messages, 110–111, 153, 203, 204, 205
  for inline-expand design pattern, 209–211
  inline validation script, 198
JIT Design, 265–266, 268
JIT Review, 265, 267–268
job application form, 93–98
Jobs, Steve, 47
JotSpot, 130
jQuery, 13, 15
Just-in-Time Design, 265–266, 268
Just-in-Time Review, 265, 267–268

K

kaizen
  benefits of, 259
  defined, 72, 273
  original purpose of, 258
  practicing, 258–261
  and use cases, 72–73
  and wireframes, 123–127
Kayak, 212
Keynote, 120, 125, 129
Keynotopia, 129
known-item search method, 164, 165
Krug, Steve, 88, 248, 250
Krug's Third Law of Usability, 88

L

labeling systems, 102, 106
layers, web, 5–6
libraries, design pattern, 231–233, 261
liking principle, 186
Lindegaard, Gitte, 218
LinkedIn, 184
links, 252–253
log-in widgets, 138
logos, 247–248

M

Macintosh
    and Internet Explorer, 197
    and online forms, 196–198
    wireframe-creation tool, 120
Macromedia
    Flash, 130 (*See also* Flash)
    weblog aggregator, 209
markup code, 221
meaning, leveraging irregularity to create, 234–242
mental maps, 228
mental models
    converting implementation models into, 111–119
    defined, 103
    designing for, 104–119
    examples of, 102–103
    helping users form, 220
    vs. implementation models, 103–104
messages
    alert, 110–111, 153, 204, 205
    confirmation, 110–111
    error (*See* error messages)
messaging, consistent, 229–230
metadata, 165
metaphors, 102–103, 107, 237. *See also* mental models
metrics, success, 32–33
Microsoft
    Excel, 59–60
    help documents, 173
    Office team, 173
    PowerPoint, 120, 231
    Visio, 120
    Word, 58–59
minimizing copy, 248–250
Mint.com, 142–145, 146, 277, 278
misaligned objects, 227
misspelled words, 201–202
"mistake-proofing" device, 191
mobile devices
    designing for, 84–87, 279
    and Flash, 31
    most popular uses of, 85
    prototyping apps for, 129
mockups, 129
modal dialog boxes, 203–204
modal errors, 203–207
modeless assistants, 205–207
modeless dialog boxes, 203
Morae, 135
motivation, 34
MSN, 171
Mullet, Kevin, 245
MySpace, 23, 178
My Yahoo, 172, 233

N

Nature.com, 218
navigation
    and card sorting, 166
    devoting too much space to, 222, 223, 224
    persistent, 132, 133, 198, 214, 244
    for search-engine sites, 172
    and spatial memory, 228
    testing, 131–133
    and user experience, 26
nested boxes, 248
Netflix, 112–119
Next button, 270–272
nice-to-have features, 88–100, 121, 279
Nielsen, Jakob, 160, 161, 247
Norman, Donald, 45, 46, 47, 49, 74
notes app, 66
note-taking tool, 193
NPR app, 224, 246
NYTimes.com, 163

O

Obama, Barack, 182–183
obvious design
    and design patterns, 171–173
    and element of familiarity, 171–173
    and featuritis, 78
    framework for, 12–16
    goals for, 10–12
    qualities of, 6–10, 219–220
    and web layers, 5–6
Odeo, 154–159
OmniGraffle, 120, 125
one-click interfaces, 170–171
organizational graphics, 248
ownership, 177–178

P

Page, Larry, 23
Pages for iPad, 102
pagination, design patterns for, 171–172, 230
Pandora, 150, 151
paper prototypes, 128–129
Paper Prototyping, 129
Pareto, Vilfredo, 92
Pareto principle, 92–93
participation, measuring, 33
passions, 18
pattern libraries, 231–233, 261
patterns, 172, 232. *See also* design patterns

peer pressure, 184
Penultimate, 66, 148, 149
people layer, 5
PeopleSoft, 40–41
perpetual intermediates, 140
persistent navigation, 132, 133, 198, 214, 244
persona descriptions, 37, 38, 43, 48, 76.
    See also personas
personal computing, 85
personal-finance management tool, 142
personality, software, 274–275
personas, 37–44
    and Activity-Centered Design, 47–48
    components of, 37
    defined, 37
    example of, 38–40
    purpose of, 37–38
    and user-centered design, 40–44
persuasion
    book about psychology of, 178, 181
    ethical, 188
    principles of, 181–188
    as quality of great application, 9
persuasive design, 176, 179. *See also*
    persuasion
persuasive statements, 180, 186
Phone app, 202
Photos app, 115–116
Photoshop, 38
pixel-to-data ratio, 247–248
podcast services, 154, 165–166
poka-yoke devices, 191–203
    defined, 191
    downside of using, 195
    examples of, 191–192
    pronunciation of, 191
    simplicity of, 195
    types of, 193
    on the web, 192
polite applications, 273–274
pop-up windows, 204, 209
portal pages, 242
"Power of Defaults" article, 160
PowerPoint, 120, 231
preferences, 163
prevention devices, error, 193–195
previewing process, iBooks, 177
pricing, 188
private beta sites, 187
problems. *See also* errors
    detecting, 195–203
    preventing, 193–195
    solving, 49, 178–179, 266
product failure, 36–37

product logos, 247–248
product research, 53–57
professional networking site, 184
profile badges, 188
progress meters, 184
project management tool, 51. *See also*
    Basecamp
promotion codes, 187
proportion, 222–224
prototypes, 127–130
    benefits of using, 127–128, 138
    defined, 127
    ways of creating, 128–130
Prototyping: A Practitioner's Guide, 41
purchase paths, 233
purchases, measuring, 33
Putorti, Jason, 142, 145

Q

quality assurance testing, 138
QuickBooks, 83
quotes, 186

R

reciprocity, 181–182
reconnaissance testing, 136
recurring activity, 33
redirecting users, 137
reducing clutter, 122
reduction, 245, 261, 280
refactoring code, 72
refinement, successive, 245
registration forms, 154–159, 203, 226.
    See also forms
regularity, 122
Remember the Milk, 200
remote user research, 66–67
requirements, project, 121
research
    situation, 54–55
    user, 66–67
responsiveness, 276–277
retention rate, 33
Retweet button, 185
rhjr.net, 282
Robertson, James, 168
round-trip interactions, 257
RP Pro, 120
RSS feeds, 152
rude behavior, 204–205, 273–274

S

sample values, 149–150
Sano, Darrell, 245
scanability, web-page, 222
scarcity principle, 187–188
screen-recording tools, 135
screen shots, 250
scrolling pages, 222
Search boxes, 234–235
search engines, 172, 230
search methods, 164
seiketsu, 261
seiri, 260, 261
seiso, 260, 261
seiton, 260, 261
self-congratulatory statements, 250
self-design, 50–52
self-tests, browserless, 131–133
semantic code, 221, 222
semantic markup, 261
settings, application, 142, 163
setup wizards, 142
shadowing, 65–66
sharing activity, 33
Shazam app, 249
shining, 260
shitsuke, 261
signposts, 237, 242
simplicity, 89, 147, 195, 245–246
Sinek, Simon, 21
site-builder tool, 161–162, 211, 213–215
situation, solving for the, 48–55
situational immersion, 52–54
situational inquiry, 63
situation-centered design, 50, 54–55, 76
situation research, 54–55
sketchbook app, 148
sketches, 124, 127, 138, 264. *See also*
     wireframes
smartphones, 85. *See also* mobile devices
Snyder, Carolyn, 129
social influence tools, 185
social networking, 23, 33, 184
social proof, 184–185
social psychology studies, 178
software. *See also* applications
     adding to *vs.* improving, 19, 259
     creating forgiving, 211–215
     detecting errors in, 195–203
     giving personality to, 274–275
     preventing errors in, 193–195
     promoting good practices with, 213–215
     qualities of great, 8–10
     testing, 130–138 (*See also* usability testing)

software designers, 230. *See also* application
     designers
Software Requirements Specification, 262
Software Usability Research Laboratory, 251
sorting
     application features, 260
     card, 166–168
Southwest Airlines app, 85–87
spatial memory, 126, 220, 227–228
specifications, 262, 263–264
spelling mistakes, 201–202
Spencer, Donna, 164
Spool, Jared, 233, 251
spread gesture, 115, 117
Spurlock, Morgan, 53
Squidoo, 201
SRS, 262
standardization, 261
standards, 278–279
Start with Why: How Great Leaders Inspire
     Everyone to Take Action, 21
stock photography sites, 135, 169
straightening, 260
strategic thinking, 34
strategists, 264
strategy
     application, 24
     company, 20
     user experience (*See* user experience
          strategy)
Strunk, William, 88, 248
style guidelines, 261
success metrics, 32–33
Super Size Me, 53
SURL, 251
SurveyMonkey.com, 67
surveys, 67–68
sustaining work, 261
system messages, 229. *See also* messages

T

tablet computers, 85, 87. *See also* mobile
     devices
tag clouds, 105–106
Target.com, 133
task-flow diagrams, 25, 74–75
task flows
     applying kaizen to, 258
     cleaning up, 255–258
     designing, 233, 258
     examples of cluttered, 244–245
task-management system, 244–245, 255, 257
tax software, 83
technology, adapting to, 44

TechSmith, 135
testimonials, 186
testing. *See also* usability testing
  with browserless self-test, 131–133
  compensating participants in, 136
  with contextual usability testing,
    136–137
  by eating your own dog food, 137–138
  with five-second test, 133–134
  with interview-style sessions, 134–135, 136
  quality assurance, 138
  recruiting testers for, 135–136
text fields, 149–150
Thaper, Sunny, 124
Things app, 151
Three Rs, 121–123
Tidwell, Jenifer, 173, 231
to-do list app, 151, 200
tooltips, 145
touchscreens, 84, 111, 115
Toyota, 72
trash metaphor, 102
travel-booking app, 212–213
trigger words, 165, 250
trust, 186, 220
Try It Now button, 250
Tumblr, 226
TurboTax, 83
tutorials, 145, 146
Twitter, 152, 185, 186, 276–277, 282
typefaces, 227. *See also* fonts
TypePad, 198–199
typography, 227

U

UCD, 40–41, 48
UI Component Set, Flash, 130
undo functions, 110–111, 205–206, 212
uniform alignment, 225–227
uniformity, 122, 220–228, 234. *See also*
  consistency
uniqueness, 234
Unnecessary Test, The, 89–90
up-to-speed aids, 141–173
  blank-slate fillers, 147–149, 168–169
  choosing good defaults, 160–163
  designing for information, 163–168
  getting rid of, 168–173
  Getting Started guides, 141–142
  instructive hints, 149–153
  and intermediate users, 140–141
  Mint.com example, 142–145
  welcome screens, 145–146, 168

URLs, 194
usability. *See also* ease of use
  and screen designs, 222
  testing (*See* usability testing)
  and white space, 251
Usability, Krug's Third Law of, 88
usability experts, 160, 280, 281
usability studies, 222. *See also* usability
  testing
usability testing, 130–138
  benefits of, 130
  with browserless self-test, 131–133
  compensating participants in, 136
  contextual, 136–137
  by eating your own dog food, 137–138
  and help documents, 173
  with interview-style sessions, 134–135,
    136
  with paper prototypes, 128–129
  recruiting testers for, 135–136
  on use of white space, 251–253
use cases, 68–74
  applying kaizen to, 72–73
  argument against, 74
  defined, 68
  exceptions for, 70–72
  refining ideas for, 74
  writing, 68–72
useit.com, 247
user-centered design, 40–41, 48
user experience
  auditing, 24–28
  elevating, 272–277, 280
  strategy (*See* user experience strategy)
user experience strategy
  core activities for developing, 24–34
  defined, 19, 20, 23
  importance of, 18
  revisiting, 32
User Interface Engineering, 133–134
User Interface Library, Yahoo, 233
user research, 45, 66–67
users
  designing for, 37–44
  getting feedback from, 99–100, 128
  how websites are judged by, 218–219
  identifying needs of, 61–68
  recruiting for usability tests, 135–136
  shadowing, 65–66
  understanding, 55–60
user surveys, 67–68

V

values, 18
VaultPress, 238, 246, 277
version tracking, 213
video tours, 141, 146
Visio, 120
vision
    and company success/failure, 19, 21,
        22–23
    defining, 28–31
    importance of, 34
Vision Document, 262
visual design, 258, 281
visual hierarchy, 219, 221–222
visual interfaces, 245
visual metaphors, 102–103, 107. *See also*
    mental models

W

walkthroughs, cognitive, 25
Warfel, Todd Zaki, 41
waste, eliminating, 262–264
*Web Anatomy: Interaction Design Frameworks
    That Work*, 233
web applications. *See also* applications
    choosing good defaults for, 160–163
    eliminating waste in, 262–264
    getting inspiration from great, 278
    process for creating, 262–263
    simplicity in, 245–246
    testing, 131–133
web-based invoicing applications, 80, 87, 246.
    See also Ballpark; Blinksale
web-based site-creation tool, 211, 213–215
web browsers, hiding tools in, 131
WebEx, 66
web forms. *See* forms
web layers, 5
webmail applications, 187, 192, 206,
    255–256
web pages. *See also* websites
    choosing colors for, 235–236, 241, 246
    hiding/displaying, 209–211
    making elements stand out on, 234–235,
        237–242
    scanability of, 222
    scrolling, 222
    surfacing bananas in, 239
    use of white space on, 222, 251–255
    visual hierarchy for, 221–222
web resources, 174
websites. *See also* web applications
    homepages for (*See* homepages)
    how users judge, 218–219

    importance of content for, 222–225
    tool for building, 211, 213–215
web standards, 261, 278–279
web usability, 88, 160, 247, 251. *See also*
    usability
"Web Users Judge Sites in the Blink of an
    Eye" article, 218
welcome screens, 145–146, 169
well-designed apps, 277
What's This? documentation, 249
White, E.B., 88, 231, 248
whiteboards, 124, 125, 266
white space, 251–255
    as alternative to graphics, 253–255
    benefits of using, 251
    as design element, 222
    and file size, 255
    separating areas of page with, 253–254
Wichita State University, 251
wikis, 141, 231
Williams, Josh, 83, 123
wireframes, 119–127
    and application process, 262
    applying kaizen to, 123–127
    benefit of using, 121
    purpose of, 119–120, 138
    revising, 127
    for simple log-in screen, 120
    Three Rs for creating, 121–123
    tools for creating, 120
    vs. coding, 127
Wireframe Toolkit, Keynote, 129
wizards, setup, 142
Woot, 275
Word, Microsoft, 58–59
Writeboard, 213
WYSIWYG editors, 129

X

X-factor, 15

Y

Yahoo
    Design Pattern Library, 232–233
    editing design patterns, 172
    pagination in search results pages, 171
    User Interface Library, 233
Yelp, 234–235
YUI Library, 233

Z

Zeldman, Jeffrey, 185
zip codes, 156